# ADVANCES IN ACCOUNTING EDUCATION: TEACHING AND CURRICULUM INNOVATIONS

# ADVANCES IN ACCOUNTING EDUCATION: TEACHING AND CURRICULUM INNOVATIONS

Series Editors: Timothy J. Rupert and Beth B. Kern

Recent Volumes:

# ADVANCES IN ACCOUNTING EDUCATION: TEACHING AND CURRICULUM INNOVATIONS

EDITED BY

## TIMOTHY J. RUPERT
*Northeastern University, USA*

## BETH B. KERN
*Indiana University South Bend, USA*

United Kingdom – North America – Japan
India – Malaysia – China

Emerald Publishing Limited
Howard House, Wagon Lane, Bingley BD16 1WA, UK

First edition 2017

**British Library Cataloguing in Publication Data**
A catalogue record for this book is available from the British Library

ISBN: 978-1-78714-181-0 (Print)
ISSN: 1085-4622 (Series)
ISBN: 978-1-78714-180-3 (Online)
ISBN: 978-1-78714-307-4 (Epub)

ISOQAR certified
Management System,
awarded to Emerald
for adherence to
Environmental
standard
ISO 14001:2004.

**ISOQAR**
REGISTERED
Certificate Number 1985
ISO 14001

INVESTOR IN PEOPLE

# CONTENTS

v

**SPECIAL SECTION ON ACCOUNTING ETHICS COURSES**

# LIST OF CONTRIBUTORS

| | |
|---|---|
| *Barbara Apostolou* | College of Business and Economics, West Virginia University, Morgantown, WV, USA |
| *Chris Bagwell* | KPMG, New York City, NY, USA |
| *Jason Bergner* | College of Business, University of Nevada, Reno, Reno, NV, USA |
| *Cynthia Blanthorne* | College of Business Administration, University of Rhode Island, Kingston, RI, USA |
| *Marcus Brooks* | College of Business, University of Nevada, Reno, Reno, NV, USA |
| *Lisa A. Burke-Smalley* | College of Business, University of Tennessee at Chattanooga, Chattanooga, TN, USA |
| *Travis Holt* | Raymond J. Harbert College of Business, Auburn University, Auburn, AL, USA |
| *Christopher Jones* | College of Business, University of Wisconsin Oshkosh, Oshkosh, WI, USA |
| *Patrick T. Kelly* | School of Business, Providence College, Providence, RI, USA |
| *Linda A. Quick* | College of Business, East Carolina University, Greenville, NC, USA |
| *Alan Reinstein* | School of Business Administration, Wayne State University, Detroit, MI, USA |
| *Michael K. Shaub* | Mays Business School, Texas A & M University, College Station, TX, USA |
| *Scott D. Vandervelde* | Moore School of Business, University of South Carolina, Columbia, SC, USA |

# CALL FOR PAPERS

Submissions are invited for forthcoming volumes. AAETCI publishes a wide variety of articles dealing with accounting education at the college and university level. AAETCI encourages readable, relevant, and reliable articles in all areas of accounting education including auditing, financial and managerial accounting, forensic accounting, governmental accounting, taxation, etc. Papers can be:

- Position papers on particular issues.
- Comprehensive literature reviews grounded in theory.
- Conceptual models.
- Historical discussions with implications for current and future pedagogical efforts.
- Methodology discussions.
- Pedagogical tools, including evidence of their effectiveness.
- Research studies with implications for improving accounting education.

AAETCI provides a forum for sharing generalizable teaching approaches from curricula development to content delivery techniques. Pedagogical research that contributes to more effective teaching in colleges and universities is highlighted. All articles must explain how teaching methods or curricula/programs can be improved. Nonempirical papers should be academically rigorous, and specifically discuss the institutional context of a course or program, as well as any relevant tradeoffs or policy issues. Empirical reports should exhibit sound research design and execution, and must develop a thorough motivation and literature review, possibly including references from outside the accounting field.

## SUBMISSION PROCESS

Send two files by e-mail: one with a manuscript copy but without a cover page, and the other solely a cover page with author information. Cover pages should list all authors' names and addresses (with telephone numbers, fax numbers, and e-mail addresses). The authors' names and addresses should not appear on the abstract. To assure anonymous review, authors should not identify themselves directly or indirectly. Also, attach a copy of any research instruments. Two reviewers assess each manuscript submitted and reviews are completed in a timely manner, usually 60–90 days.

Send manuscripts to aiae@neu.edu

# WRITING GUIDELINES

1. Write your manuscript using active voice. Therefore, you can use the pronouns "we" and "I." Also, please avoid using a series of prepositional phrases. We strongly encourage you to use a grammar and spell checker on manuscripts before you submit to our journal. Parsimony is a highly desirable trait for manuscripts we publish. Be concise in making your points and arguments. The text of typical manuscripts (exclusive of references, tables, and appendices) are no longer than 30 pages.

2. Each paper should include a cover sheet with names, addresses, telephone numbers, fax numbers, and e-mail address for all authors. The title page also should include an abbreviated title that you should use as a running head (see item 7 below). The running head should be no more than 70 characters, which includes all letters, punctuation, and spaces between words.

3. The second page should consist of a Structured Abstract of no more than 250 words. Guidance for the Structured Abstract may be found at: http://www.emeraldgrouppublishing.com/authors/guides/write/abstracts.htm. Abstracts from recent issues of *Advances in Accounting Education* function as helpful examples.

4. You should begin the first page of the manuscript with the manuscript's title. DO NOT use the term "Introduction" or any other term at the beginning of the manuscript. Simply begin your discussion.

5. Use uniform margins of 1 1/2 inches at the top, bottom, right and left of every page. Do not justify lines, leave the right margins uneven. Do not hyphenate words at the end of a line; let a line run short or long rather than break a word. Type no more than 25 lines of text per page.

6. Double space all lines of text, which includes title, headings, and quotations.

7. All citations within your text should be formatted with the author(s) name and the year of publication. An appropriate citation is Catanach (2004) or Catanach and Feldmann (2005), or Gaffney, Ryan, and Wurst (2010) when there are three or more authors. You do not need to cite six or seven references at once, particularly when the most recent

references refer to earlier works. Please try to limit yourself to two or three citations at a time, preferably the most recent ones.

8. You should place page numbers for quotations along with the date of the material being cited. For example: According to Beaver (1987, 4), "Our knowledge of education research ... and its potential limitations for accounting ...."

9. Headings: Use headings and subheadings liberally to break up your text and ease the reader's ability to follow your arguments and train of thought.
   - First-level headings should be ***UPPER CASE ITALICS***, bold face, and flush to the left margin.
     - Second level headings should be in ***Bold Face Italics***, flush to the left margin with only the first letter of each primary word capitalized.
       - Third-level headings should be flush to the left margin, in *Italics* (but not bold face), with only the first letter of each primary word capitalized.

10. Notes or Endnotes should be used only if absolutely necessary. Try to incorporate endnote/footnote material into the body of the manuscript. Notes must be identified in the text by consecutive numbers, then enclosed in square brackets and listed at the end of the article. Place them on a separate section before your references. Begin notes on a separate page, with the word "Notes" centered at the top of the page. All notes should be double-spaced; indent the first line of each note five spaces.

11. Your reference pages should appear immediately after your "Notes" section (if any) and should include only works cited in the manuscript. The first page of this section should begin with the word "References" centered on the page. References to working papers are normally not appropriate. All references must be available to the reader; however, reference to unpublished dissertations is acceptable.

**Sample Book References**

Runkel, P. J. & McGrath, J. E. (1972). *Research on human behavior: A systematic guide to method.* New York, NY: Holt, Rinehart and Winston.

Smith, P. L. (1982). Measures of variance accounted for: theory and practice. In Keren (Ed.), *Statistical and methodological issues in psychology and social science research* (pp. 101–129), Hillsdale, NJ: Erlbaum.

### Sample Journal References

Abdolmohammadi, M. J., Menon, K., Oliver, T. W., & Umpathy, S. (1985). The role of the doctoral dissertation in accounting research careers. *Issues in Accounting Education, 22*, 59–76.

Thompson, B. (1993). The use of statistical significance tests in research: Bootstrap and other methods. *Journal of Experimental Education, 61*, 361–377.

Simon, H. A. (1980). The behavioral and social sciences. *Sciences,* (July), 72–78.

### Electronic Sources

If available online, the full URL should be supplied at the end of the reference.

American Institute of Certified Public Accountants (AICPA). (1999). *Core competency framework for the accounting profession.* Retrieved from http://www.aicpa.org/edu/corecomp.htm

12. You should label TABLES and FIGURES as such and number them consecutively (using Arabic numerals) in the order in which you mention them first in the text. Indicate the approximate placement of each table/figure by a clear break in the text, inserting:

   **TABLE (or FIGURE) 1 ABOUT HERE**

   Figures should be placed after your References section and tables should follow figures. Begin each table and figure on a separate page.

13. You should list any acknowledgments on a separate page in a separate electronic file to preserve author anonymity. Type the word "Acknowledgment," centered, at the top of the page and type the acknowledgment itself as a double-spaced, single paragraph. Once the editorial review process is complete, your acknowledgments will be

inserted immediately after the last page of text (before the Notes and References Sections).

14. The proper order for sections of your manuscript should be: title page, structured abstract, main text, acknowledgments (once editorial process is complete), appendix, references, figures and finally tables.

15. After you have arranged the manuscript pages in correct order, number them consecutively, beginning with the title page. Number all pages. Place the number in the upper right-hand corner using Arabic numerals. Identify each manuscript page by typing an abbreviated title (header) above the page number.

# EDITORIAL REVIEW BOARD

# STATEMENT OF PURPOSE

*Advances in Accounting Education: Teaching and Curriculum Innovations* is a refereed academic journal whose purpose is to meet the needs of individuals interested in the educational process. We publish thoughtful, well-developed articles that are readable, relevant, and reliable.

Articles may be nonempirical or empirical. Our emphasis is pedagogy, and articles MUST explain how instructors can improve teaching methods or accounting units can improve curricula/programs.

Nonempirical manuscripts should be academically rigorous. They can be theoretical syntheses, conceptual models, position papers, discussions of methodology, comprehensive literature reviews grounded in theory, or historical discussions with implications for current and future efforts. Reasonable assumptions and logical development are essential. All manuscripts should discuss implications for research and/or teaching.

Sound research design and execution are critical for empirical reports. All articles should have well-articulated and strong theoretical foundations, and establishing a link to the non-accounting literature is desirable.

# REVIEW PROCEDURES

*Advances in Accounting Education: Teaching and Curriculum Innovations* will provide authors with timely reports that clearly indicate the review status of the manuscript. Authors will receive the results of initial reviews normally within eight to twelve weeks of manuscript submission, if not earlier. We expect authors to work with a co-editor who will act as a liaison between the authors and the reviewers to resolve areas of concern.

# AN EMPIRICAL INVESTIGATION OF STUDENT CAREER INTERESTS IN AUDITING USING THE BIG FIVE MODEL OF PERSONALITY

Travis Holt, Lisa A. Burke-Smalley and Christopher Jones

## ABSTRACT

*In this study, we use the well-researched and validated Big Five model of personality traits to examine accounting students' career interests in auditing. Using the person-job fit literature as a springboard for our study, we investigate the influence of accounting students' personality traits on their career interests in auditing using a research survey. We uncover a general "trait gap" (i.e., lack of fit) between accounting students' own personality traits and their perceptions of the ideal auditor, which presents implications for workplace readiness. Additionally, analysis focusing on students who particularly want to work in auditing indicates that those with more auditing work experience are more likely to identify auditing as their preferred job. Furthermore, results indicate*

Advances in Accounting Education: Teaching and Curriculum Innovations, Volume 20, 1–31
ISSN: 1085-4622/doi:10.1108/S1085-462220170000020002

*that accounting students higher on openness to experience tend to view auditing jobs as more desirable. Finally, accounting students who prefer the auditing career path perceive the ideal auditor as extroverted, agreeable, and open to experience. We extend prior findings in the accounting education literature surrounding personality traits and their impact on student career choices. Because advising students for a career path suiting their traits and talents is important for each student and the accounting profession, our study's insights into the "matching process" add value to career advising.*

**Keywords:** Auditing; Big Five personality model; career choice

As business evolves, so do the expectations for workplace entrants across career fields. The accounting profession has seen important and significant shifts over the last several decades, such as challenging ethical dilemmas, dramatic consequences for those engaged in fraudulent reporting, increased regulations, and changes in reporting standards. All of these factors can have an influence on those choosing to become an accounting major as well as the factors that affect their choice of various jobs in the field. The auditing profession is of particular importance given the integral and growing role that internal and external auditors play in ensuring the fair portrayal of a firm's financial position and compliance with important regulations. Indeed, a persistent challenge facing the accounting profession continues to be the recruitment of high-quality employees who are a good fit for jobs in the accounting field (Dalton, Buchheit, & McMillan, 2014).

Using the person-job fit literature as a springboard, we investigate the relationship between accounting students' personality traits and their career interests in auditing. Our goal is to illuminate and extend prior findings surrounding the critically important "matching process" between employers and college recruits. To contribute to the literature, we explore how personality factors influence job fit. While prior literature such as Dalton et al. (2014) have incorporated one aspect of personality and its relationship to job fit, our study explores personality and job fit using a multi-faceted view of personality operationalized with the Big Five model. Indeed, the Big Five model is the most widely accepted taxonomy of personality in the behavioral sciences (Digman, 1990; Goldberg, 1992), explaining about 75% of the variance in behavioral traits (Costa & McCrae, 1992). By invoking this contemporary personality model, we aim to add to the accounting education literature as well as generate meaningful practical implications for career services staff, academic advisors, faculty, and corporate recruiters who facilitate students' career choices and enhance person-job fit. Further, there is high relevance and value for external and internal recruiters in this stream of research as they desire to glean best practices for new hire interventions designed to create positive employee attitudes and enhanced person-job fit perceptions.

The next section describes the person-job fit and Big Five personality literature, and interweaves relevant prior accounting education findings when possible to develop the study's over-arching research questions. Then, we describe the design, method, and results of the study. The final section identifies study limitations and directions for future research.

# LITERATURE REVIEW AND RESEARCH QUESTIONS

## *Person-Job Fit*

The concept of person-job fit is foundational to the career management literature. Simply stated, the concept of person-job fit in the matching process refers to the relationship between individual characteristics and those of the job or tasks that are performed at work (Kristof, 1996). Conceptualizations of person-job fit usually address whether a worker's personality, preferences, and abilities fit with the career or vocation he/she is in or desires (Edwards, 1991). A recent meta-analysis to include enhanced work attitudes (i.e., higher organizational commitment, job performance and job satisfaction and lower intentions to quit) (Oh, Guay, Kim, Harold, & Lee, 2014) shows the valuable organizational outcomes associated with workers experiencing high fit. The concept originated out of Schneider's (1987) work done in the organizational behavior literature on the attraction-selection-attrition (ASA) cycle in organizations. He argued that individuals in organizations are a direct byproduct of that organization's processes used to attract, select, and retain workers. Kristof-Brown's (2000) follow-up empirical work using field data verified that person-job fit is a discernible factor used by recruiters in the hiring process and that recruiters can discriminate between applicants' person-job fit.

Bipp's (2010) research suggests individuals are motivated uniquely for work on the basis of their individual differences, which has numerous practical implications for recruiting, selection, and career management decisions. Bipp studied two different samples, students on the verge of graduation and full-time employees, and found that there were relationships between personality traits and individual preferences for certain jobs. He concluded that personality constructs in particular have applied relevance in the arena of workplace fit, which lends credence to our adaptation of the fit construct in the present research to examine accounting students' career-related perceptions. For example, based on a study of accounting interns, Tong and Tong (2012) found that person-job fit affects accounting students' career decisions (even more than perceptions of person-organization fit). Similar research utilizing the concept of fit has been done in marketing education based on a stated need to improve the recruiting process for sales students (Agnihotri, Bonney, Dixon, Erffmeyer, & Pullins, 2014).

*Research Question #1*

To explore the matching process we wanted to better understand students' self-perceived traits versus those they associate with "ideal auditors" in the workplace. Again, practical implications associated with any gap in these perceptions are important for universities to consider (as discussed later). To this end, it is notable that the Institute of Internal Auditors (IIA) and Robert Half recently published an investigation of successful auditor attributes in the contemporary workplace (Chambers & McDonald, 2013). In their report, based on in-depth interviews of chief audit executives across global companies, Chambers and McDonald (2013) conclude highly effective auditors must be naturally inquisitive and strive to continuously learn, be successful at building relationships and communicating, espouse integrity, and have a service orientation in order to respond to diverse thinking/learning styles in a team-based environment. One of the interviewed auditing executives in their study even concluded that in the recruiting and retention of successful auditing professionals "soft skills are the new hard skills" (p. 2). Thus, our first research question investigates the person-job fit process by looking for any gap in students' self-versus-other perceptions.

**Research Question 1.** For students expressing a higher interest in auditing work, are their personality traits congruent with those they perceive of ideal auditors?

## *The Big Five Personality Model*

Given that personality constructs have significant relevance in the fit literature (Schneider, 1987), next we provide background information on the widely acclaimed Big Five model of personality used in our study. Prior studies of personality in accounting education largely have used the Myers-Briggs Type Indicator (MBTI, http://www.myersbriggs.org) (see Wheeler, 2001 for a review) instead of the currently accepted Big Five model from the behavioral sciences. The MBTI includes extroversion/introversion, sensing/intuition, thinking/feeling, and perceiving/judging as personality traits that are used to classify individuals into 16 personality types. The instrument has been used in accounting education literature. For example, Laribee (1994) examined undergraduate accounting students and found that students possessed the traits of sensing, thinking, and judging. Wolk and Nikolai (1997) found accounting students to be significantly more extroverted, sensing, and feeling than accounting faculty. Swain and Olsen (2012) conducted a longitudinal study of personality types of accounting students as they progressed into the accounting profession; similar to prior work, their results indicated that accounting students/professionals tend to exhibit sensing and judging traits, suggesting they pay attention to information coming through their senses (versus looking for patterns) and like having things decided rather than staying open to new information. More recently, Dalton et al. (2014) compared students' perceptions versus practitioners' perceptions — in accounting as well as tax — using the theory of planned behavior and included one personality trait, extroversion/introversion, which is a trait that the MBTI and the Big Five model share. They found that students choosing the audit profession perceived greater client interaction, career advancement opportunities, and understanding of how businesses work than those students electing tax careers.

Nonetheless, most scholars in the behavioral sciences have embraced the Five-Factor Model of personality (Big Five) as a replicable and unifying taxonomy of personality (e.g., Digman, 1990; Goldberg, 1992). This model has received evidence of validity across different occupations, cultures, and sources of ratings (De Raad & Doddema-Winsemius, 1999;

John & Srivastava, 1999), and as such, is widely used in contemporary organizational research. In this framework, conscientiousness, emotional stability (often referred to in terms of negative emotional stability or neuroticism), agreeableness, openness to experience, and extroversion/introversion are five distinct traits that predict workplace attitudes and behaviors. Several studies indicate that personality tests can account for significant incremental validity when predicting employee performance, beyond that accounted for by biodata (e.g., McManus & Kelly, 1999), mental ability (McHenry, Hough, Toquam, Hanson, & Ashworth, 1990), and interviews (e.g., Cortina, Goldstein, Payne, Davison, & Gilliland, 2000).

Meta-analytic studies have shown that two of the Big Five constructs, conscientiousness and (to a somewhat lesser extent) emotional stability, predict job performance across most jobs (e.g., Barrick, Mount, & Judge, 2001; Salgado, 1997). Other Big Five constructs tend to be more relevant in specific jobs; for example, extroversion tends to predict success in sales careers (Barrick et al., 2001). As such, it is possible that the specialized or niche career field of auditing may allow for other components of the Big Five (e.g., agreeableness, openness, and extroversion) to evidence themselves. Next, each of the five-factor model variables is reviewed.

### Conscientiousness

Workers high in conscientiousness are predisposed to be organized, exacting, disciplined, diligent, dependable, and methodical (McCrae & Costa, 1989). They are likely to perform work tasks thoroughly, to take initiative in solving problems, to remain committed to work performance, to comply with policies, and to stay focused on work tasks. Conscientiousness tends to be associated with more advantages in the workplace (e.g., reliability, dependability, work ethic) than disadvantages (e.g., lower adaptability to new situations, Viswesvaran, Deller, & Ones, 2007). Prior research supports the conscientiousness–performance link, including the classic Barrick and Mount (1991) meta-analysis conducted across five occupational groups that showed the stable predictive power of conscientiousness across three performance variables. Gellatly (1996) also illustrated that conscientiousness relates to job performance, although mean validity coefficients typically are moderate (e.g., $r = .02$ to $.23$, depending on the criteria; Hough, Eaton, Dunnette, Kemp, & McCloy, 1990). Research has revealed that managers perceive cognitive ability and conscientiousness as the most important attributes related to applicant hirability (Dunn, Mount, Barrick, & Ones, 1995).

*Neuroticism (Emotional Stability)*

Neuroticism taps an individual's degree of emotional stability. Emotionally unstable people tend to be anxious, tense, and prone to worry; they also can be moody and have irrational and perfectionistic beliefs (McCrae & John, 1992). They are more likely to report distress over time even in the absence of any overt or objective source of stress (Watson & Clark, 1984). Two meta-analytic reviews have indicated a positive relationship between emotional stability and job performance (Salgado, 1997; Tett, Jackson, & Rothstein, 1991). Emotionally stable people tend to be better overall job performers, be more effective leaders, exhibit lower turnover, and report higher levels of job satisfaction (Viswesvaran et al., 2007). However, they also tend to be less capable of identifying threats in their environment and more likely to engage in risky behaviors (Berry, Ones, & Sackett, 2007).

*Agreeableness*

Agreeableness (Hogan, 1986) refers to such traits as selflessness, cooperativeness, helpfulness, tolerance, flexibility, generosity, sympathy, and courtesy (Digman, 1990). "Agreeableness contrasts a prosocial and communal orientation toward others with antagonism and includes traits such as altruism, tender-mindedness, trust, and modesty" (John & Srivastava, 1999, p. 121). Individuals high in agreeableness believe in cooperation, and have forgiving attitudes (McCrae & Costa, 1999). This Big Five variable appears to be most relevant to job performance in situations where joint action and collaboration are needed (Mount, Barrick, & Stewart, 1998), such as in audit teams (Dalton et al., 2014). Work contexts having a fairly high level of interpersonal interaction require selflessness, tolerance, and flexibility, and agreeable persons tend to deal with conflict cooperatively or collaboratively, strive for common understanding and maintain social affiliations (Digman, 1990). There are however several potential downsides of being too agreeable at work; for example, individuals high in agreeableness may experience lower career success and generally are less able to deal directly with conflict (Berry et al., 2007).

*Openness to Experience*

The conceptual nature of openness suggests a close relationship with such other dispositional traits such as creativity, inquisitiveness, unconventionality, autonomy, intellectance, and change acceptance (Goldberg, 1992; McCrae & John, 1992). Persons who are more open to experience are likely to exhibit tendencies of particular value in contemporary work environments, such as positively viewing workplace transitions (Wanberg & Banas,

2000), creatively thinking of ideas in dynamic ways, and remaining open to alternatives. Furthermore, openness has been demonstrated as predictive of training proficiency (e.g., Salgado, 1997). Not being stifled by tradition or social conformity norms (Judge, Higgins, Thoresen, & Barrick, 1999), individuals who are more open to experience prefer to generate insights independently. However, they also may be less committed to an employer (Berry et al., 2007).

Ones and Viswesvaran (1999) studied a sample of 96 managers with expatriate staffing experience, who made judgments about 32 expatriates based on Big Five characteristics; openness to experience was perceived to be important for the completion of overseas assignments. Bing and Lounsbury (2000) researched 113 team leaders and supervisors in a U.S.-based Japanese manufacturing firm, which emphasized team-building, and they found that openness predicted unique variance in job performance, above-and-beyond both cognitive aptitude and the other Big Five traits. These findings suggest the importance of openness in certain settings, particularly when work is not "black and white." Given that audit work is often ambiguous (Dalton et al., 2014), openness may be perceived as important in the audit profession.

*Extroversion/Introversion*

Extroversion is predictive of performance in jobs and tasks steeped in social contact (Frei & McDaniel, 1998; Mount et al., 1998), such as sales. Individuals high in extroversion tend to become energized in social settings, whereas introverts lose energy in social situations. Extroverts tend to be more likely to emerge as leaders and report higher levels of job satisfaction, but they also may tend to have higher absenteeism in the workplace (Berry et al., 2007). Trainees who were highly sociable (extroverted) in Barrick and Mount's classic work (1991) also exhibited higher training performance. For example, Lemke, Leicht, and Miller (1974) found in a study of 64 undergraduates – stratified by ability and extroversion – that a low-ability trainee is not likely to develop a solution strategy on his or her own, and thus the presence of an extrovert in a training group may increase the verbalization of training transfer strategies.

Interestingly, Dalton et al. (2014) found that neither auditing students nor auditing professionals reported being significantly more extroverted than their tax counterparts. This finding goes against the stereotype of auditors as extroverted so perhaps the present exploration will shed light on the role of extroversion/introversion in accounting students' career perceptions of auditing professionals.

Since our accounting education study is one of the first to use the Big Five model, our investigation into personality traits is largely exploratory. Nonetheless, in our literature review we tried to interweave (when available) prior accounting education findings to help make predictions of what we may uncover regarding our research questions. More specifically, to take a deeper dive into the matching process, we examine the Big Five personality traits associated with accounting students' interest in auditing work, and to get a sense of accounting students' fit for professional auditing work we examine their perceptions of "ideal" auditor traits.

**Research Question 2.** Are there certain Big Five personality traits associated with accounting students who desire a career in auditing?

**Research Question 3.** Are there certain Big Five personality traits accounting students associate with their perception of an ideal auditor?

# METHODOLOGY

*Sample and Procedures*

We surveyed anonymously a sample of 139 students enrolled in intermediate accounting classes across two AACSB-accredited business schools, located in the Southeastern and Midwestern United States, to enhance the generalizability of our findings.[1] We administered the research survey to accounting majors[2] over the course of four semesters, but any student who took the survey previously was asked not to complete it again. The survey garnered both universities' Human Subjects approval and was voluntary. Across all administrations, students completed the surveys and placed them in an envelope without the instructor present.

*Measures*

*Personality Measures*
We measured each of the Big Five factors of personality using the International Personality Item Pool (Goldberg, 1999; IPIP, 2001), a scale commonly used in other behavioral science research (e.g., Aguinis,

Mazurkiewicz, & Heggestad, 2009; Liao, Joshi, & Chuang, 2004).[3] We assessed each dimension on a five-point Likert scale via 10 items anchored by "very inaccurate" to "very accurate." The Cronbach alphas found in prior research are as follows: Conscientiousness: 0.79; Openness to Experience: 0.84; Emotional Stability: 0.86; Extroversion: 0.87; and Agreeableness: 0.82 (Goldberg, 1999).

We first asked students to assess the 50-item personality questionnaire based on the question: "To what extent do the following statements accurately describe you?" The questionnaire is included in the appendix. The first 10 items assessed the extroversion dimension, with subsequent groupings of 10 items measuring agreeableness, conscientiousness, neuroticism, and openness to experience, respectively. We reverse-worded multiple items within each personality dimension to test for measure consistency. We used the averages of the 10 items within each personality dimension for data analysis.

After assessing the students' Big Five personality traits, we presented students with a summary of the job responsibilities auditors perform, which stated: "Auditors examine the financial information of a company to ensure that the information is reasonably stated. In addition, auditors often provide recommendations to management to improve operations, risk management, and internal controls." After reading the information, students assessed an additional 50-item personality questionnaire that tapped their perceptions of auditors' personality traits, in response to the question: "To what extent would the following statements describe the ideal auditor?"

We present descriptive statistics for the personality measures in Table 1. We found evidence of internal consistency for the Big Five personality measures with Cronbach's alpha exceeding 0.70 for all of the traits, consistent with prior research (e.g., Goldberg, 1999). The mean measures for students' Big Five personality traits were 3.05, 3.89, 3.94, 2.65, and 3.63 for extroversion, agreeableness, conscientiousness, neuroticism, and openness to experience, respectively. The mean measure for student perceptions of the personality traits of the "ideal auditor" were 3.42, 3.31, 4.67, 2.26, and 3.91 for extroversion, agreeableness, conscientiousness, neuroticism, and openness to experience, respectively.

*Auditing Job Interest Measure*
We also surveyed students' view of auditing as a preferred career choice. Specifically, students were asked to what extent auditing would describe their "ideal job." We assessed this measure (IdealJobAud) on a five-point Likert scale anchored by "strongly disagree" (1) to "strongly agree" (5), with a mean, as reported in Table 1, of 3.57. This assessment indicated that

***Table 1.*** Descriptive Statistics.

|  | Mean | Std. Deviation | Cronbach's $\alpha$ |
|---|---|---|---|
| YouExt | 3.05 | 0.772 | 0.879 |
| YouAgr | 3.89 | 0.667 | 0.858 |
| YouCon | 3.94 | 0.649 | 0.838 |
| YouNeur | 2.65 | 0.842 | 0.898 |
| YouOpen | 3.63 | 0.537 | 0.730 |
| AudExt | 3.42 | 0.724 | 0.864 |
| AudAgr | 3.31 | 0.655 | 0.807 |
| AudCon | 4.67 | 0.448 | 0.826 |
| AudNeur | 2.26 | 0.699 | 0.866 |
| AudOpen | 3.91 | 0.588 | 0.813 |
| AudWorkExp | 0.06 | 0.400 | |
| AcctWorkExp | 0.80 | 1.627 | |
| IdealJobAud | 3.57 | 1.214 | |

Variables are defined as follows:

YouExt, YouAgr, YouCon, YouNeur, YouOpen are the averages of students' personality self-assessments of questions related to the extroversion, agreeableness, conscientiousness, neuroticism, and openness personality dimensions, respectively.

AudExt, AudAgr, AudCon, AudNeur, AudOpen are the averages of students' personality assessments of questions related to the extroversion, agreeableness, conscientiousness, neuroticism, and openness personality dimensions, respectively, of the ideal auditor.

AudWorkExp is the number of years of auditing work experience.

AcctWorkExp is the number of years of accounting work experience.

IdealJobAud is a measure of to what extent (1−5) auditing describes the student's ideal job.

students overall agreed that auditing described their ideal job, as the mean was significantly greater than the "neutral" position of three ($p < 0.001$).

To test our Research Questions, we divided the sample into two groups based upon the degree to which auditing represented students' ideal job (IdealJobAud). For testing purposes, we placed accounting students with an IdealJobAud < 3 ($n = 26$) in the group of students not desiring a job in auditing, and we placed students with an IdealJobAud > 2 ($n = 113$) in the group of students desiring a job in auditing.[4]

*Demographic Measures*

We collected demographic variables for sample description and exploring differences in personality measures. In terms of demographics, 46% of respondents were female and 54% were male, with a student mean age of 23.8 years. Students in the sample reported on average a 3.44 overall cumulative GPA and a 3.50 major GPA. Additionally, respondents had an average of around six years of total work experience, with less than a year on average of both audit and accounting work experience. One-sample $t$-tests revealed that the means for both audit work experience and accounting work experience were significantly greater than zero ($p < 0.05$). Statistical tests revealed no significant differences in the means of the demographic variables among students across the different universities involved in the study.

# RESULTS

## *Correlations*

Table 2 reports the Spearman correlations for the study's measures. Pearson correlations (not reported) yielded similar results. The correlations indicate that age and gender had no statistically significant relationship to students' desire to work in auditing. Students exhibiting higher ratings for openness to experience had a greater desire to work in auditing ($r = 0.196$, $p = 0.02$). Students with a higher desire to work in auditing perceived an ideal auditor as open to experience, agreeable, conscientious, low on neuroticism, and extroverted — which we note is compatible with the description of successful auditors in the aforementioned IIA and Robert Half report (Chambers & McDonald, 2013).

The correlational results also indicate relationships between students' prior accounting and auditing work experience and their desire to work in auditing. Students with work experience specifically in auditing were more likely to view auditing as an ideal job ($r = 0.266$, $p = 0.002$); however, it is important to note that students with general accounting work experience (e.g., bookkeeping, payroll clerk) were significantly less likely to view auditing as their ideal job.

## *Person-Job Fit Differences*

### *Research Question 1*

Research Question 1 focuses on those students expressing a higher interest in audit work and assesses if this desire is congruent with the personality traits they perceive for an ideal auditor. For Research Question 1, we focused on a subset of our sample who expressed a notably higher interest

**Table 2.** Bivariate Correlation Matrix.

| | (1) | (2) | (3) | (4) | (5) | (6) | (7) | (8) | (9) | (10) | (11) | (12) | (13) | (14) |
|---|---|---|---|---|---|---|---|---|---|---|---|---|---|---|
| (1) Age | | | | | | | | | | | | | | |
| (2) Gender | -0.010<br>0.905 | | | | | | | | | | | | | |
| (3) YouExt | -0.015<br>0.858 | -0.328<br>*<0.001* | | | | | | | | | | | | |
| (4) YouAgr | -0.144<br>0.093 | 0.376<br>*<0.001* | 0.162<br>0.057 | | | | | | | | | | | |
| (5) YouCon | 0.011<br>0.901 | 0.157<br>0.066 | 0.005<br>0.952 | 0.192<br>*0.023* | | | | | | | | | | |
| (6) YouNeur | 0.075<br>0.384 | 0.251<br>*0.003* | -0.320<br>*<0.001* | -0.078<br>0.361 | -0.108<br>0.205 | | | | | | | | | |
| (7) YouOpen | 0.053<br>0.537 | -0.144<br>0.090 | 0.175<br>*0.040* | 0.054<br>0.525 | 0.176<br>*0.038* | -0.232<br>*0.006* | | | | | | | | |
| (8) AudExt | 0.088<br>0.302 | 0.090<br>0.100 | 0.023<br>0.785 | 0.095<br>0.267 | -0.045<br>0.597 | 0.033<br>0.696 | -0.006<br>0.942 | | | | | | | |
| (9) AudAgr | 0.085<br>0.320 | 0.100<br>0.240 | 0.028<br>0.744 | 0.082<br>0.336 | 0.128<br>0.133 | -0.054<br>0.528 | 0.205<br>*0.016* | 0.294<br>*<0.001* | | | | | | |
| (10) AudCon | 0.103<br>0.232 | 0.169<br>*0.047* | -0.154<br>*0.070* | 0.133<br>0.118 | 0.276<br>*0.001* | -0.105<br>0.217 | 0.268<br>*0.001* | -0.035<br>0.684 | 0.112<br>0.190 | | | | | |
| (11) AudNeur | -0.029<br>0.734 | 0.013<br>0.878 | 0.019<br>0.824 | 0.024<br>0.781 | -0.008<br>0.922 | 0.328<br>*<0.001* | -0.138<br>0.105 | -0.319<br>*<0.001* | -0.249<br>*0.003* | -0.251<br>*0.003* | | | | |
| (12) AudOpen | 0.022<br>0.800 | 0.139<br>0.103 | -0.032<br>0.712 | 0.123<br>0.151 | 0.201<br>*0.018* | 0.002<br>0.984 | 0.332<br>*<0.001* | 0.395<br>*<0.001* | 0.366<br>*<0.001* | 0.341<br>*<0.001* | -0.321<br>*<0.001* | | | |
| (13) AudWorkExp | 0.056<br>0.519 | 0.060<br>0.483 | 0.027<br>0.753 | 0.004<br>0.962 | -0.032<br>0.715 | -0.042<br>0.629 | 0.110<br>0.202 | 0.129<br>0.134 | 0.004<br>0.960 | 0.166<br>0.053 | -0.143<br>0.096 | 0.055<br>0.526 | | |
| (14) AcctWorkExp | 0.181<br>*0.034* | 0.240<br>*0.005* | -0.069<br>0.422 | 0.072<br>0.399 | 0.119<br>0.166 | -0.009<br>0.918 | 0.056<br>0.517 | -0.086<br>0.318 | -0.073<br>0.397 | 0.026<br>0.758 | 0.004<br>0.966 | -0.091<br>0.288 | 0.159<br>0.064 | |
| (15) IdealJobAud | -0.102<br>0.234 | -0.091<br>0.288 | 0.054<br>0.531 | 0.024<br>0.780 | 0.054<br>0.526 | -0.080<br>0.352 | 0.196<br>*0.021* | 0.187<br>*0.028* | 0.242<br>*0.004* | 0.171<br>*0.045* | -0.291<br>*0.001* | 0.370<br>*<0.001* | 0.266<br>*0.002* | -0.195<br>*0.022* |

*Notes:* Spearman correlations are reported. Pearson correlations (not reported) yield qualitatively similar results. Two-tailed significance levels are reported below the correlation coefficients. Significant *p*-values are in bolded italics. See Table 1 for variable definitions. Gender is coded as 1 for male, 2 for female.

in an auditing career path ($n$ = 113). We examined whether their self-reported individual personality traits were different from their perceptions of model auditors' personality traits. We report the paired sample $t$-test results in Panel A of Table 3, and results indicate significant differences for all five personality traits. More specifically, our results indicate that those accounting students who particularly desire to work in auditing are more agreeable and neurotic ($p < 0.001$) than their perceptions of the model auditor, as well as less extroverted, less conscientious, and less open to experience ($p < 0.001$). Similar results were found when running the test with only accounting students who had work experience and when running the test with accounting students who had work experience and were interested in auditing. The gap between their personal perceptions and their perceptions of ideal auditors were significant for all five traits at the 0.05 significance-level in each of these additional tests.

To explore this research question further, we performed a multivariate analysis to test whether students' perceptions of the Big Five personality traits of the ideal auditor are related to their interest in auditing. We used the following multivariate regression model:

$$IdealJobAud_i = b_0 + b_1 AudExt + b_2 AudAgr + b_3 AudCon + b_4 AudNeur \\ + b_5 AudOpen + b_6 AudWork + b_7 AcctWork + e_i$$

IdealJobAud = extent that auditing would describe students' ideal job (3–5)
AudExt = mean student perceptions of ideal auditor extroversion
AudAgr = mean student perceptions of ideal auditor agreeableness
AudCon = mean student perceptions of ideal auditor conscientiousness
AudNeur = mean student perceptions of ideal auditor neuroticism
AudOpen = mean student perceptions of ideal auditor openness
AudWorkExp = number of years of audit work experience
AcctWorkExp = number of years of accounting work experience.

We present the regression results in Panel B of Table 3. The model is significant ($F = 4.55$; $p < 0.001$), indicating that students who perceived auditors as more open to experience ($p = 0.009$), and less neurotic ($p = 0.008$), had a greater desire to work in auditing. Interestingly, although overall accounting work experience was *not* significantly related to student desires to work in auditing, students with more auditing work experience reported a higher desire to work in auditing ($p = 0.044$).

***Table 3.*** Analysis of Personality Traits of Students Desiring Auditing Jobs.

Panel A: Differences between Students' Personality Traits and Their Perceptions of Ideal Auditor

| | Student | Ideal Auditor | *t*-Stat. | *p*-Value |
|---|---|---|---|---|
| Extroversion | 3.07 | 3.50 | −4.968 | *<0.001* |
| Agreeableness | 3.91 | 3.37 | 6.875 | *<0.001* |
| Conscientiousness | 3.96 | 4.66 | −10.541 | *<0.001* |
| Neuroticism | 2.62 | 2.21 | 5.005 | *<0.001* |
| Openness | 3.66 | 3.99 | −5.473 | *<0.001* |

Panel B: Multivariate Regression Analysis: Perceptions of Auditors

$$\text{IdealJobAud}_i = b_0 + b_1\text{AudExt} + b_2\text{AudAgr} + b_3\text{AudCon} + b_4\text{AudNeur} + b_5\text{AudOpen} + b_6\text{AudWorkExp} + b_7\text{AcctWorkExp} + e_i$$

| Variable | Coeff. | *t*-Stat. | *p*-Value |
|---|---|---|---|
| Intercept | 3.167 | 3.36 | *0.001* |
| AudExt | −0.195 | −1.73 | 0.087 |
| AudAgr | 0.087 | 0.80 | 0.425 |
| AudCon | 0.085 | 0.54 | 0.591 |
| AudNeur | −0.291 | −2.70 | *0.008* |
| AudOpen | 0.364 | 2.66 | *0.009* |
| AudWorkExp | 0.311 | 2.04 | *0.044* |
| AcctWorkExp | 0.061 | 0.93 | 0.354 |
| Observations | 109 | | |
| *F*-value/*p* | 4.55 | *<0.001* | |
| Adjusted $R^2$ (%) | 18.5 | | |

Panel C: Multivariate Regression Analysis: Student Self-Assessments

$$\text{IdealJobAud}_i = b_0 + b_1\text{YouExt} + b_2\text{YouAgr} + b_3\text{YouCon} + b_4\text{YouNeur} + b_5\text{YouOpen} + b_6\text{AudWorkExp} + b_7\text{AcctWorkExp} + e_i$$

| Variable | Coeff. | *t*-Stat. | *p*-Value |
|---|---|---|---|
| Intercept | 3.871 | 4.70 | *<0.001* |
| YouExt | −0.085 | −0.82 | 0.416 |
| YouAgr | −0.007 | −0.06 | 0.950 |
| YouCon | −0.123 | −1.08 | 0.282 |
| YouNeur | −0.018 | −0.92 | 0.848 |
| YouOpen | 0.255 | 1.85 | 0.067 |
| AudWorkExp | 0.335 | 2.05 | *0.043* |
| AcctWorkExp | 0.047 | 0.65 | 0.517 |
| Observations | 109 | | |
| *F*-value/*p* | 1.51 | 0.172 | |
| Adjusted $R^2$ (%) | 3.2 | | |

*Notes*: Panel A tests for differences in means are based on paired sample *t*-tests. Nonparametric Wilcoxon rank sum tests (not reported) yield qualitatively similar results. Reported *p*-values signify two-tailed significance levels. *p*-values below 0.05 are in bolded italics. See Table 1 for variable definitions.

*Personality Trait Differences*

*Research Question 2*

Research Question 2 ascertains what personality traits are associated with accounting students who desire a career in auditing. To test this question, we first performed a multivariate analysis on our sample subset of students wanting a job in auditing to test whether students' Big Five personality traits of the ideal auditor are related to their interest in auditing. We used the following multivariate regression model:

$$\text{IdealJobAud}_i = b_0 + b_1\text{YouExt} + b_2\text{YouAgr} + b_3\text{YouCon} + b_4\text{YouNeur} \\ + b_5\text{YouOpen} + b_6\text{AudWork} + b_7\text{AcctWork} + e_i$$

IdealJobAud = extent that auditing would describe students' ideal job (3–5)
YouExt = mean student extroversion
YouAgr = mean student agreeableness
YouCon = mean student conscientiousness
YouNeur = mean student neuroticism
YouOpen = mean student openness
AudWorkExp = number of years of audit work experience
AcctWorkExp = number of years of accounting work experience.

We present the regression results in Panel C of Table 3. While the results indicate significant coefficients for student openness and audit work experience ($p = 0.067$ and $0.043$, respectively), the overall model is not significant ($F = 1.51$; $p = 0.172$).

Next, we conducted analysis on our entire sample of accounting students. Panel A of Table 4 reports comparisons among the Big Five personality traits of the sample of accounting students not desiring to work in auditing versus those students that do want a job in auditing. The independent sample $t$-test results suggest that students wanting to work in auditing tend to be more open to experience ($p = 0.07$) than those who do not want to work in auditing (although not at the 0.05 convention). Interestingly, there were no statistical differences in conscientiousness or emotional stability (i.e., the two traits that are most predictive in Big Five studies), and so it appears our study of this niche career field is revealing other differences.

*Research Question 3*

Research Question 3 ascertains if perceived personality traits of an ideal auditor differ for those students who express a higher desire for a career as auditors than those students who do not. To test Research Question 3, we

***Table 4.*** Personality Trait Comparisons of All Students.

Panel A: Personality Differences between Students Desiring to Work in Auditing versus Those Who Do Not

|  | Not Desiring Audit Job | Desiring Audit Job | $t$-Stat. | $p$-Value |
|---|---|---|---|---|
| Extroversion | 2.96 | 3.07 | −0.688 | 0.492 |
| Agreeableness | 3.83 | 3.91 | −0.638 | 0.527 |
| Conscientiousness | 3.85 | 3.96 | −0.743 | 0.462 |
| Neuroticism | 2.81 | 2.62 | 1.005 | 0.321 |
| Openness | 3.47 | 3.66 | −1.844 | *0.072* |

Panel B: Differences in Perceived Auditor Personality Traits between Students Desiring to Work in Auditing versus Those Who Do Not

|  | Not Desiring Audit Job | Desiring Audit Job | $t$-Stat. | $p$-Value |
|---|---|---|---|---|
| Extroversion | 3.07 | 3.50 | −2.863 | *0.005* |
| Agreeableness | 3.10 | 3.37 | −2.246 | *0.029* |
| Conscientiousness | 4.69 | 4.66 | 0.276 | 0.783 |
| Neuroticism | 2.45 | 2.21 | 1.570 | 0.125 |
| Openness | 3.57 | 3.99 | −3.332 | *0.002* |

*Notes*: Tests for differences in means are based on independent sample $t$-tests. Nonparametric Mann-Whitney U tests (not reported) yield qualitatively similar results. Reported $p$-values signify two-tailed significance levels. $p$-values below 0.05 are in bolded italics. See Table 1 for variable definitions.

compared how students between the two groups perceived the personality traits of auditors. Panel B of Table 4 reports the results of those independent sample $t$-test comparisons. Specifically, students desiring a job in auditing perceived auditors as being more agreeable ($p = 0.029$), more open to experience ($p = 0.002$), and more extroverted ($p = 0.005$), compared to students not wanting to work in auditing. Again, students' perceptions of successful auditors seem largely to mimic the portrait painted by chief auditing executives (Chambers & McDonald, 2013).

# CONCLUSION

## *Discussion and Implications*

The objective of this chapter was to explore the influence of personality traits on accounting students' career interest in auditing. The tests we performed indicated that for those accounting students who particularly desire a career in auditing, there exists a notable gap in how they perceive their *own* personality traits versus those of successful auditors. Additionally, we found that students with more auditing experience were more likely to desire to work in auditing.

We also found in the overall sample that students who were higher on openness to experience more highly viewed auditing as their ideal job. Finally, we examined how accounting students view the model or "ideal" auditor based on the Big Five personality traits. Students desiring a job in auditing perceived auditors as more open to experience, agreeable, and extroverted — a portrait that is again consistent with the IIA report on successful auditors (Chambers & McDonald, 2013).

Interesting practical implications based on these findings begin to emerge for advisers, faculty, recruiters, and employers regarding accounting students. Although students appear to have compatible views with top audit executives regarding successful auditor attributes, they do not (yet) view *themselves* as espousing such traits. Furthermore, we find that audit work experience does not ameliorate these results. These findings suggest colleges of business may have notable work to do in terms of accounting students' career preparation to enhance students' overall workplace readiness, an observation well-established in the extant literature (Casner-Lotto, Rosenblum, & Wright, 2009; McLester & McIntire, 2006). Indeed, those accounting programs that incorporate relevant experiences (Kolb, 2014) and learning centered on the skills and attributes necessary for success in the workplace could garner a competitive advantage in placing top accounting students.

More specifically, to enhance the possibility of person-job fit, we contend that exposing students to auditing internships as well as to a range of auditing professionals during their education, as mock interviewers, business mentors, intern supervisors, adjunct or part-time instructors, etc., could help effectively shape students' experiential learning (Kolb, 2014). This recommendation is consistent with the long-supported social learning theory (Bandura, 1963), which claims that much of human behavior is learned from modeling others, and the concept of socialization, in which we internalize the attitudes, values, and beliefs from our immediate context to develop our "sense of self." It is worth noting that prior accounting education studies have found superficial exchanges between recruiters and accounting students may not be "strong" enough to have lasting impact on student attitudes (e.g., Bundy & Norris, 1992); thus, accounting programs should target the most immersive experiences possible to develop their students effectively. For example, an auditing guest speaker will likely have a lesser impact on a student's career perceptions than a longer term mentoring relationship would provide.

Based on our findings, we also suggest that recruiters and employers seeking to fill auditing positions aim to design internship programs and other socialization practices (e.g., onboarding, job shadowing, and realistic job previews) that inculcate congruent values and attitudes to prospective full-time hires. That is, from the first encounter employers have with interns, mentees and job applicants, employers should be mindful of the influence they have on shaping students' career interests. This recommendation is notably reinforced by our finding that students with previous *auditing* work experience are more likely to view auditing as their ideal career choice. In other words, consistent with other accounting education studies that report on the critical influence prior experience has on accounting students' job choices (e.g., Bundy & Norris, 1992), the type of preprofessional work experience students acquire appears to have a key influence on their career interests, which is of particular concern to employers and recruiters.

Our personality trait results have practical implications for CPA firms who wish to identify accounting students who are interested in auditing. Because researchers have found that organizational socialization tactics are positively related to students' person-job fit perceptions (Saks & Gruman, 2011), employers who work to emphasize openness during the recruiting and onboarding processes should enhance worker fit and subsequent workplace outcomes. For example, recruiters could look for accounting students who demonstrate traits associated with openness to experience in structured behavioral interviews or on Big Five personality assessments (such as http://ipip.ori.org/) administered during the initial selection process (Seol & Sarkis, 2005). Behavioral interviews (see Fernández-Aráoz, Groysberg, & Nohria, 2009) could attempt to tap students' degree of willingness to tackle new problems or willingness to learn new skills, as those students likely will view the auditing profession more positively, and according to auditing executives, be more successful in their auditing careers (Chambers & McDonald, 2013).

Our personality trait findings also have implications for campus advising and career services staff, as it suggests which students might be a better match for an auditing career. For example, upon administering available personality inventories and career values assessments in the career advising process (Gordon, 2007), advisors could better identify those students who envision their work life to include socially interacting with others, closely collaborating with others (inside and outside the firm), and continuous learning opportunities. This finding also may have implications for recruiters and managers in auditing functions who initially solicit campus job seekers, as they may want to provide students with examples from their organization of auditing tasks that provide new hires various opportunities for interacting with various stakeholders and working cooperatively on tasks.

### Limitations and Future Research Ideas

As with any study, there are several potential limitations as well as un-answered questions that could be explored in future research. One potential limitation is a paper-based instrument that asked participants their version of an ideal auditor after asking the participants questions about their own personality traits. It is possible that students were biased when responding to their ideal view of the auditor in light of their own self-assessed personality traits. A second potential limitation is that this study examined only the auditing career choice. We do not know whether the potential links between personality attributes and desire to work in auditing hold for those students who wished to pursue accounting careers in tax, managerial/cost, govern-mental, or academia. Future research could examine links between personal-ity attributes and the desire to work in fields of accounting other than audit.

Further, the cross-sectional survey was administered only at one point in time to the students. Future research could administer a similar question-naire at multiple points in time to see when students begin to form their opinions of model auditors and their desire to work in auditing. In terms of other future research opportunities, researchers have investigated the potential interaction of several different personality measures. According to Armstrong and Rounds (2010, p. 143):

> In recent years, there has been a call for integration across domains of individual differ-ences measurement. Although researchers who study an individual differences domain, such as interests, personality, abilities, or values, tend to focus on only one set of con-structs at a time, they have also realized that a more effective understanding of how individuals adjust to their environments will emerge when multiple areas are assessed simultaneously.

Employers have a vested interest in identifying and developing their new hires' person-job fit and so future research in the accounting literature could explore how students' desire for work/life flexibility or their value of advance-ment potential interacts with their personality traits when deciding to pursue auditing as a career choice. Other research ideas include investigating stu-dents' perceptions of campus recruiters' interviewing and branding strategies to ascertain whether certain strategies affect accounting students' initial and lasting impressions, or ultimate job selection decisions. Researchers also could interview students before and after they select their first auditing job to determine whether the students logically considered recruiter messaging, or more spontaneously responded to recruiters' sales attempts. Any of these studies would be of value to faculty, college career services and placement staff, and employers to better understand accounting students' career choices in the highly competitive contemporary labor market.

# NOTES

1. Five of the 139 intermediate accounting students reported that they were not accounting majors. The study's results were statistically similar when those students were excluded.
2. Although we located research that suggests gender (Luzzo, 2011) may influence career attitudes and career decision making, we did not uncover research that implied the same for masters/undergraduate status. Thus, gathering data from both levels of students broadens the generalizability of our findings.
3. The IPIP is a website that has scales for measuring numerous personality traits. The website address is ipip.ori.org
4. The results are statistically similar when students with the neutral position of an IdealJobAud of 3 ($n = 29$) are removed from the analysis.

# REFERENCES

Agnihotri, R., Bonney, L., Dixon, A., Erffmeyer, R., & Pullins, E. (2014). Developing a stakeholder approach for recruiting top-level sales students. *Journal of Marketing Education*, *36*(1), 75.

Aguinis, H., Mazurkiewicz, M., & Heggestad, E. (2009). Using web-based frame-of-reference training to decrease biases in personality-based job analysis: An experimental field study. *Personnel Psychology*, *62*, 405–438.

Armstrong, P. I., & Rounds, J. (2010). Integrating individual differences in career assessment: The atlas model of individual differences and the strong ring. *The Career Development Quarterly*, *59*(2), 143–153.

Bandura, A. (1963). *Social learning and personality development*. New York, NY: Holt, Rinehart, and Winston.

Barrick, M. R., & Mount, M. K. (1991). The Big Five personality dimensions and performance: A meta-analyses. *Personnel Psychology*, *44*, 1–26.

Barrick, M. R., Mount, M. K., & Judge, T. A. (2001). Personality and performance at the beginning of the new millennium: What do we know and where do we go next? *International Journal of Selection and Assessment*, *9*(1), 9–30.

Berry, C., Ones, D., & Sackett, P. (2007). Interpersonal deviance, organizational deviance, and their common correlates: A review and meta analysis. *Journal of Applied Psychology, 92,* 410–424.

Bing, M. N., & Lounsbury, J. W. (2000). Openness and job performance in U.S.-based Japanese manufacturing companies. *Journal of Business and Psychology, 14,* 515–522.

Bipp, T. (2010). What do people want from their jobs? The Big Five, core self-evaluations and work motivation. *International Journal of Selection and Assessment, 18*(1), 28–39.

Bundy, P., & Norris, D. (1992). What accounting students consider important in the job selection process. *Journal of Applied Business Research, 8*(2), 1–6.

Casner-Lotto, J., Rosenblum, E., & Wright, M. (2009). *The ill-prepared US workforce: Exploring the challenges of employer-provided workforce readiness training.* New York, NY: The Conference Board, Inc.

Chambers, R., & McDonald, P. (2013). *Succeeding as a 21st century internal auditor: 7 Attributes of highly effective internal auditors* (pp. 1–12). Menlo Park, CA: Robert Half International Inc. and The Institute of Internal Auditors.

Cortina, J. M., Goldstein, N. B., Payne, S. C., Davison, H. K., & Gilliland, S. W. (2000). The incremental validity of interview scores over and above cognitive ability and conscientiousness scores. *Personnel Psychology, 53,* 325–352.

Costa, P., & McCrae, R. (1992). Four ways five factors are basic. *Personality and Individual Differences, 13,* 653–665.

Dalton, D. W., Buchheit, S., & McMillan, J. J. (2014). Audit and tax career paths in public accounting: An analysis of student and professional perceptions. *Accounting Horizons, 28*(2), 213–231.

De Raad, B., & Doddema-Winsemius, M. (1999). Instincts and personality. *Personality & Individual Differences, 27,* 293–305.

Digman, J. (1990). Personality structure: Emergence of the five-factor model. *Annual Review of Psychology, 41,* 417–440.

Dunn, W. S., Mount, M. K., Barrick, M. R., & Ones, D. S. (1995). Relative importance of personality and general mental ability in managers' judgments of applicant qualifications. *Journal of Applied Psychology, 80,* 500–510.

Edwards, J. (1991). Person–job fit: A conceptual integration, literature review, and methodological critique. In CooperCLRIT (Ed.), *International review of industrial and organizational psychology* (Vol. 6, pp. 283–357). Chichester: Wiley.

Fernández-Aráoz, C., Groysberg, B., & Nohria, N. (2009). The definitive guide to recruiting in good times and bad. *Harvard Business Review, 87*(5), 74–84.

Frei, R. L., & McDaniel, M. A. (1998). Validity of customer service measures in personnel selection: A review of criterion and construct evidence. *Human Performance, 11,* 1–27.

Gellatly, I. R. (1996). Conscientiousness and task performance: Test of a cognitive process model. *Journal of Applied Psychology, 81,* 474–482.

Goldberg, L. R. (1992). The development of markers for the Big Five factor structure. *Psychological Assessment, 4,* 26–42.

Goldberg, L. R. (1999). A broad-bandwidth, public domain, personality inventory measuring the lower-level facets of several five-factor models. In I. Mervielde, I. Deary, F. De Fruyt, & F. Ostendorf (Eds.), *Personality psychology in Europe* (pp. 7–28). Tilburg: Tilburg University Press.

Gordon, V. N. (2007). *The undecided college student: An academic and career advising challenge.* Springfield, IL: Charles C. Thomas Publisher.

Hogan, R. (1986). *Manual for the Hogan personality inventory.* Minneapolis, MN: National Computer Systems.

Hough, L. M., Eaton, N. K., Dunnette, M. D., Kemp, J. D., & McCloy, R. A. (1990). Criterion-related validities of personality constructs and the effect of response distortion on those validities. *Journal of Applied Psychology*, 75, 581−595.

International Personality Item Pool (IPIP). (2001). *A scientific collaboratory for the development of advanced measures of personality traits and other individual differences.* Retrieved from http://ipip.ori.org/

John, O. P., & Srivastava, S. (1999). The Big Five trait taxonomy: History, measurement, and theoretical perspectives. In L. A. Pervin & O. P. John (Eds.), *Handbook of personality: Theory and research* (pp. 102−138). New York, NY: The Guilford Press.

Judge, T. A., Higgins, C. A., Thoresen, C. J., & Barrick, M. R. (1999). The Big Five personality traits, general mental ability, and career success across the life span. *Personnel Psychology*, 52, 621−652.

Kolb, D. (2014). *Experiential learning: Experience as the source of learning and development.* Upper Saddle River, NJ: Pearson.

Kristof, A. (1996). Person−organization fit: An integrative review of its conceptualizations, measurement, and implications. *Personnel Psychology*, 49(1), 1−49.

Kristof-Brown, A. (2000). Perceived applicant fit: Distinguishing between recruiters' perceptions of person-job and person-organization fit. *Personnel Psychology*, 53(3), 643−671.

Laribee, S. F. (1994). The psychological types of college accounting students. *Journal of Psychological Type*, 28, 27−42.

Lemke, E. A., Leicht, K. L., & Miller, J. C. (1974). Role of ability and extroversion in concept attainment of individuals trained in heterogeneous or homogeneous personality groups. *Journal of Educational Research*, 67(5), 202−204.

Liao, H., Joshi, A., & Chuang, A. (2004). Sticking out like a sore thumb: Employee dissimilarity and deviance at work. *Personnel Psychology*, 57, 969−1000.

Luzzo, D. A. (2011). Gender differences in college students' career maturity and perceived barriers in career development. *Journal of Counseling & Development*, 73(3), 319−322.

McCrae, R. R., & Costa, P. T., Jr. (1989). Reinterpreting the Myers-Briggs type indicator in terms of the five-factor model of personality. *Journal of Personality*, 57, 17−40.

McCrae, R. R., & Costa, P. T., Jr. (1999). A five-factor theory of personality. In L. Pervin & O. P. John (Eds.), *Handbook of personality: Theory and research* (2nd ed., pp. 139−153). New York, NY: The Guilford Press.

McCrae, R. R., & John, O. P. (1992). An introduction to the five-factor model and its applications. *Journal of Personality*, 60, 175−216.

McHenry, J. J., Hough, L. M., Toquam, J. L., Hanson, M. A., & Ashworth, S. (1990). Project A validity results: The relationship between predictor and criterion domains. *Personnel Psychology*, 43, 335−354.

McLester, S., & McIntire, T. (2006). The workforce readiness crisis: We're not turning out employable graduates nor maintaining our position as a global competitor − Why? *Technology & Learning*, 27(4), 22.

McManus, M. A., & Kelly, M. L. (1999). Personality measures and biodata: Evidence regarding their incremental predictive value in the life insurance industry. *Personnel Psychology*, 52, 137−148.

Mount, M. K., Barrick, M. R., & Stewart, G. L. (1998). Five-factor model of personality and performance in jobs involving interpersonal interactions. *Human Performance*, 11, 145−165.

Myers-Briggs. Retrieved from http://www.myersbriggs.org/my-mbti-personality-type/mbti-basics/. Accessed on March 3, 2015.

Oh, I., Guay, R., Kim, K., Harold, C., & Lee, J. (2014). Fit happens globally: A meta-analytic comparison of the relationships of person-environment fit dimensions with work attitudes and performance across east Asia, Europe, and North America. *Personnel Psychology, 67,* 99–121.

Ones, D. S., & Viswesvaran, C. (1999). Relative importance of personality dimensions for expatriate selection: A policy capturing study. *Human Performance, 12,* 275–294.

Saks, A., & Gruman, J. (2011). Getting newcomers engaged: The role of socialization tactics. *Journal of Managerial Psychology, 26*(5), 383–402.

Salgado, J. F. (1997). The five factor model of personality and job performance in the European community. *Journal of Applied Psychology, 82,* 30–43.

Schneider, B. (1987). The people make the place. *Personnel Psychology, 40*(3), 437–453.

Seol, I., & Sarkis, J. (2005). A multi-attribute model for internal auditor selection. *Managerial Auditing Journal, 20*(8), 876–892.

Swain, M. R., & Olsen, K. J. (2012). From student to accounting professional: A longitudinal study of the filtering process. *Issues in Accounting Education, 27*(1), 17–52.

Tett, R. P., Jackson, D. N., & Rothstein, M. (1991). Personality measures as predictors of job performance: A meta-analytic review. *Personnel Psychology, 44,* 703–742.

Tong, D., & Tong, X. (2012). Negative opinion of company environment mediates career choice of accountancy students. *Education & Training, 54,* 534–557.

Viswesvaran, C., Deller, J., & Ones, D. (2007). Personality measures in personnel selection: Some new contributions. *International Journal of Selection and Assessment, 15,* 354–358.

Wanberg, C. R., & Banas, J. T. (2000). Predictors and outcomes of openness to changes in a reorganizing workplace. *Journal of Applied Psychology, 85,* 132–142.

Watson, D., & Clark, L. A. (1984). Negative affectivity: The disposition to experience aversive emotional states. *Psychological Bulletin, 96,* 465–490.

Wheeler, P. (2001). The Myers-Briggs type indicator and applications to accounting education and research. *Issues in Accounting Education, 16*(1), 125–150.

Wolk, C., & Nikolai, L. (1997). Personality types of accounting students and faculty: Comparisons and implications. *Journal of Accounting Education, 15,* 1–17.

# APPENDIX

# PERSONALITY MEASURES

I. **To what extent do the following statements accurately DESCRIBE YOU? Insert the appropriate number, using the scale below, for each factor.**

*1 = Very Inaccurate, 2 = Somewhat Inaccurate, 3 = Neutral,*
*4 = Somewhat Accurate, 5 = Very Accurate*

_____ Am the life of the party.

_____ Don't talk a lot.

_____ Feel comfortable around people.

_____ Start conversations.

_____ Keep in the background.

_____ Have little to say.

_____ Don't like to draw attention to myself.

_____ Talk to a lot of different people at parties.

_____ Don't mind being the center of attention.

_____ Am quiet around strangers.

_____ Am interested in people.

_____ Sympathize with others' feelings.

_____ Have a soft heart.

_____ Insult people.

_____ Am not really interested in others.

_____ Am not interested in other people's problems.

_____ Take time out for others.

_____ Feel others' emotions.

_____ Feel little concern for others.

_____ Make people feel at ease.

_____ Am always prepared.

_____ Leave my belongings around.

_____ Pay attention to details.

_____ Get chores done right away.

_____ Make a mess of things.

_____ Shirk my duties.

_____ Often forget to put things back in their proper place.

_____ Follow a schedule.

_____ Like order.

_____ Am exacting in my work.

_____ Am relaxed most of the time.

_____ Get stressed out easily.

_____ Seldom feel blue.

_____ Worry about things.

_____ Am easily disturbed.

_____ Have frequent mood swings.

_____ Get upset easily.

_____ Change my mood a lot.

_____ Get irritated easily.

_____ Often feel blue.

_____ Have a rich vocabulary.

_____ Have difficulty understanding abstract ideas.

_____ Have a vivid imagination.

_____ Spend time reflecting on things.

_____ Have excellent ideas.

_____ Am quick to understand things.

_____ Do not have a good imagination.

_____ Use difficult words.

_____ Am not interested in abstract ideas.

_____ Am full of ideas.

II. **Auditors examine the financial information of a company to ensure that the information is reasonably stated. In addition, auditors often provide recommendations to management to improve operations, risk management, and internal controls.**

**To what extent would the following statements describe "THE IDEAL AUDITOR"? Insert the appropriate number, using the scale below, for each factor.**

*1 = Very Inaccurate, 2 = Somewhat Inaccurate, 3 = Neutral,*
*4 = Somewhat Accurate, 5 = Very Accurate*

_____ Am the life of the party.

_____ Don't talk a lot.

_____ Feel comfortable around people.

_____ Start conversations.

_____ Keep in the background.

_____ Have little to say.

_____ Don't like to draw attention to myself.

_____ Talk to a lot of different people at parties.

_____ Don't mind being the center of attention.

_____ Am quiet around strangers.

_____ Am interested in people.

_____ Sympathize with others' feelings.

_____ Have a soft heart.

_____ Insult people.

_____ Am not really interested in others.

_____ Am not interested in other people's problems.

_____ Take time out for others.

_____ Feel others' emotions.

_____ Feel little concern for others.

_____ Make people feel at ease.

_____ Am always prepared.

_____ Leave my belongings around.

_____ Pay attention to details.

_____ Get chores done right away.

_____ Make a mess of things.

_____ Shirk my duties.

_____ Often forget to put things back in their proper place.

_____ Follow a schedule.

_____ Like order.

_____ Am exacting in my work.

_____ Am relaxed most of the time.

_____ Get stressed out easily.

_____ Seldom feel blue.

_____ Worry about things.

_____ Am easily disturbed.

_____ Have frequent mood swings.

_____ Get upset easily.

_____ Change my mood a lot.

_____ Get irritated easily.

_____ Often feel blue.

_____ Have a rich vocabulary.

_____ Have difficulty understanding abstract ideas.

_____ Have a vivid imagination.

_____ Spend time reflecting on things.

_____ Have excellent ideas.

_____ Am quick to understand things.

_____ Do not have a good imagination.

_____ Use difficult words.

_____ Am not interested in abstract ideas.

_____ Am full of ideas.

**Please answer the following demographic questions by filling in the blank or circling the appropriate response.**

1. What is your major (*circle one*)?

   Accounting   *or*   Entrepreneurship   *or*   Finance   *or*

   Management   *or*   Marketing   *or*   MAcc   *or*   MBA

2. What is your sex (*circle one*)?

   Male   or   Female

3. What is your class standing (*circle one*)?

   Junior   *or*   Senior   *or*   MAcc   *or*   MACC

4. What is your age? _____

5. How many years of *total* work experience do you have?

   _____

6. How many years of work experience in *Auditing* do you have?

   _____

7. How many years of work experience in *Accounting* do you have?

   _____

8. How many years of *supervisory* experience do you have?

   _____

9. What Professional Certification(s) listed below do you possess?

   CPA   CFA   CMA   Other, please describe

   _____

10. What is your current *overall GPA*?

    _____

    *[please do not round up & be as precise as possible]*

11. What is your current *GPA in your major?*

_____

*[please do not round up & be as precise as possible]*

12. To what extent do the following job titles describe your "ideal job"?

| | Strongly Disagree | Somewhat Disagree | Neutral | Somewhat Agree | Strongly Agree |
|---|---|---|---|---|---|
| Auditor | 1 | 2 | 3 | 4 | 5 |
| Tax accountant | 1 | 2 | 3 | 4 | 5 |
| Management accountant | 1 | 2 | 3 | 4 | 5 |

13. For the following courses, indicate the final course grade you earned if you've already taken the class **OR** your anticipated course grade if currently enrolled in the class.

| | *Grade Earned* (if You Already Took the Course) | *Grade Anticipated* (if You're Currently Enrolled in the course) |
|---|---|---|
| Intermediate accounting 1 | | |
| Intermediate accounting 2 | | |
| Intermediate accounting 3 | | |
| Individual tax accounting | | |
| Corporate tax accounting | | |
| Management accounting | | |
| Auditing | | |

# THE EFFICACY OF USING *MONOPOLY* TO IMPROVE UNDERGRADUATE STUDENTS' UNDERSTANDING OF THE ACCOUNTING CYCLE

Jason Bergner and Marcus Brooks

## ABSTRACT

*We investigate how different methods of instructor-led reviews for an introductory accounting exam may affect student achievement. We compare two review groups: students who review for the exam by playing* Monopoly *versus those engaged a more traditional review. We also include a third group (no formal review). We conducted an experiment by examining students' test scores on an accounting cycle exam. The students were placed into three groups: those who played* Monopoly *to review for the exam, those who participated in a more traditional exam review, and those who did not participate in any formal review. Our results indicate that, as expected, reviewing for an*

Advances in Accounting Education: Teaching and Curriculum Innovations, Volume 20, 33–50
Copyright © 2017 by Emerald Publishing Limited
ISSN: 1085-4622/doi:10.1108/S1085-462220170000020003

*exam significantly improves students' exam scores when compared to peers that did not review. However, this result is driven by the students in the* Monopoly *condition. Students in the traditional review did not score statistically significantly higher than those in the control (no review) group. Also, we did not find that students playing* Monopoly *as a review scored significantly higher than students actively working in a more traditional review. This study contributes to the literature by informing professors about the efficacy of using* Monopoly *to review the accounting cycle. This is the first paper to directly test the effects of using* Monopoly *on student achievement.*

**Keywords:** Accounting cycle; *Monopoly*; Introductory financial accounting; active learning; business games

We report the results of an experiment designed to test whether students who review for an introductory financial accounting exam by playing *Monopoly* outperform two other groups of students: those who do an active but more traditional, instructor-led review and those who do not participate in a formal review at all. Well-chosen pedagogical methods have been identified as one of five critical components of effective teaching (AECC, 1993), and since many professors choose to review for their exams, the question of whether different review methods would be more effective than others is important. We chose to test the efficacy of *Monopoly*, as Knechel (1989) originally argued that it would be a theoretically superior alternative over regular practice sets for introductory accounting students. Knechel (1989) argues that *Monopoly*, when used as a business simulation game, should provide a richer context for students to practice accounting and review the accounting cycle since students playing *Monopoly* are engaged in active learning, recording transactions that occur organically, and are unable to copy off of other students in the class since everyone's game will have slightly different economic events.

To investigate this issue, we conduct an experiment using a single large section of introductory accounting students ($N = 169$). Students were given the opportunity to sign up (voluntarily) for one of two different review groups, with each group meeting twice outside of normal class time the week prior to the exam. Students did not know which of the two review groups was *Monopoly* versus a traditional review, so they could not self-select into a preferred review group. Rather, students were told that both were simply review sessions being offered on different days in order to try and accommodate as many students as possible.

The first review group played *Monopoly* to practice accounting sets (analyzing/recording transactions; posting entries to T-accounts; and generating trial balances, adjusting entries, and financial statements) as review for the upcoming exam. The second review group also reviewed for the exam by doing practice sets, but an instructor led these sessions by having students work problems out of a textbook (what we term the *traditional* condition).[1] Students who chose not to sign up for either session comprised the third group (*control* condition).

Our results indicate that students who reviewed by playing *Monopoly* did not score significantly higher on the classroom exam than students in the traditional review. However, *Monopoly* students scored significantly higher on the exam than those who did not review at all, while we detected no significant difference between the traditional review and control groups. These results indicate that professors should consider the structure and mechanisms for reviewing for exams; that is, not all methods of review are equally as effective.

The remainder of this chapter is organized into four sections: background and hypothesis, methodology, results and analysis, and a conclusion.

# BACKGROUND AND HYPOTHESIS

## *Background*

It is argued that active learning techniques, such as using games in the classroom, can achieve greater student learning than traditional lecture approaches (Shanahan, Hermans, & Haytko, 2006). Accordingly, games have commonly been used to try to engage students and improve their understanding of course content in business classes (e.g., Arora, 2012; Klotz, 2011). The use of games is also common in programs outside of business, such as pharmacy (Aburahma & Mohamed, 2015) and statistics (Chow, Woodford, & Maes, 2011). In general, the use of games in both business and nonbusiness courses has shown to be effective in increasing student understanding and/or retention.

In business courses, games have been used in a variety of areas, including marketing (Arora & Arora, 2015), management (Piercy, 2010), and accounting (Mastilak, 2012). Proponents of using games to help students learn accounting concepts goes back at least 50 years. Bruns (1965) argued that the potential efficacy of using business games in accounting courses is obvious considering that accounting plays a central role in nearly all management decisions. Additionally, business games are often characterized by sequential decision-making and interim reporting, facets that are crucial in accounting.

Early evidence on the efficacy of using games to teach accounting was questioned. DeCoster and Prater (1973) provided an early investigation as to whether games could be successfully adapted to an introductory managerial accounting course. The authors posited three specific advantages for using games in the classroom: students' *attitudes* should be more positive, their *ability* to understand the material should be improved, and they should be able to *integrate* a number of learning experiences and thus have a broader understanding of the subject. However, the authors did not find significant differences in either attitude or ability as a result of implementing the game and concluded that the use of games would not likely make a difference in student understanding.

Knechel (1989) supported the idea of using games, and specifically *Monopoly*, in an introductory financial accounting course because students would not be able to collude as easily as they might from a traditional practice set and because the practice would be done in a richer context than the sterile environments typically provided in textbooks. Using *Monopoly* in the classroom could potentially make students take something they know (i.e., how to play *Monopoly*) and connect it to something they have trouble understanding (i.e., the accounting cycle). By using the game in the course of instruction, an accounting professor could help students better understand the accounting cycle, show the link between accounting and the decisions made in the game (i.e., running their "business"), and potentially find a very effective method for teaching a complex concept.

However, Knechel (1989) did not attempt to answer the efficacy question. Instead, he sought to explain the concept and implementation of using the game in class. His conclusions, therefore, do not report data, but rather make broad statements such as "the approach is more interesting to the students" and "the experiment ... was considered successful by the students and the instructor."

Other researchers have investigated *Monopoly*, but they have done so in the frame of how students and/or instructors *perceive* the activity rather than assessing its impact on students' learning. These subsequent papers have described alternative uses of *Monopoly* in teaching introductory accounting, including the demand for accounting information (Mastilak, 2012) and distinguishing between accounting and economic income (Shanklin & Ehlen, 2007). Other studies have focused on the first of DeCoster and Prater's (1973) three attributes of benefit to students: *attitude*.

Albrecht (1995) expanded Knechel's idea beyond the accounting cycle, with students preparing financial statements and then investing in the "market" of the *Monopoly* businesses based on their evaluation of companies' financials. Results showed that students' attitudes (both graduate and undergraduate) were positive toward the exercises. However, no data was collected that might reveal if students actually learned more as a result of the activity. Tanner and Lindquist (1998) used *Monopoly* in a cooperative learning environment. Although they also found students' attitudes to be positive toward the simulation, they admit that could not separate the incremental benefits of using *Monopoly* without a control group.

## *Hypotheses*

We have optimism about the efficacy of using *Monopoly* as a review mechanism for two reasons. First, *Monopoly* is a game that, even if unfamiliar to students, contains rules that are easily understood when played for a short time. Second, *Monopoly* seems to be a great fit for learning accounting. The game revolves around typical accounting transactions: earning revenue, incurring expenses, investing in assets, etc. These transactions can be recorded and used to produce a trial balance and financial statements. Thus, the use of *Monopoly* in a financial accounting classroom would appear to be a natural fit for conveying and reinforcing accounting cycle concepts. However, we cannot presume that this particular method would be superior to a more traditional review method. Accordingly, we state our first hypothesis in the null:

**H1.** Students who review for an accounting cycle exam by playing Monopoly will not score higher than those participating in a traditional review.

However, we believe that regardless of whether students review for the exam by playing *Monopoly* or by participating in a more traditional review, those who review will score higher than students who choose not to participate.

> **H2.** Students who review for an accounting cycle exam will score higher than students who do not participate in a formal review.

# METHOD

## *Participants and Design*

A total of 197 students in a single section of introductory financial accounting at a public, western university participated in the experiment.[2] This section was taught during the morning two days a week and thus contained a large percentage of traditional prebusiness majors. One author taught this section as part of the normal teaching load for the department.

Students were offered an opportunity to participate in extra review sessions for the initial exam in the course which included material that predominantly covered the accounting cycle. Accordingly, students ended up in one of three experimental conditions: those who reviewed for the exam by playing *Monopoly* (*Monopoly* condition), those who participated in an instructor-led review (traditional condition), and those who did not participate in either structured review (control condition). We then collected students' exam scores and analyzed the data.

In order to be included in the main analysis, students who participated in either review (*Monopoly* or traditional) had to attend both sessions for their respective groups. There were 26 students (18 in the *Monopoly* condition and 8 in the traditional condition) who only attended one of the two review sessions. Further, two of the students enrolled in the course did not sit for the first exam. Thus, in the main analysis, we exclude these 28 students[3] or a final sample of 169 participants.[4]

## *Procedure*

We conducted an experiment with three conditions (*Monopoly*, traditional review, control). About three weeks prior to the exam, the professor (one of the authors) announced to the students that they would have the opportunity to participate in an additional review for the upcoming exam. Students could sign up for one of two review groups via an emailed link. Each group would meet for 90 minutes on two separate days in the week prior to the exam, and the sign-up sheet contained the days, times, and classrooms where the reviews would take place. The review sessions took place on either Tuesday/Thursday or Wednesday/Friday the week prior to the exam. All sessions were scheduled for the late afternoon/early evening in order to reduce the chance that the review sessions would conflict with the students' other classes.

Students were not told which group would correspond to which experimental condition (*Monopoly* vs. traditional), and students were not informed of any of the specific differences between the two review groups. Since the reviews were held in smaller classrooms, the creation of two review groups allowed more students the opportunity to review for the exam. Thus, students had no way of self-selecting into a particular experimental condition in terms of *Monopoly* versus traditional. Students did self-select into reviewing versus not reviewing (control). We explore and attempt to control for potential differences between these particular groups in the analysis section.

The two review groups (*Monopoly* and traditional) met twice for 90 minutes per session the week prior to the exam, and the author who was not the class's instructor led both review sessions for both groups. Thus, all three conditions (*Monopoly*, traditional, and control) had the same instructor for the regular course material (one author), and both review conditions (*Monopoly* and traditional) had the same instructor for the review (the other author).

For both review groups, students reviewed the accounting cycle. Students in both groups practiced analyzing transactions, recording journal entries, posting entries to T-accounts, calculating trial balances, preparing adjusting journal entries, and preparing financial statements. In the *Monopoly* condition, students practiced these steps while playing the game. In the traditional condition, students practiced these steps within a traditional instructor-led review. In both conditions, students were encouraged to ask the instructor questions as needed.

The *Monopoly* review began with students receiving instructions how to play the game to review the accounting cycle. Students were not allowed to use the play money that came with the game but were required to keep track of all transactions and T-accounts on paper. Because of the record keeping involved, students played in teams of two, with one student responsible for making the journal entries and the other for posting to

T-accounts and maintaining balances. Each team of two students played against another team of two, creating a game with only two teams. Games were restricted to only two teams in order to increase the number of transactions each team would have to record, thereby providing the participants with additional practice.

Students playing *Monopoly* were free to create their own "house" rules, since it didn't matter if different games were being played by different rules. The point of the activity was to have students practice analyzing and recording transactions (as well as the rest of the cycle). However, certain accounting-specific rules were required for all games, and these rules were introduced prior to the beginning of play. These accounting-specific rules included the following:

- Students earned 5% interest on their cash each time they passed Go, rounded to the nearest dollar.
- Students could buy houses and hotels without owning a monopoly.
- Students had a line of credit on which they could draw for any reason. However, interest would accrue on the debt at 10% and was charged each time the students passed Go. The minimum required payment on the debt was the lower of $50 or 10% of the balance and was also due when passing Go.

The point of the above rules was to force students to think about accruals (interest) and depreciation (buildings) and thus review certain types of adjusting entries.

In the first session, the instructor encouraged students to focus on making the proper journal entries from the transaction. Students asked many questions initially, but the quantity of questions lessened over time and students became familiar with frequent entries (passing Go, paying rent, etc.). Students often asked questions about interesting transactions, which gave rise to discussions about how to treat them. For instance, students drawing a "get out of jail free" card often did not know how to record it. An instructor-led discussion helped the students realize that they did receive something of value (an asset) that had a specific dollar worth (the amount they would normally have to pay to get out of jail).

At the end of the first session, students completed a trial balance, made adjusting entries (buildings, railroads, and utilities were depreciated), and prepared financial statements. Nearly all groups failed in getting trial balances and balance sheets to balance. Thus, in the second session, the instructor encouraged the students to focus on accuracy.

The second *Monopoly* session went much smoother from a transaction analysis point of view. Students were already familiar with analyzing and recording transactions from the first session, and they remembered the frustration of not being able to get trial balances and balance sheets to balance. Thus, the instructor observed a determined effort to be precise in recording transactions and maintaining balances. Students also asked questions in this session, but the questions were overwhelmingly related to nonjournal entry questions, such as how to put accounts in their proper order for a trial balance, what financial statement should a particular account appear on. By the end of the second session, nearly all students were able to get the trial balance and balance sheet to balance. The instructor observed many instances of students expressing satisfaction at being able to do it "on their own."

The traditional review was intentionally structured in a similar fashion to the *Monopoly* sessions in order to maintain consistency in content coverage between the two review groups. The traditional review also focused on analyzing and recording transactions in the first session, using several sample problems out of a textbook.[5] In the review, the instructor provided an example of working through transaction analysis and journal entries, and then gave sample problems for the students to complete. Students were permitted to work in groups of their choosing in order to allow for discussion. As with the *Monopoly* group, students asked many questions about how to make journal entries, and students also experienced frustration with balancing items at the end of the session.

In the second session, students in the traditional review were also encouraged to focus on accuracy. As with the first session, the instructor provided an example of how to work through the accounting cycle and then gave practice problems for the students to complete. As with the *Monopoly* group, nearly all of the students were able to get items to balance by the end and likewise expressed satisfaction at their ability to do so.

## Variables and Model

Our three review conditions comprise the main independent variable, Review Group: those students who reviewed for the exam by playing *Monopoly*, those students who reviewed for the exam in a more traditional manner, and those students who did not review.

Students' scores on the accounting exam are our dependent variable. The accounting exam covered mainly the accounting cycle. However, other questions appeared on the exam unrelated to the accounting cycle.[6] Those questions were appropriately excluded from our analysis. Questions used for our analysis included 14 multiple-choice questions (out of 20 total) and four open-ended response questions (each with multiple parts).

We also include two variables in our model as potential covariates. First, since students self-selected by either signing up to review for the exam or not, we consider the possibility that perhaps the more successful students elected to participate in the review. Since this is the first exam in the semester (and occurs relatively early in the course), we use students' overall GPA to proxy for student success.

Second, it may be that students who carried a larger credit load may not have been able to review for the exam due to commitments for other courses. In this case, students with larger credit loads may not have been able to commit as much time studying for the exam as other students, so a larger credit load may be correlated with not participating in the review. In order to avoid this potentially correlated omitted variable, we use students' credit load for the current semester (Load) in the model.

## RESULTS AND ANALYSIS

Table 1 reports our main dependent variable (exam scores) and our two control variables (GPA and Load) by experimental condition. Participants in the three conditions marginally differed by exam scores ($p < 0.07$) and significantly by GPA ($p < 0.01$). We explore these differences in subsequent analysis.

We conduct post hoc tests (Tukey) to compare the means of each individual condition (*Monopoly*, traditional, and no review) with the other two conditions. One individual comparison (Monopoly vs. traditional) is used to evaluate H1, testing whether students in the *Monopoly* condition scored higher than those in a more traditional review.

The results displayed in Table 1, Panel B, show that while students playing *Monopoly* scored higher than those who did not review formally ($p < 0.00$), the *Monopoly* students did not score higher than the traditional reviewers ($p < 0.78$). Thus, we cannot reject H1.

Interestingly, students in the traditional review did not score higher than those under no formal review ($p < 0.23$). Thus, this preliminary analysis

***Table 1.*** Descriptive Statistics for Independent/Dependent Variables and Post Hoc Tests.

Panel A: Means for Independent and Dependent Variables by Experimental Condition

| *Condition*[a] | | | | | | |
|---|---|---|---|---|---|---|
| Variables | *Monopoly* ($n = 29$) | Traditional ($n = 16$) | Control ($n = 129$) | SD | *F*-stat. | *p*-Value |
| Exam scores | 87.03 | 83.88 | 77.25 | 15.70 | 2.58 | 0.07* |
| GPA | 3.12 | 3.10 | 2.87 | 0.51 | 52.91 | 0.00** |
| Load | 14.06 | 14.31 | 14.06 | 2.26 | 0.81 | 0.36 |

Panel B: Post Hoc (Tukey) Tests, H1

| Test | *t* | *p*-Value |
|---|---|---|
| *Monopoly* versus no review | 3.10 | 0.00** |
| Traditional versus no review | 1.63 | 0.23 |
| Traditional versus *Monopoly* (H1) | −0.66 | 0.78 |

Variable definitions: GPA = student cumulative GPA at the beginning of the financial accounting course, Load = student credit hours taken during the semester of the financial accounting course.

[a]*Monopoly*: Students reviewed for the exam by playing *Monopoly* for two 90-minute sessions; *Traditional*: Students reviewed for the exam by working accounting cycle-related problems in a more traditional format; *Control*: Students did not participate in a formal review.

*Significant at the $p < 0.10$ level.

**Significant at the $p < 0.05$ level.

appears to imply that simply reviewing for exams may not significantly improve student exam performance. Therefore, H2 is only supported when a review is conducted using *Monopoly*. A traditional review session did not show a statistically significant difference in exam scores.

To further assess the differences in the exam scores by exam review treatments (Monopoly vs. Traditional vs. No Review), we perform an ANCOVA. Table 2 reports the results of our ANCOVA analysis with our main independent variable (Review Group) and our two control variables (GPA and Load).[7] The results show a marginally significant Review Group variable ($p < .07$) indicating a relationship between the type of review session and exam score even after controlling for course load and grade point average.

*Table 2.*   Effect of Exam Review Type on Student Exam Scores
(ANCOVA).

| Source | Sum of Squares | df | Mean Square | F | p-Value |
|---|---|---|---|---|---|
| Model | 13503.72 | 4 | 3375.93 | 19.83 | 0.00 |
| Review group | 877.11 | 2 | 438.55 | 2.58 | 0.07* |
| GPA | 9007.78 | 1 | 9007.78 | 52.91 | 0.00** |
| Load | 136.67 | 1 | 136.67 | 0.81 | 0.36 |

Variable definitions:
Student exam scores = students score on the financial accounting exam covering the accounting cycle, Review group = whether students reviewed for exam by (1) playing *Monopoly*, (2) participating in a more traditional review, or (3) did not participate in a formal review, GPA = student cumulative GPA at the beginning of the financial accounting course, Load = student credit hours taken during the semester of the financial accounting course.
*Significant at the $p < 0.10$ level.
**Significant at the $p < 0.05$ level.

## Additional Analyses

Since two types of questions were asked on the exam (multiple-choice and open-ended), it could be that differences observed in the main analyses are being driven by one type of the question over the other. We thus performed an ANCOVA for each question type, using the same main independent variable and covariates but limiting our dependent variable to students' results on each specific question type. The results are reported in Table 3.

The results in Table 3, Panel A, show that open-ended question performance ($p < 0.01$) is significantly different across experimental condition. As with our main analysis, we repeated our post hoc (Tukey) tests to examine the data for potential differences between experimental conditions. Panel B of Table 3 shows that students in the *Monopoly* condition scored higher than those who did not review ($p < 0.01$), as they did in main analysis. The difference that existed between the *Monopoly* and "no review" groups for open-ended questions but not MC questions may be due to the nature of the review. Playing *Monopoly* is not an exercise in practicing MC questions but rather an open-ended format. Thus, we find that reviewing by playing *Monopoly* helps students score better on open-ended questions, and it is these questions which often require a higher level of thinking.

To further assess the differences in the exam scores by exam review treatments (Monopoly vs. Traditional vs. No Review), we perform an ANCOVA. Table 4, Panels A and B, reports the results of our ANCOVA

***Table 3.*** Descriptive Statistics for Independent/Dependent Variables and Post Hoc Tests (Multiple-Choice and Open-Ended Questions).

Panel A: Means for Independent and Dependent Variables by Experimental Condition

| Variables | *Monopoly* (*n* = 29) | Traditional (*n* = 16) | Control (*n* = 129) | SD | *F*-stat. | *p*-Value |
|---|---|---|---|---|---|---|
| MC questions | 39.22 | 39.41 | 38.42 | 5.44 | 0.01 | 0.98 |
| Open-ended | 47.81 | 44.47 | 38.83 | 12.20 | 4.42 | 0.01** |

Panel B: Post Hoc (Tukey) Tests, Open-Ended Questions

| Test | *t* | *p*-Value |
|---|---|---|
| *Monopoly* versus no review | 3.71 | 0.00** |
| Traditional versus no review | 1.81 | 0.17 |
| Traditional versus *Monopoly* | −0.91 | 0.63 |

Variable definitions:
MC questions = student score on the multiple-choice accounting cycle questions, Open-ended = student score on the open-ended accounting cycle questions, GPA = student cumulative GPA at the beginning of the financial accounting course, Load = student credit hours taken during the semester of the financial accounting course.
[a] *Monopoly*: Students reviewed for the exam by playing *Monopoly* for two 90-minute sessions; *Traditional*: Students reviewed for the exam by working accounting cycle-related problems in a more traditional format; *Control*: Students did not participate in a formal review.
**Significant at the $p < 0.05$ level.

analysis with our main independent variable (Review Group) and our two control variables (GPA and Load) for each type of question.[8] The results show a statistically significant relationship between the type of review session and exam score even after controlling for course load and grade point average.

We also analyzed whether student performance on the nonaccounting-related exam questions were different by experimental condition. The exam consisted of 20 MC questions and four open-ended questions. Of these, six MC questions were not related to the accounting cycle. Since both review conditions were focused on the accounting cycle, we had no reason to believe that differences would exist between conditions for these nonaccounting cycle MC questions. An ANCOVA similar to the analysis described above resulted in a lack of significance for the Review Group variable.

**Table 4.** Analysis of Student Exam Scores by Question Type (ANCOVA).

Panel A: ANCOVA, Multiple-Choice Questions

| Source | Sum of Squares | df | Mean Square | $F$ | $p$-Value |
|---|---|---|---|---|---|
| Model | 823.45 | 4 | 205.86 | 8.11 | 0.00 |
| Review group | 0.73 | 2 | 0.36 | 0.01 | 0.98 |
| GPA | 604.17 | 1 | 604.17 | 23.80 | 0.00** |
| Load | 30.44 | 1 | 30.44 | 1.20 | 0.27 |

Panel B: ANCOVA, Open-Ended Questions

| Source | Sum of Squares | df | Mean Square | $F$ | $p$-Value |
|---|---|---|---|---|---|
| Model | 7958.23 | 6 | 1989.55 | 19.12 | 0.00 |
| Review group | 919.31 | 2 | 459.65 | 4.42 | 0.01** |
| GPA | 4946.21 | 1 | 4946.21 | 47.53 | 0.00** |
| Load | 39.17 | 1 | 39.17 | 0.38 | 0.54 |

Variable definitions:
Student exam scores = students score on the financial accounting exam covering the accounting cycle, Review group = whether students reviewed for exam by (1) playing *Monopoly*, (2) participating in a more traditional review, or (3) did not participate in a formal review, GPA = student cumulative GPA at the beginning of the financial accounting course, Load = student credit hours taken during the semester of the financial accounting course.
**Significant at the $p < 0.05$ level.

Finally, we analyzed whether students who attended a particular review session (either *Monopoly* or traditional) were more likely to get questions related to that particular session correct on the exam. We focused on the open-ended questions, since those questions are where the differences lie.[9]

We believe our review of the accounting cycle over two sessions can be divided equally across the two sessions. The first review session (for both review groups) had a focus on making journal entries and recording adjusting entries at the end of the period. The second review session (while necessarily having review of the first session's content) had a focus on calculating account balances, placing accounts on the correct financial statement, and creating a classified balance sheet.

In order to test whether students attending a session did better on the corresponding exam questions, we took the open-ended questions from the exam as our dependent variable. There were four open-ended questions on the exam, and each one fell into one of our four categories (journal entries, adjusting entries, etc.). Since we compare only two groups (review vs. no review), we use a regression to test for differences. For our regression, the Review variable is coded as "1" if the student participated in the related review session and "0" if the student did not participate. We also included the covariates of GPA and Load, as with the other analyses. The results for these tests are reported in Table 5.

Panel 5, Table 4 shows that students from the first session did not score significantly better on the related exam questions ($p < 0.56$), while those from the second session displayed in Table 5, Panel B outscored their counterparts ($p < 0.01$). The lack of results for session 1 could be due to the fact that a professor other than the course instructor was conducting the review. Students may have needed time to become comfortable with the reviewing professor, his way of explaining things, and general style of teaching. Another reason may be that accounting, in general, is difficult for many students in an introductory course. Thus, it may simply be a case of students needing more time and repetition to learn the material.

***Table 5.*** Analysis of Student Performance on Open-Ended Exam Problems by Type of Review Session (Model: Score $= \beta_0 + \beta_1 \times$ Review $+ \beta_2 \times$ GPA $+ \beta_3 \times$ Load $+ \varepsilon$).

| Panel A: Regression Results, 1st Session | Score | $t$ | $p$-Value |
|---|---|---|---|
| Review | 0.234 | 0.57 | 0.56 |
| GPA | 2.158 | 6.01 | 0.00** |
| Load | −0.037 | −0.46 | 0.64 |
| Number of observations | 169 | | |
| Adjusted $R^2$ | 0.188 | | |
| Panel B: Regression Results, 2nd Session | | | |
| Review | 4.851 | 2.99 | 0.00** |
| GPA | 8.888 | 6.23 | 0.00** |
| Load | 0.251 | 0.77 | 0.44 |
| Number of observations | 169 | | |
| Adjusted $R^2$ | 0.274 | | |

Variable definitions:
Score = student's score on the open-ended exam questions, Review = 1 if student participated the review session, 0 if not, GPA = student cumulative GPA at the beginning of the financial accounting course, Load = student credit hours taken during the semester of the financial accounting course.
**Significant at the $p < 0.05$ level.

# CONCLUSION

While we show that reviewing for an exam by playing *Monopoly* results in students having higher exam scores compared to those who do not review, our results do not confirm Knechel's (1989) belief that *Monopoly* can be used in introductory financial accounting classes to increase students' understanding in comparison to more traditional methods. Our research adds to the body of literature demonstrating the effects of using *Monopoly* in the classroom. Future research should investigate other specific games that can be used for other concepts in introductory, intermediate, and advanced financial accounting courses, as well as other accounting courses (e.g., managerial).

Additionally, future research could focus on whether different types of learning in reviews (active vs. passive) affect students' exam scores. We also used students from a general service course (an introductory accounting class). Future research could examine review effects for upper-level accounting majors and/or graduate students.

Our research has some limitations. First, our data comprises a single large section of accounting students at a particular university. Students at other universities in different size classrooms may not necessarily experience the same results. Our results are also based on 45 out of 169 students participating in a review. This represents less little more than 25% of the students. This smaller sample could have affected the power of our statistical tests and resulted in a lack of significance for some of the analysis.

Another significant limitation is a potential self-selection bias. While students could not self-select into either of the two review groups, they could self-select into review versus no review groups by choosing to sign up (or not) for the reviews. We note that student GPA is significant throughout our results. This makes sense. Students with higher GPA's have been more successful at getting good grades and are thus more likely to do well on exams. However, the students with higher GPA's also seem to have chosen to review. Although we did find significance for the review groups even after controlling for GPA, this issue of self-selection is one we admit remains a distinct possibility within the study.

The GPA question points to a larger issue. The students who chose to review for the exams are those who have been more successful in school to date. Thus, those with lower GPA's (the students who are more likely to need the help) were less likely to seek the help. Future research may focus on seeing if reviewing with these "less motivated" students would benefit them as well.

# NOTES

1. We recognize that different professors have different opinions/definitions of what constitutes a practice set and that our usage of the term may be broader than some would prefer.

2. The authors received the necessary approval from the appropriate IRB office.

3. We include these students and analyze the full sample in the additional analysis section.

4. We examine effects of attending at least one session later in the chapter.

5. The instructor leading the traditional review purposefully used a different text than that the students used in the regular class in order to avoid covering problems the students may had already seen or had access to solutions.

6. These questions included items on such topics as business formations (e.g., partnerships).

7. We tested the model using an interaction term for GPA × Review Group. The interaction was not statistically significant ($p = 0.35$). The inclusion of this interaction terms resulted in a drop in our Review Group variable's significance from being marginally significant to dropping below conventionally accepted levels of statistical significance.

8. We tested the model using an interaction term for GPA × Review Group. The interaction was not statistically significant for either MC questions ($p = 0.95$) or open-ended questions ($p = 0.14$). The inclusion of this interaction terms resulted in a drop in our Review Group variable's significance from being marginally significant to dropping below conventionally accepted levels of statistical significance.

9. We ran the tests for the multiple-choice questions and found no significant difference, as expected. Those results are not tabulated.

# ACKNOWLEDGMENT

We thank Beth Kern (editor) and the two anonymous reviewers for their insights and helpfulness with this chapter.

# REFERENCES

Aburahma, M. H., & Mohamed, H. M. (2015). Educational games as a teaching tool in pharmacy curriculum. *American Journal of Pharmaceutical Education*, *79*, Article 59.

Accounting Education Change Commission (AECC). (1993). Evaluating and rewarding effective teaching: Issues statement no. 5. *Issues in Accounting Education*, *8*, 436–439.

Albrecht, W. D. (1995). A financial accounting and investment simulation game. *Issues in Accounting Education*, *10*, 127–141.

Arora, A., & Arora, A. S. (2015). "Supply chain – Marketing shark tank" experiential lab game in interdisciplinary business education: Qualitative and quantitative analyses. *Decision Sciences Journal of Innovative Education, 13*, 21–43.

Arora, A. S. (2012). The "organization" as an interdisciplinary learning zone: Using a strategic game to integrate learning about supply chain management and advertising. *The Learning Organization, 19*, 121–133.

Bruns, W. (1965). Business games in accounting education. *The Accounting Review, 40*, 650–653.

Chow, A. F., Woodford, K. C., & Maes, J. (2011). Deal or no deal: Using games to improve student learning, retention, and decision-making. *International Journal of Mathematical Education in Science & Technology, 42*, 259–264.

DeCoster, D., & Prater, G. (1973). An experimental study of the use of a business game in elementary accounting. *The Accounting Review, 48*, 137–142.

Klotz, D. (2011). The bicycle line assembly game. *Decision Sciences Journal of Innovative Education, 9*, 371–377.

Knechel, W. R. (1989). Using a business simulation game as a substitute for a practice set. *Issues in Accounting Education, 4*, 411–424.

Mastilak, C. (2012). First-day strategies for millennial students in introductory accounting courses: It's all fun and games until something gets learned. *Journal of Education for Business, 87*, 48–51.

Piercy, N. (2010). Experiential learning: The case of the production game. *Decision Sciences Journal of Innovative Education, 8*, 275–280.

Shanahan, K. J., Hermans, C. M., & Haytko, D. L. (2006). Overcoming apathy and disconnect in marketing courses: Employing karaoke jeopardy as a content retention tool. *Marketing Education Review, 16*, 85–90.

Shanklin, S. B., & Ehlen, C. (2007). Using the *Monopoly* board game as an efficient tool in introductory financial accounting instruction. *Journal of Business Case Studies, 3*, 17–22.

Tanner, M. M., & Lindquist, T. M. (1998). Using *Monopoly* and teams-games-tournaments in accounting education: A cooperative learning teaching resource. *Accounting Education, 7*, 139–162.

# ANALYTICAL PROCEDURES: AN IN-CLASS EXERCISE

Chris Bagwell, Linda A. Quick and
Scott D. Vandervelde

## ABSTRACT

*We have designed this in-class exercise to benefit undergraduate or grad-uate students enrolled in courses in auditing. This in-class exercise involves six short independent analytical procedures scenarios, two each for three different accounts: Payroll Expense; Depreciation Expense; and Interest Expense. The scenarios require students to perform substan-tive analytical procedures for each of the financial statement accounts. Students must use their accounting knowledge, analytical thinking skills, and problem-solving ability in order to compute an estimated expectation for an account balance. Following computing an estimate of the expected balance, students must then compare the result to the client-recorded balance and determine if the difference is within tolerable limits*

Advances in Accounting Education: Teaching and Curriculum Innovations, Volume 20, 51–78
Copyright © 2017 by Emerald Publishing Limited
ISSN: 1085-4622/doi:10.1108/S1085-462220170000020004

*established for the audit. The primary learning objectives for the in-class analytical procedures exercise involve the following:*

1. *Understanding when it might be appropriate for the auditor to perform substantive analytical procedures,*
2. *Understanding how to form an expectation of an account balance when performing analytical procedures, and*
3. *Understanding how to evaluate the results of a substantive analytical procedure.*

*In cooperation with KPMG, we believe that the analytical procedures exercise gives students a better understanding of performing substantive analytical procedures.[1] As identified by Auditing Standard AU-C 520, PCAOB Standard AS 2305, and in the academic literature (e.g., Hirst & Koonce, 1996), analytical procedures are an important part of the audit process. Understanding when and how to perform substantive analytical procedures, combined with how to evaluate the results, will aid in student knowledge of the audit process.*

**Keywords:** Analytical procedures; substantive testing; undergraduate auditing

While analytical procedures have been part of a financial statement audit for decades (e.g., PCAOB AS 2305, effective for audits of financial statements for periods beginning on or after January 1, 1989), Public Company Accounting Oversight Board inspections from 2004 to 2007 revealed that auditors need to improve the performance of analytical procedures (PCAOB, 2008). In the report, the board stated:

Inspection teams have identified deficiencies in firms' performance of analytical procedures that the firms intended to be substantive tests, including the failure to (a) develop appropriate expectations, including in some instances the failure to appropriately disaggregate data in order to obtain the necessary level of precision for the expectation, (b) establish a threshold for differences that the firm could accept without further investigation, (c) establish a threshold for differences that was low enough to provide the level of assurance that the firm planned to achieve from the test, (d) test the data that the firm used in the analytical procedures, (e) investigate significant unexpected differences from the firm's expectations, and (f) examine other evidence to obtain corroboration of management's explanations regarding significant unexpected differences. (PCAOB, 2008, p. 15)

As indicated by the inspection report, auditors make errors when performing analytical procedures, thus highlighting the need for continued learning at all levels.

The importance of performing substantive analytical procedures is highlighted in the recent guidance in AU-C 520 (AICPA, 2012; effective for audits of financial statements for periods ending on or after December 15, 2012). AU-C 520.05 provides steps the auditor is to take when performing analytical procedures either in conjunction with other substantive procedures or as substantive procedures.[2] The analytical procedures the students perform during this in-class exercise are consistent with what is proscribed in the standard.

A significant amount of accounting research has been performed related to analytical procedures.[3] In a field study, Hirst and Koonce (1996) find that the techniques being used in practice to estimate balances when performing substantive analytical procedures are regularly used and they are used to decrease other substantive testing which is more time-consuming (Trompeter & Wright, 2010). Additionally, analytical procedures are frequently being performed by lower level staff auditors (Trompeter & Wright, 2010). Moreno, Bhattacharjee, and Brandon (2007) found that students who were trained in certain ways performed as well as practicing auditors on analytical procedure tasks. One of those training methods was using "worked-out examples." Therefore, substantive analytical procedure techniques are important for students to learn, in order to increase the likelihood of performing high quality audit procedures.

This in-class exercise involves six short independent analytical procedures scenarios, two each for three different accounts: Payroll Expense; Depreciation Expense; and Interest Expense. The scenarios require students to perform substantive analytical procedures for each of these financial statement accounts. Students must use their accounting knowledge, analytical thinking skills, and problem-solving ability in order to compute an estimated expectation for an account balance. After computing an estimate of the expected balance, students must then compare the result to the client-recorded balance and determine if the difference is within tolerable limits established for the audit. While these scenarios have been very effective for the authors as an in-class exercise, instructors could also assign any or all of them as out-of-class work; however, some of the benefit of the in-class exercise is having practicing auditors act as facilitators during the class period. The original scenarios were designed for KPMG firm-wide training, thus having KPMG personnel facilitating provides valuable insight for the students in addition to providing further opportunity for students to interact with professionals and continue to refine interpersonal communication skills. The KPMG personnel also add credibility to the use of analytical procedures that is not always achieved by just being covered by accounting faculty.

# LEARNING OBJECTIVES AND IMPLEMENTATION GUIDANCE

While we have experienced great success in using these scenarios during class with a KPMG professional leading the discussion, instructors can use these scenarios without any assistance from a representative from the profession. KPMG representatives (including one of the co-authors on this chapter) have been coming to our Audit 1 class for eight years to participate in the in-class learning case scenarios presented in this chapter. Students have regularly responded very favorably to this exercise and greatly appreciate the involvement of representatives from the profession (typically alumni from the participating school) during the class period in leading the exercise discussion. Having accounting firm professionals involved increases the credibility of the procedures from the student's perspective. Although professional communication skills are not one of the initial primary objectives, it also continues to help them develop these skills by interacting with professionals. Even without assistance from a representative from the profession in class, the nature of the scenarios lends themselves to active discussion, thus enhancing professional communication skills of the students. KPMG personnel originally created the case scenarios for in-house training related to analytical procedures.

*Learning Objectives*

The primary learning objectives for the in-class exercise involve the following:

1. Understanding when it might be appropriate for the auditor to perform substantive analytical procedures,
2. Understanding how to form an expectation of an account balance when performing analytical procedures, and
3. Understanding how to evaluate the results of a substantive analytical procedure.

*Understanding When to Perform Substantive Analytical Procedures*
AU-C 520.05 identifies when to perform substantive analytical procedures and the general approach to performing such procedures:

When designing and performing analytical procedures, either alone or in combination with tests of details, as substantive procedures in accordance with section 330, the auditor should (Ref: par. A7-.A9)

    a. Determine the suitability of particular substantive analytical procedures for given assertions, taking into account the assessed risks of material misstatement and tests of details, if any, for these assertions; (Ref: par. A10-.A16)
    b. Evaluate the reliability of data from which the auditor's expectation of recorded amounts or ratios is developed, taking into account the source, comparability, and nature and relevance of information available and controls over preparation; (Ref: par. A17-.A20)

As seen in the exercise, we incorporated some of this information into the exercise in the "required" section for the task and in telling the students the criteria that have been met which leads to the substantive analytical procedures being performed over the given accounts. Additionally, there are PowerPoint slides that the KPMG personnel used at the beginning of the class period to discuss when substantive analytical procedures might be appropriate to be performed in lieu of or in conjunction with test of details as a substantive procedure.[4]

*Understanding How to Form an Expectation of an Account Balance When Performing Analytical Procedures*
The authoritative guidance on "how" to form an expectation for an account balance starts with the definition of an analytical procedure in stating the following (AU-C 520.04)[5]

.04 For the purposes of generally accepted auditing standards, the following term has the meaning attributed as follows:

Analytical procedures. Evaluations of financial information through analysis of plausible relationships among both financial and nonfinancial data. Analytical procedures also encompass such investigation, as is necessary, of identified fluctuations or relationships that are inconsistent with other relevant information or that differ from expected values by a significant amount. (Ref: par. A2-. A6)

*Understanding How to Evaluate the Results of a Substantive Analytical Procedure*
    a. Develop an expectation of recorded amounts or ratios and evaluate whether the expectation is sufficiently precise (taking into account whether substantive

analytical procedures are to be performed alone or in combination with tests of details) to identify a misstatement that, individually or when aggregated with other misstatements, may cause the financial statements to be materially misstated; and (Ref: par. A21-.A23)

b. Determine the amount of any difference of recorded amounts from expected values that is acceptable without further investigation as required by paragraph .07 and compare the recorded amounts, or ratios developed from recorded amounts, with the expectations. (Ref: par. A24)

When evaluating the results of substantive analytical procedures, the auditor must complete the following decision process:

.07 If analytical procedures performed in accordance with this section identify fluctuations or relationships that are inconsistent with other relevant information or that differ from expected values by a significant amount, the auditor should investigate such differences by

a. inquiring of management and obtaining appropriate audit evidence relevant to management's responses and

b. performing other audit procedures as necessary in the circumstances. (Ref: par. A28-.A29) (AU-C 520.07)

## Implementation

In collaboration with KPMG, we have always had audit personnel from the local KPMG office lead the discussion of the analytical procedures in-class exercises with our Audit 1 class.[6] Typically there is at least one auditor at the manager level or above supported by one or two senior or staff level auditors.[7] The first part of class is designed for the KPMG representative(s) to utilize the PowerPoint presentation to guide a discussion in a predominantly lecture format about the use of analytical procedures, including the important role that they play, how to perform substantive analytical procedures, and the implications of the results.[8]

Following the slides covering substantive analytical procedures, the remainder of the time is spent working on the exercise scenarios. The exercise includes background information and instructions along with six short scenarios that require students to conduct analytical procedures on one of three financial statement accounts. Table 1 includes the background information and instructions that we distribute to the students. The instructions note that the student is acting as the auditor for a US-based client; the accounts in question are considered low risk, and thus substantive analytical procedures are considered sufficient evidence; and the precision level for

## *Table 1.* Background and Instructions.

*Background*

You are the auditor of a United States client. You are entering the preliminary testing phase of the audit work program which instructs you to perform substantive analytical procedures in order to perform substantive test work over some previously identified low risk financial statement accounts. The internal controls testing surrounding these accounts have not uncovered any deficiencies that would preclude a lower control risk being included in the auditor's risk assessment for the accounts. The financial statement accounts for which you are going to perform substantive analytical procedures meet all of the following criteria:

1. The transactions within the account are routine and the results are reasonably predictable,

2. The transactions within the account do not involve complex accounting standards or complex judgments by management, and

3. There are relationships among data that exist and continue in the absence of known conditions to the contrary.[a]

Given the low levels of risk of material misstatement surrounding these accounts, it has been indicated to you that performing a substantive analytical procedure over the accounts will provide sufficient appropriate audit evidence in order to conclude on the account balances and respective assertions. For the purposes of this exercise, it is assumed that the data you have received that will be used to form your expectations of the account has been separately subjected to sufficient appropriate audit procedures and is therefore reliable for use in the substantive analytical procedure to be performed. Following the determination of your expectation for the account balance, you are to compare any difference between what you calculate and the client-recorded account balance. It has been determined that the level of precision to be used in this comparison is ±5% of the expected balance that you calculate. If any difference between the expected balance and the recorded balance is within the ±5% precision, then no further investigation will be necessary. If the difference is greater than the ±5% precision level, then additional investigation will be necessary for an audit team in practice. For this exercise, you should consider the types of additional testing, but you will not be asked to actually perform it as it is beyond the scope of this activity. You will need to determine how the expected balance was calculated, what might have led to the difference, and what (if any) additional substantive testing might be necessary.

*Instruction*

Use the information provided in the exercise scenarios for each of the accounts to determine an expectation for the current year balance for each of the following scenarios. Compare the expected balance you calculate to the client-recorded balance. Conclude on whether the difference is within the ±5% level of precision and think about the implications of your findings for the audit. You should consider each scenario as independent of the other scenarios.

[a]These criteria are consistent with AU-C 520.5 and 520.A8.

the analytical procedures is ±5% of the expected balance. The KPMG representative(s) first goes through a very brief introduction of each scenario. While each of the scenarios could be completed individually or in groups, we have always used groups of 3–5 students. We assign each group one of the scenarios and give them time to compute an expected value of the assigned account balance using the facts provided in each scenario. During this time the KPMG personnel (and professor) walk around and help groups as needed. We provide the solutions for all of the scenarios to the students following class for them to be able to review each scenario that was not assigned to their group. However, another option is to include the rest of the scenarios as an out-of-class assignment and provide the solutions at some later date.

The first two scenarios, shown in Table 2 and Table 3 (with corresponding solutions in Table 4 and Table 5, respectively), test payroll expense. We provide information regarding the number of workers per store, the number of new and existing stores, the average wage per hour, the regular and overtime hours worked, and the prior year's payroll expense. Students can calculate the number of hours worked based on the number of employees per store, the number of stores existing at the beginning of the year, and the number of stores opened during the current year. In Scenario 1, the client opened all new stores on October 1. In Scenario 2, the client opened new stores evenly throughout the year.

The third and fourth scenarios, shown in Table 6 and Table 7 (with corresponding solutions in Table 8 and Table 9, respectively), test depreciation expense. We provide information regarding asset categories and the cost basis, accumulated depreciation, and expected life for each category, along with new assets purchased in the current year and service dates for all assets (new and old). The primary difference between Scenario 3 and Scenario 4, besides the acquisition date for new assets, is that in Scenario 4, we note that the company's policy is to begin depreciating the assets at the beginning of the quarter *after* they are put in service. Because this is a non-GAAP policy, we expect students to ignore this policy when calculating their expected depreciation expense.

The final two scenarios, shown in Table 10 and Table 11 (with corresponding solutions in Table 12 and Table 13, respectively), test interest expense. We provide information regarding balances and terms (including interest rates) for outstanding debt, as well as the amount outstanding at the beginning of the year and amounts paid on the debt throughout the year. Scenario 5 includes three bonds with various interest rates and terms. Scenario 6 includes three bonds with various interest rates and terms, as

***Table 2.***    Analytical Procedure Scenario 1.

Payroll Testing 1

ABC Restaurant Company

Payroll Testing Fact Sheet

December 31, 2016

ABC Restaurant Company owned 133 stores in 2015. Each store employs 32 hourly employees on average and each employee worked approximately 8 hours of overtime per week. In 2015, we performed tests of details over hourly payroll expense. The procedures performed in 2015 included selecting a statistical sample of 134 employees. For each employee we recalculate five weekly paychecks. To accomplish this, we obtained five different weekly timecards for each employee, recalculated payroll expense for each employee, and traced that amount to the weekly payroll summary report. Then, each weekly payroll report was traced to the general ledger.

In 2016, we would like to determine a more efficient method to test payroll expense for hourly employees. Below are a summary of facts that were obtained from the 2015 audit workpapers:

1. Employees in 2015 = 4,250

2. Average wage per hour = $14.50

3. Average employee hours per week = 48

4. 2015 regular hourly payroll expense = $128,180,000

5. 2015 overtime hourly payroll expense = $38,454,000

6. 2015 total payroll expense = $166,634,000

Below are a summary of facts obtained from inquiries of the corporate controller and the payroll manager related to the 2016 audit of payroll expense:

1. 43 new stores were obtained on October 1.

2. Each store employs 32 hourly workers.

3. Overtime pays time and a half.

4. Management implemented a strategy that reduces overtime by 50% per employee compared to 2015.

5. There were no raises for hourly employees.

6. Assume each employee works 40 regular hours per week.

7. Assume 52 weeks per year.

8. 2016 client-recorded payroll expense = $161,253,989.

***Table 3.***    Analytical Procedure Scenario 2.

| Payroll Testing 2 |
| --- |

DEF Restaurant Company

Payroll Testing Fact Sheet

December 31, 2016

DEF Restaurant Company owned 133 stores in 2015. Each store employs 32 hourly employees on average and each employee worked approximately 8 hours of overtime per week. In 2015, we performed tests of details over hourly payroll expense. The procedures performed in 2015 included selecting a statistical sample of 134 employees. For each employee we recalculate 5 weekly paychecks. To accomplish this, we obtained five different weekly timecards for each employee, recalculated payroll expense for each employee, and traced that amount to the weekly payroll summary report. Then, each weekly payroll report was traced to the general ledger.

In 2016, we would like to determine a more efficient method to test payroll expense for hourly employees. Below are a summary of facts that were obtained from the 2015 audit work papers:

1. Employees in 2015 = 4,250

2. Average wage per hour = $14.50

3. Average employee hours per week = 48

4. 2015 regular hourly payroll expense = $128,180,000

5. 2015 overtime hourly payroll expense = $38,454,000

6. 2015 total payroll expense = $166,634,000

Below are a summary of facts obtained from inquiries of the corporate controller and the payroll manager related to the 2016 audit of payroll expense:

1. 43 new stores were obtained evenly throughout the year.

2. Each store employs 32 hourly workers.

3. Overtime pays time and a half.

4. Management implemented a strategy that reduces overtime by 50% per employee compared to 2015.

5. There were no raises for hourly employees.

6. Assume each employee works 40 regular hours per week.

7. Assume 52 weeks per year.

8. 2016 client-recorded payroll expense = $170,125,987.

***Table 4.*** Analytical Procedure Scenario 1 Suggested Solution.

Payroll Testing 1

| *ANSWER* | | |
|---|---|---|
| Average wage per hour | 14.5 | *A* |
| Overtime hours per employee | 4 | *B* |
| 2015 employees | 4,250 | *C* |
| Regular hours (existing employees) | 8,840,000 | $D = C*40*52$ |
| OT hours (existing employees) | 884,000 | $E = C*B*52$ |
| New employees | 1,376 | $F = 43*32$ |
| Regular hours (new employees) | 715,520 | $G = F*40*52*.25$ |
| OT hours (new employees) | 71,552 | $H = F*B*52*.25$ |
| 2016 regular payroll – existing employees | 128,180,000 | $= D*A$ |
| 2016 regular payroll – new employees | 10,375,040 | $= G*A$ |
| 2016 OT payroll – existing employees | 19,227,000 | $= E*A*1.5$ |
| 2016 OT payroll – new employees | 1,556,256 | $= H*A*1.5$ |
| Total expected payroll | 159,338,296 | |
| Actual payroll expense | 161,253,989 | |
| Difference | (1,915,693) | |
| % difference | −1.20% | |
| Test result | *PASS* | |

***Table 5.*** Analytical Procedure Scenario 2 Suggested Solution.

Payroll Testing 2

| *ANSWER* | | |
|---|---|---|
| Average wage per hour | 14.5 | *A* |
| Overtime hours per employee | 4 | *B* |
| 2015 employees | 4,250 | *C* |
| Regular hours (existing employees) | 8,840,000 | $D = C*40*52$ |
| OT hours (existing employees) | 884,000 | $E = C*B*52$ |
| New employees | 1,376 | $F = 43*32$ |
| Regular hours (employees) | 1,431,040 | $G = F*40*52*.5$ |
| OT hours (existing employees) | 143,104 | $H = F*B*52*.5$ |
| 2016 regular payroll – existing employees | 128,180,000 | $= D*A$ |
| 2016 regular payroll – new employees | 20,750,080 | $= G*A$ |
| 2016 OT payroll – existing employees | 19,227,000 | $= E*A*1.5$ |
| 2016 OT payroll – new employees | 3,112,512 | $= H*A*1.5$ |
| Total expected payroll | 171,269,592 | |
| Actual payroll expense | 170,125,987 | |
| Difference | 1,143,605 | |
| % difference | 0.67% | |
| Test result | *PASS* | |

*Table 6.* Analytical Procedure Scenario 3.

Depreciation Expense 1

GHI Restaurant Company

Depreciation Expense Fact Sheet
December 31, 2016

Below are a summary of facts obtained from inquiries of the corporate controller and the fixed asset manager related to the 2016 audit of depreciation expense:

1. The Company opened all of its old restaurants on June 30, 2008.

2. The Company's accounting policy requires that assets begin to be depreciated using the straight-line method as soon as they are put into service.

3. The Company opened three new stores on April 1, 2016.

4. Total new store costs include $1,500,000 for land, $9,400,000 for buildings, $8,500,000 for equipment, and $3,200,000 for furniture and fixtures.

5. 2016 client-recorded depreciation expense = $4,752,396.

Below is the existing cost basis and accumulated depreciation information (not including the new assets).

Existing Assets

| Asset Category | Cost Basis | Accumulated Depreciation | Net Cost Basis | Economic Expected Life |
|---|---|---|---|---|
| Land | $2,500,000 | — | $2,500,000 | |
| Building | 19,500,000 | $5,362,500 | 14,137,500 | 20 |
| Equipment | 15,242,003 | 11,975,860 | 3,266,143 | 7 |
| Furniture/fixtures | 8,259,650 | 8,259,650 | — | 5 |
| Totals | $45,501,653 | $25,598,010 | $19,903,643 | |

***Table 7.*** Analytical Procedure Scenario 4.

Depreciation Expense 2

JKL Restaurant Company

Depreciation Expense Fact Sheet
December 31, 2016
Below are a summary of facts obtained from inquiries of the corporate controller and the fixed asset manager related to the 2016 audit of depreciation expense:

1. The Company opened all of its old restaurants on June 30, 2008.

2. The Company's accounting policy requires that assets begin to be depreciated using the straight-line method at the beginning of the following quarter after they are placed into service.

3. The Company opened three new stores on October 2, 2016.

4. Total new store costs include $1,500,000 for land, $9,400,000 for buildings, $8,500,000 for equipment, and $3,200,000 for furniture and fixtures.

5. 2016 client-recorded depreciation expense = $3,148,430.

Below is the existing cost basis and accumulated depreciation information (not including the new assets).

Existing Assets

| Asset Category | Cost Basis | Accumulated Depreciation | Net Cost Basis | Economic Expected Life |
|---|---|---|---|---|
| Land | $2,500,000 | — | $2,500,000 | |
| Building | 19,500,000 | $5,362,500 | 14,137,500 | 20 |
| Equipment | 15,242,003 | 11,975,860 | 3,266,143 | 7 |
| Furniture/fixtures | 8,259,650 | 8,259,650 | — | 5 |
| Totals | $45,501,653 | $25,598,010 | $19,903,643 | |

***Table 8.*** Analytical Procedure Scenario 3 Suggested Solution.

Depreciation Expense 1

Existing Assets

| Asset Category | Cost Basis | Accumulated Depreciation | Net Cost Basis | Expected Economic Life | Depreciation Expense |
| --- | --- | --- | --- | --- | --- |
| Land | 2,500,000 | – | 2,500,000 | | |
| Building | 19,500,000 | 5,362,500 | 14,137,500 | 20 | 975,000 |
| Equipment | 15,242,003 | 11,975,860 | 3,266,144 | 7 | 2,177,427 |
| Furniture/fixtures | 8,259,650 | 8,259,650 | – | 5 | – |
| Totals | 45,501,653 | 25,598,010 | 19,903,644 | | 3,152,429 |

Expected depreciation expense – Existing assets    3,152,429

New Assets

| Asset Category | Cost Basis | Accumulated Depreciation | Net Cost Basis | Life | Depreciation Expense |
| --- | --- | --- | --- | --- | --- |
| Land | 1,500,000 | – | 1,500,000 | | |
| Building | 9,400,000 | – | 9,400,000 | 20 | 352,500 |
| Equipment | 8,500,000 | – | 8,500,000 | 7 | 910,714 |
| Furniture/fixtures | 3,200,000 | – | 3,200,000 | 5 | 480,000 |
| Total | 22,600,000 | | | | 1,743,214 |

Expected depreciation expense – New assets    1,743,214
Total expected depreciation expense    4,895,643
Actual depreciation expense    4,752,396
$$ Difference    143,247
% Difference    293%
Result    *PASS*

***Table 9.*** Analytical Procedure Scenario 4 Suggested Solution.

**Depreciation Expense 2**

**Existing Assets**

| Asset Category | Cost Basis | Accumulated Depreciation | Net Cost Basis | Expected Economic Life | Depreciation Expense |
|---|---|---|---|---|---|
| Land | 2,500,000 | – | 2,500,000 | | |
| Building | 19,500,000 | 5,362,500 | 14,137,500 | 20 | 975,000 |
| Equipment | 15,242,003 | 11,975,860 | 3,266,144 | 7 | 2,177,429 |
| Furniture/fixtures | 8,259,650 | 8,259,650 | – | 5 | – |
| Total | 45,501,653 | 25,598,010 | 19,903,644 | | 3,152,429 |

Expected depreciation expense – Existing assets 3,152,429

**New Assets**

| Asset Category | Cost Basis | Accumulated Depreciation | Net Cost Basis | Life | Depreciation Expense | (See Note) |
|---|---|---|---|---|---|---|
| Land | 1,500,000 | – | 1,500,000 | | | |
| Building | 9,400,000 | – | 9,400,000 | 20 | 117,500 | |
| Equipment | 8,500,000 | – | 8,500,000 | 7 | 303,571 | |
| Furniture/fixtures | 3,200,000 | – | 3,200,000 | 5 | 160,000 | |
| Total | 22,600,000 | | | | 581,071 | |

Expected depreciation expense – New assets 581,071

Total expected depreciation expense 3,733,500

Actual depreciation expenses 3,148,430

$$ Difference 585,070

% Difference 15.67%

Result *FAIL*

*Note:* The Company's depreciation policy is a non-GAAP policy; the calculation is performed in accordance with GAAP.

*Table 10.* Analytical Procedure Scenario 5.

Interest Expense 1

MNO Restaurant Company

Interest Expense Fact Sheet

December 31, 2016

Below are a summary of facts obtained from inquiries of the CFO related to the 2016 audit of interest expense:

1. The Company made scheduled, quarter-end principle payments of $2,000,000 on its Series A notes.

2. The Company issued Series D, 7.25% subordinated debentures for $103,000,000 at par on July 1, 2016, due January 1, 2023.

3. The Company made an unscheduled principle payment of $78,000,000 to retire the Series B notes on July 1, 2016, using the proceeds obtained from the sale of the Series D notes.

4. 2016 client-recorded interest expense = $21,023,412.

Below is the existing debt schedule from the beginning of the current year.

| Issuance | Terms | Collateral | Balance January 1, 2016 |
|---|---|---|---|
| Series A | 7.75% bonds, due in quarterly installments beginning June 30, 2016 | Unsecured | $125,000,000 |
| Series B | 11.25% bonds, due in full on December 1, 2024 | Unsecured | 78,000,000 |
| Series C | 6.0% bonds, due in full on January 31, 2026 | All land and buildings | 52,600,000 |
| | | Total outstanding debt | $255,600,000 |

**Table 11.** Analytical Procedure Scenario 6.

Interest Expense 2

PQR Restaurant Company

Interest Expense Fact Sheet

December 31, 2016

Below are a summary of facts obtained from inquiries of the CFO related to the 2016 audit of interest expense:

1. The Company made scheduled, quarter-end principle payments of $2,000,000 on its Series A notes.

2. The Company issued Series D, 7.25% subordinated debentures for $103,000,000 at par on July 1, 2016, due on January 1, 2023.

3. The Company made an unscheduled principle payment of $78,000,000 to retire the Series B notes on July 1, 2016, using the proceeds obtained from the sale of the Series D notes.

4. The revolver balance remained steady during the year, but the actual (prime) rate fluctuated throughout the year from 5% to 11%.

5. 2016 client-recorded interest expense = $23,723,412.

Below is the existing debt schedule from the beginning of the current year.

| Issuance | Terms | Collateral | Balance January 1, 2016 |
|---|---|---|---|
| Series A | 7.75% bonds, due in quarterly installments beginning June 30, 2016 | Unsecured | $125,000,000 |
| Series B | 11.25% bonds, due in full on December 1, 2024 | Unsecured | 78,000,000 |
| Series C | 6.0% bonds, due in full on January 31, 2026 | All land and buildings | 52,600,000 |
| Revolver | Variable rate revolving line of credit, bearing interest at prime + 1.25% | Unsecured | 25,000,000 |
| | | Total outstanding debt | $280,600,000 |

Table 12. Analytical Procedure Scenario 5 Suggested Solution.

Interest Expense 1

| Issuance | Terms | Collateral | Balance | Expected Interest Expense |
|---|---|---|---|---|
| Series A | 7.75% bonds, due in quarterly installments beginning June 30, 2016 | Unsecured | 125,0000,000 | 4,843,750 |
| Series A | | | 123,000,000 | 2,383,125 |
| Series A | | | 121,000,000 | 2,344,375 |
| Series A | | | 119,000,000 | - |
| Series B | 11.25% bonds, due in full on December 1, 2024 | Unsecured | 78,000,000 | 4,387,500 |
| Series C | 6.0% bonds, due in full on January 31, 2026 | All land and buildings | 52,600,000 | 3,156,000 |
| Series D | 7.25% debentures, due on January 1, 2023 | Subordinated | 103,000,000 | 3,733,750 |
| | Total outstanding debt at December 31, 2016 | | 274,600,000 | |
| | Total expected interest expense | | | 20,848,500 |
| | Actual interest expense | | | 21,023,412 |
| | $$ Difference | | | (174,912) |
| | $ Difference | | | −0.84% |
| | Result | | | PASS |

*Table 13.* Analytical Procedure Scenario 6 Suggested Solution.

Interest Expense 2

| Issuance | Terms | Collateral | Balance | Expected Interest Expense |
|---|---|---|---|---|
| Series A | 7.75% bonds, due in quarterly installments beginning June 30, 2016 | Unsecured | 125,000,000 | 4,843,750 |
| Series A | | | 123,000,000 | 2,383,125 |
| Series A | | | 121,000,000 | 2,344,375 |
| Series A | | | 119,000,000 | — |
| Series B | 11.25% bonds, due in full on December 1, 2024 | Unsecured | 78,000,000 | 4,387,500 |
| Series C | 6.0% bonds, due in full on January 31, 2026 | All land and buildings | 52,600,000 | 3,156,000 |
| Series D | 7.25% debentures, due on January 1, 2023 | Subordinated | 103,000,000 | 3,733,750 |
| Revolver | Unsecured, variable rate revolving line of credit, bearing interest at prime + 1.25% | Unsecured | 25,000,000 | 2,312,500 |
| | | Total outstanding debt at December 31, 2016 | 299,600,000 | |
| | | Total expected interest expense | | 23,161,000 |
| | | Actual interest expense | | 23,723,412 |
| | | | $$ Difference | (562,412) |
| | | | $ Difference | −2.43% |
| | | | Result | *PASS* |

well as one revolving line of credit with a variable interest rate based on the prime rate.

The final 15–20 minutes of class is spent debriefing, including having groups present their assessment of the assigned scenario.[9] This allows the students to practice presenting their work, while also providing the KPMG representatives the opportunity to discuss the process of how the students arrived at their assessment. This is followed by the KPMG representatives providing feedback on how it "should" be approached, using the suggested solutions available for each scenario as a guide, and discussing the next step in the process based on the results.

## Assessment of Effectiveness

Three other faculty members (not co-authors on this chapter) have used the scenarios in class, with great success from an unsolicited student feedback standpoint. While we have repeatedly received very positive feedback from students regarding the day in class when we have gone through the substantive analytical procedure scenarios, we have recently obtained formal feedback from two sections of Audit 1 students ($n = 41$). We obtained the feedback during the next class period following when the KPMG representative was in class. Table 14 shows the questions asked and mean responses. Each response was given on a 5-point scale: 1 = strongly disagree, 2 = disagree, 3 = neutral, 4 = agree, 5 = strongly agree. A simple $t$-test indicates that each of the mean responses is significantly greater than the mid-point of the scale ($p$-value $< 0.01$).

While we do not have any before measures for understanding of substantive analytical procedures (consistent with Nicholls & Mastrolia, 2015), in addition to the question response data reported here, we have both anecdotal evidence and exam question results. Prior to the use of the substantive analytical procedure exercises presented in this manuscript the students complete a "simple" exercise from the text book in class in being introduced to substantive analytical procedures. The students regularly struggle with the exercise until the professor discusses how to complete the exercise. This indicates that their level of understanding prior to the exercises is limited and is consistent with the responses to the question indicating that the exercises increased their overall understanding (mean = 4.10). From exam questions following the coverage of analytical procedures the students did very well (from a different semester than the question responses included

***Table 14.*** Student Feedback.

| Question | Mean Response |
|---|---|
| 1. The scenarios increased my understanding of how to perform substantive analytical procedures. | 4.26 |
| 2. The scenarios increased my overall understanding of analytical procedures. | 4.10 |
| 3. The scenarios and presentation of the slides increased my understanding of when to perform substantive analytical procedures. | 3.98 |
| 4. The scenarios and related discussion increased my understanding of how to evaluate the results of substantive analytical procedures. | 3.95 |
| 5. The scenarios and related discussion increased my understanding of how to proceed with the audit based on the results of substantive analytical procedures. | 3.90 |
| 6. The scenarios required me to use critical thinking skills in performing the substantive analytical procedures. | 4.34 |
| 7. I found the scenarios to be challenging. | 3.83 |
| 8. I found the scenarios involving substantive analytical procedures to be interesting and enjoyable. | 3.76 |

in the manuscript). For three questions involving calculations out of 100 students 97, 85, and 98, performed the analytical procedures correctly, respectively. Also, 96 out of 100 students reached the proper conclusion based on the substantive analytical procedures performed. On a more complex exam problem on a comprehensive final exam, the same group of students performed three substantive analytical procedures, with 31, 65, and 79, calculating the estimate correctly, and 83 arriving at the proper conclusion based on the analytical procedures performed.[10,11]

Based on the various forms of evidence gathered, we conclude that the in-class exercises are effective in teaching students how to perform substantive analytical procedures.

# NOTES

1. This chapter is published with the full support of KPMG. If at any time in the future the AICPA and PCAOB determine that analytical procedures are no longer a valid procedure for obtaining audit evidence, then KPMG will no longer

support these in-class exercises as acceptable ways to teach analytical procedures and request that they no longer be used for such a purpose.

2. Similar importance placed on substantive analytical procedures can be seen in PCAOB AS 2305: Substantive Analytical Procedures.

3. See Messier, Simon, and Smith (2013) for a synthesis of the research post-1996. See Hirst and Koonce (1996) for a synthesis of the research pre-1996.

4. These PowerPoint slides are available in Appendix B.

5. The PCAOB authoritative guidance is similar in AS No. 12.48, as is the IAASB guidance in ISA 520.5. This applies to the references in understanding how to form expectations and how to evaluate results.

6. While we have experienced great success following this format, instructors can implement the scenarios without a representative from the profession in attendance. Through the remainder of the implementation guidance we present the information as if a representative(s) from the profession will be present; however, any of it can also be done without any outside assistance.

7. The number of representatives from the profession could depend on how many students are in the class. In order for the auditors to provide guidance to the student groups while working on the exercise scenarios, the larger the class size the more helpful a larger number of auditors would be. The professor can also be involved in providing guidance either with or instead of using representatives from the profession.

8. The slides used by KPMG are available in Appendix B, with KPMG branding removed.

9. Our class period is 75 minutes.

10. There were 99 who completed the final exam questions, as one student did not take the final exam.

11. The lower score on one of the exam questions was due to one question/calculation being intentionally more challenging than the other questions/calculations.

# REFERENCES

American Institute of Certified Public Accountants (AICPA). (2012). *AICPA professional standards*. New York, NY: AICPA.

Hirst, D. E., & Koonce, L. (1996). Audit analytical procedures: A field investigation. *Contemporary Accounting Research, 13*(2), 457–486.

Messier, W. F., Simon, C. A., & Smith, J. L. (2013). Two decades of behavioral research on analytical procedures: What have we learned? *Auditing: A Journal of Practice & Theory, 32*(1), 139–181.

Moreno, K. K., Bhattacharjee, S., & Brandon, D. M. (2007). The effectiveness of alternative training techniques on analytical procedures performance. *Contemporary Accounting Research, 24*(3), 983–1014.

Nicholls, C. M., & Mastrolia, S. A. (2015). Second chance homeless shelter: A fraud exercise for introductory and survey courses in accounting. *Advances in Accounting, 17*, 1–24.

Public Company Accounting Oversight Board (PCAOB). (2008). *Report on the PCAOB's 2004, 2005, 2006, and 2007 inspections of domestic annually inspected firms.* Retrieved from http://pcaobus.org/Inspections/Documents/2008_12-05_Release_2008-008.pdf

Public Company Accounting Oversight Board (PCAOB). *AS 2305: Substantive analytical procedures.* Retrieved from http://pcaobus.org/Standards/Auditing/Pages/AS2305.aspx

Trompeter, G., & Wright, A. (2010). The world has changed — Have analytical procedure practices? *Contemporary Accounting Research, 27*(2), 669–700.

# APPENDIX A: AUDITING STANDARD REFERENCES TO ANALYTICAL PROCEDURES

PCAOB:

1. Auditing Standard No. 12.5, 46-48, 57: Identifying and Assessing Risks of Material Misstatement

2. Auditing Standard No. 14.4-9: Evaluating Audit Results

3. Auditing Standard No. 15.13-14, 21: Audit Evidence

4. AU section 316.10-.11, .53-56, .83: Consideration of Fraud in a Financial Statement Audit

5. AU section 329.01-.05, .09-.22: Substantive Analytical Procedures

6. AU section 332.21-22, .27: Auditing Derivative Instruments, Hedging Activities, and Investments in Securities

7. AU section 339, Appendix A and Appendix B: Audit Documentation

8. AU section 341.05: The Auditor's Consideration of an Entity's Ability to Continue as a Going Concern

9. AU section 9312.03: Audit Risk and Materiality in Conducting an Audit: Auditing Interpretations of *Section 312*

AICPA:

1. AU-C section 240.22, .34,.A24-.A27,.A43,.A58, Appendix B, Appendix C.A77: Consideration of Fraud in a Financial Statement Audit

2. AU-C section 300.A2: Planning an Audit

3. AU section 314.03, .06, .09, .38, .50: Understanding the Entity and Its Environment and Assessing the Risks of Material Misstatement

4. AU-C section 315.06,.A1,.A7−A.10,.A64: in Understanding the Entity and Its Environment and Assessing the Risks of Material Misstatement

5. AU-C section 330.04,.A5,.A9,.A11,.A16,.A26,.A46−.A47,.A60,.A63,. A73: Performing Audit Procedures in Response to Assessed Risks and Evaluating the Audit Evidence Obtained

6. AU-C section 500.A2,.A10,.A20−.A22,.A31−.A33,.A52: Audit Evidence

7. AU-C section 520.03−.08,.A1−.A30: Analytical Procedures

IAASB:

1. ISA 240.22, .34,.A22,.A37,.A50, Appendix C: The Auditor's Responsibilities Relating to Fraud in an Audit of Financial Statements

2. ISA 300.A2: Planning an Audit of Financial Statements

3. ISA 315.5-.6,.A1,.A14-.17: Identifying and Assessing the Risks of Material Misstatement Through Understanding the Entity and Its Environment.

4. ISA 330.A5,.A10,.A15,.A43-.A44,.A55,.A57,.A60: The Auditor's Responses to Assessed Risks

5. ISA 500.A2,.A10,.A21,.A30,.A51: Audit Evidence

6. ISA 520.1-.7,.A1-.A21: Analytical Procedures


# APPENDIX B: KPMG SLIDES USED TO DISCUSS ANALYTICAL PROCEDURES

Below are the slides used by the KPMG representatives to guide the discussion of analytical procedures prior to the exercise scenarios. As noted previously, it is not necessary to have a representative from the profession to implement this exercise. While the slides were originally created by a KPMG professional, none of the information in the slides is proprietary, therefore, the slides below are generic and can be used with or without a KPMG professional presenting. Note that there is typically very little time spent on discussion of analytical procedures used in the audit planning and audit completion ("final") phases as that is covered separately during class and is not the primary objective of the KPMG case scenarios. The primary objective of the scenarios is analytical procedures utilized during the substantive phase of the audit.

# Analytical Procedures in Auditing

## Analytical Procedures in an Audit

Three general types of analytical procedures:

- Analytical procedures for planning purposes

- Substantive analytical procedures

- Final analytical procedures

## Analytical procedures for planning purposes

- General purpose: to identify areas of risk and changes in the business that should be addressed in the audit

- Example procedures

  - Trend analysis

  - Ratio analysis

  - Review of press releases, statements or other public information

  - Comparison of interim results to budget

  - Review of analyst or other third party company and industry analysis

## Analytical procedures for planning purposes

- Examples

- Interim results through 9 months resulted revenue in excess of budget by 14%

    - Analysis: Potentially increased risk over revenue recognition

- Analysts reports reach a consensus that EPS should exceed budgeted EPS by 7%

    - Analysis: Potentially pervasive risk that may increase the audit risk overall

- Net fixed assets increased by $186 million through September 30. Expected capital spending for entire year was $200 million.

    - Analysis: Potentially inappropriate capitalization of operating expenses

## Final analytical procedures

- General purpose: to perform analytical procedures near the end of the audit that assist in forming an overall conclusion as to whether the financial statements are consistent with your understanding of the entity

- Example procedures

    - Comparison of financial trending information

    - Comparison of actual results to expected results

    - Review of accounting policies and footnote disclosure

## Substantive analytical procedures

We perform substantive analytical procedures alone or in conjunction with test of details in order to conclude on certain audit objectives

- Circumstances when substantive analytical procedures may be appropriate:

    - Class of transactions are routine and the results are reasonably predictable

    - Transactions not involving complex accounting standards or judgment by management

    - Relationships among data exist and continue in the absence of known conditions to the contrary

    - Also should consider results of internal control testing, if performed

## Substantive analytical procedures

Examples of accounts typically tested via substantive analytical procedures:

- Depreciation expense

- Payroll expense

- Interest income/expense

- Revenue (dependent upon risk assessment and nature of revenue)

## Class Exercises

- Payroll expense substantive analytical
- Depreciation expense substantive analytical
- Interest expense substantive analytical

    - **Precision: $\pm$ 5% of expectation

## Questions ?

# JOURNAL LISTS AND STEPS TO DEVELOP THEM

Alan Reinstein and Barbara Apostolou

## ABSTRACT

*Association to Advance Collegiate Schools of Business (AACSB) member schools often compare their faculties' research records to journal lists of their "peer and aspirational" programs. They often survey faculty and administrators' perceptions of journal quality; number of Social Sciences Citation Index downloads; or "count" the number of faculty publications — but rarely analyze accounting programs' actual journal quality lists. To examine this issue, we use a survey of national accounting programs. We identify a set of quality-classified journal lists by sampling 38 programs nationwide, varying by mission (e.g., urban or research), degrees granted (e.g., doctoral degrees in accounting), and national ranking (e.g., classified as a Top 75 Research Program) — from which we derive 1,436 data points that classify 359 journals that appear on these 38 programs' journal lists. We also describe a case study that an accounting program used to revise its old journal list. We also find that while programs generally use generally accepted "bright lines" among the top three categories (A+, A, A−), they tailor their listings*

Advances in Accounting Education: Teaching and Curriculum Innovations, Volume 20, 79–132
ISSN: 1085-4622/doi:10.1108/S1085-462220170000020005

*from the wide variety of B or C classified journals to create their own sets of acceptable journals in these categories. The study provides guidance and data for accounting programs who wish to develop or revise their own journal lists. While many studies have examined journal rankings, this is the first study to document the use of journal lists by accounting programs with a wide array of missions.*

**Keywords:** Research productivity; benchmarks; accounting faculty assessment

This study has two objectives. The first is to provide a methodology for accounting programs to compile a broad journal list. To accomplish this objective we sampled 38 accounting programs with and without doctoral programs, including nationally and non-nationally ranked schools. The second objective of this research is to describe a case study in which Wayne State University (WSU) — an accounting-non-doctoral-granting program, located in an "urban" location with many commuter students — used to revise its own journal list.[1]

As the number of journals has skyrocketed in recent years, many accounting programs have developed, or are currently developing their own quality journal lists. While prior studies (e.g., Glover, Prawitt, & Wood, 2006; Hasselback, Reinstein, & Abdolmohammadi, 2012) have used various methods to develop and assess journal quality, differences of opinion remain about how accounting programs (e.g., Chan, Chen, & Cheng, 2007; Everett, Klamm, & Stoltzfus, 2004) and individuals (e.g., Brown & Gardner, 1985; Coyne, Summers, Williams, & Wood, 2010; Hasselback, Reinstein, & Schwan, 2000, 2003) assess accounting journal quality. Examining how 1,230 international accounting faculty ranked 58 listed journals, Ballas and Theoharakis (2003) found that researcher's geographic origin, research orientation, and journal affiliation affect journal quality perceptions. Finding that journal quality does not always reflect research quality they warn against using monolithic research evaluation practices to assess accounting faculty research at various types of accounting programs.

Other studies have focused on only a few, "quality" journals or highly ranked accounting programs. Using Trieschmann, Dennis, Northcraft, and Niemi (2000) rankings of publications in 11 top accounting journals,

Glover et al. (2006) and Glover, Prawitt, Summers, and Wood (2012) examine the promotion and tenure (P & T) research standards at the nation's top 75 accounting programs. Not surprisingly, the more highly ranked schools in this set had higher average publication records than those in lower level programs. Using a small sample, Reinstein and Calderon (2006) find general consensus among accounting faculty about the top three journals, which normally consist of *Journal of Accounting and Economics* (JAE), *Journal of Accounting Research* (JAR), and *The Accounting Review* (TAR). When examining journal rankings below the top three journals, less consensus arises. For example, doctoral-granting accounting programs ranked some journals (e.g., *Auditing: A Journal of Practice & Theory* (AJPT)) higher than did non-doctoral programs.

Journal lists provide many benefits, including adding objectivity to assess colleagues' research productivity — especially for non-experts on the quality of accounting journals. Such lists also reduce differences between faculty members who evaluate colleagues for promotion and tenure (P & T) decisions and merit raises. Moreover, such lists provide a basis for recruiting new faculty, and for a faculty member to assess his/her own research record to help decide whether or not to apply for P & T. Journal lists also help allocate resources, or otherwise enable external bodies such as the Association to Advance Collegiate Schools of Business (AACSB, 2013) to assess the quality of a school's programs. For example, accounting programs with "highly research active" as their mission would normally use more exclusive journal lists than "teaching-focused programs." Finally, accounting departments can use journal list benchmarks derived from masters and doctoral programs to assess whether or not they have adequate faculty scholarly productivity to offer masters or doctoral programs. With all these benefits, we believe that journal lists should be used primarily as a decision aid — an input to the decision — but not the decision itself.

The number of accounting programs using journal lists as part of their peer-review process has increased greatly over the last decade. Reinstein and Calderon (2006) asked all 295 members of Accounting Program Leadership Group consisting of nationwide department chairs and directors of accounting programs to forward their journal lists and other information to the researchers. Of the 145 respondents, only 19 accounting programs had such lists. Two years later, Lewis (2008) noted that the AACSB International found that about 40 percent of its members had created journal lists to assess their programs' research quality. Walker, Fleishman, and Stephenson (2010) found that about 15% of schools use journal lists, of which about two-thirds have explicitly documented journal lists. However, we found no study examining a broad range of schools' actual journal lists. Also, while some studies have provided journal lists, they have not explained how their accounting programs developed such lists. Using a case study approach we demonstrate steps that one university took to update its journal list.

Faculty at schools wishing to attain or maintain AACSB accreditation status must produce intellectual contributions that are congruent with their mission. As the then-AACSB Chair Williams (2012) noted, such benchmarks should significantly relate to the individual program's peer and aspirational schools. Prior studies provide evidence on this issue. For example, several studies have measured tenured and promoted faculty members' research records (e.g., Campbell & Morgan, 1987; Glover et al., 2006; Hasselback & Reinstein, 2011; Hasselback, Reinstein, & Reckers, 2011; Street, Baril, & Benke, 1993) to help individual faculty members gauge their own research progress.

Developing valid journal lists based on peer and aspirational programs involves many of the same techniques and associated problems as benchmarking faculty research productivity. These methods can include surveying department chairs, deans or faculty members, reviewing the published literature of ranking studies, citation studies, or using other techniques — each with its own set of challenges.

## NEED FOR BROADER LISTS OF JOURNALS

While the literature reviewed above finds near unanimity in ranking premier journals, the limited faculties publishing there indicate a need for broader, valid sets of journal lists — especially when a research mission states that a program seeks to publish in a diverse set of journals. Hasselback et al. (2012) indicate that since a relatively small percentage of accounting faculty consistently publish in the top 40 journals, accounting programs should develop realistic research benchmarks. Moreover, Attaway, Baxendale, Foster, and Karcher (2008) measure the proportion of articles from 38 journals written by faculty from four types of programs: (1) U.S. accounting doctoral-granting programs, (2) U.S. non-accounting doctoral-granting programs, (3) non-U.S. programs, and (4) business, government, association, or other institutions. They find much variation in the proportion of articles in 40 journals of faculty output among these four types of programs. For example, faculty at U.S. accounting doctoral-granting programs generate 79.3% of all

JAR articles, but only 32.6% of all *Accounting, Organizations & Society* (AOS) articles. They thus conclude that accounting programs should create more realistic journal lists.

In contrast to the potentially positive effects of journal lists, Sangster (2015) stresses that journal lists negatively impact accounting education. They can impact academic freedom, merit pay, P & T standards, and teaching loads. Since most faculty do not publish in the top journals listed in most journal lists, distinguishing the remaining faculty can be difficult. Parker (2011) found many universities increasingly using convergent and homogenized research missions, reflecting their obsession with misapplying single sets of rankings across all business disciplines. Such uniform methods to rank research often stifle imagination, innovation, and critique; hence the need for dynamic journal lists across the academic environment.

Moore (2015) claims an improper search for symbolic markers of prestige or the implied demands of the accrediting body led to the journal list adoption processes more than any well-thought out mission-driven focus on solving a functional public interest problem related to poor-quality research. Such lists too often have participants unable to define the attributes of high-quality research on an a-priori basis. Thus, the faculty should gather broad input to develop journal lists that reflect their programs' research missions.

Analyzing articles that Spanish academics wrote from 1998 to 2015, Moya, Prior, and Rodríguez-Pérez (2015) found that journal list pressures caused a major shift from publishing in professional to academic journals. This change impaired the transmission of knowledge from university to society and jeopardized the relationship between accounting research and professional practice. This trend contradicts the primary demand of the Pathways Commission (Behn et al., 2012) — to bridge the gap between accounting academe and practice. Thus, broad and objective journal lists — using faculty input — can help minimize the above objections to this assessment method, and help accounting programs meet their individual research assessment goals.

## RESEARCH METHOD

### *Journal List Sample*

Glover et al.'s (2012) research benchmark study of the Top 75 U.S. accounting programs formed a starting point to define nationally ranked schools for our study. We also used their definition of the top 27 accounting journals as a baseline upon which our study expands. Rather than ranking accounting programs, we generated a broad journal list to reflect the consensus of our convenience sample of 38 programs. We initially surveyed 40 accounting programs, asking for copies of their journal lists in order to help WSU update its journal rankings. Of the 40 inquiries we received 37 responses – three of whom stated that they had no lists,[2] deriving 34 usable responses. Our Internet search for other accounting programs with journal lists found three additional schools. Adding WSU's own journal list, we derived a total sample of 38 programs consisting of: five urban programs (including WSU), 20 non-top 75 programs that Glover et al. (2012) identified (including 15[3] that offered doctoral degrees in accounting and five that did not), and 13 top 75 programs of which three did not offer doctoral degrees in accounting.

# RESULTS

## *A Broad Journal List*

We used 38 sampled schools to develop our journal dataset, also generating a list of 1,436 data points of 359 journals ranked A+, A, A−, B, or C. These journal rankings match Glover et al.'s (2012) journal ranking method that listed the highest ranked journals as "A+" journals and the lowest ones as "C" journals – and included no rankings below "C." Given the efforts to develop individual journal lists, we assume that programs give little, if any, credit to journals not on their lists. We matched our responses onto the above five journal categories by interpreting the response rankings into the Glover et al. (2012) ranking system. For example, we ranked "A+" journals that our sample schools placed in their highest category – as *elite*, *best*, or *A*. While different programs often value the same journal differently, our approach used a uniform coding to assess how different schools assess various journals.

While near unanimity exists in schools classifying top journals, divergence often arises in ranking lower level ones – with perceived top schools generally ranking fewer journals than lower ranking ones. Upon examining 16 studies, Bonner, Hesford, Van der Stede, and Young (2006) found that *Contemporary Accounting Research* (CAR), AOS, JAE, JAR, and TAR most consistently rank among the top five in accounting, while many programs give some credit to high-level journals published in top journals in such specialty areas as auditing (e.g., *Auditing: A Journal of Practice and*

*Theory* (AJPT)), management accounting (e.g., *Journal of Management Accounting Research* (JMAR)) and taxation (e.g., *Journal of the American Taxation Association* (JATA)).

Other studies have examined alternate methods to assess the quality of a broad set of journals. For example, Chan, Seow, and Tam (2009) ranked journals using citation counts from 1999 to 2003 indicating JAR, AOS, TAR, and JAE as top journals. Brown (2003) and Brown and Laksmana (2004) ranked journals based on the frequency of articles downloaded on the Social Science Research Network (SSRN), finding five journals that many elite ranking studies often ignore: *Journal of Financial Economics, Review of Accounting Studies, Review of Quantitative Finance and Accounting, Journal of Corporate Finance,* and *Journal of International Financial Management and Accounting.* However, Chow, Haddad, Singh, and Wu (2007) found many highly cited SSCI-cited articles do not appear in the top three accounting journals, supporting the need to evaluate each article on its own merit, rather than abdicating this responsibility by using journal ranking as a key proxy for quality. While alternate measures of quality exist, each with their own advantages and disadvantages, our study uses a method to develop a consensus ranking process congruent with a school's mission.

Upon examining the data, we segregated the 359 sampled journals that appeared in at least five sampled schools' journal lists and the remaining 286 journals from four or fewer of such schools. At the end of our deliberations, we asked the 34 responding schools (including WSU, but ignoring the ones on the Internet) for permission to list their names in our study. Twelve programs denied this permission or did not respond to our request.

Next, accounting programs usually tailor their journal lists to their research missions. For example, given their usually rigorous research missions, flagship public institutions and preeminent private universities generally place many more resources and resultant high research expectations than do most regional and urban programs — which often have more modest research missions congruent with a greater emphasis on teaching or service to their regions and urban areas. Exhibit 1 lists the 26 programs that allowed us to use their names plus journal lists that we found on the Internet, which we classify into four school types: (1) urban non-doctoral-granting programs typically located in a large city with many commuter students; (2) non-nationally ranked per Glover et al. (2012) not offering doctoral programs; (3) non-nationally ranked programs offering doctoral degrees in Accounting; and (4) nationally ranked programs named in Glover et al.'s (2012) list of Top 75 Accounting Programs, of which ten do and three do not offer doctoral degrees in Accounting.

***Exhibit 1.*** Listing by Program Type of All 26 Respondents Who Allowed
Their Names to Be Identified, Plus Programs Whose Journal Rankings
Were Found on the Internet.[a]

Type I (*n* = 5):
Urban non-doctoral-granting programs typically located in a large city with many
commuter students
University of Alabama-Birmingham
University of Louisville
University of Missouri-St. Louis
Wayne State University
Other[b] (*n* = 1)

Type II (*n* = 5):
Non-nationally ranked per Glover et al. (2012) not offering doctoral programs
Auburn University
DePaul University
Marquette University
Other[b] (*n* = 2)

Type III (*n* = 15):
Non-nationally ranked programs offering Doctoral Degrees in Accounting
Case Western Reserve University
Cleveland State University
Drexel University
Georgia Tech University
SUNY Buffalo
University of Central Florida
University of Kentucky
University of Memphis
University of North Texas
University of Texas-Dallas
University of Texas-San Antonio
Other[b] (*n* = 4)

Type IV (*n* = 13):
Nationally ranked programs named in Glover et al.'s (2012) list of Top 75 Accounting
Programs, of which 10 do and three do not offer Doctoral Degrees in Accounting
Boston College
Brigham Young University
University of Illinois at Urbana-Champaign
University of Iowa
University of Notre Dame
Pennsylvania State University
Syracuse University
University of Texas-Austin
Other[b] (*n* = 5)

[a]Some schools requested us to note that they were updating their journal ranking lists or that
these were informal lists.
[b]Other programs are those that did not allow us reveal their names.

Adapting Glover et al.'s (2012) methodology, Exhibit 2 lists their top 27 journals under Top 6 (A+), Next 9 (A) and Next 12 (A−). Appendix provides journal rankings for the 38 analyzed schools, plus Glover et al.'s (2012) top 27 journals as well as additional journals on lists provided by our sample of 38 schools resulting in an expanded ranking of 359 journals for the four types of programs. The rankings are grouped by type of school with individual school rankings so that the data can be aggregated in a manner which is compatible with a user's mission. The 38 schools listed 73 top journals, of which we placed the top 27 in Exhibit 2 and the remaining 46 in Exhibit 4.

In Exhibit 2, we use Glover et al.'s (2012) labels in the first column, followed by the list of journals in Column 2. The current study's ratings are presented under five columns headed by A+, A, A−, B, and C, where the highest proportions of journal selections are presented to show the journals that received the largest selections by our sample. The next column provides the total number of journal selections, followed by the final column that presents a weighted average ranking for each journal. We calculated the weighted averages by assigning a weight of five to A+ journals, four to A journals, and three, two, and one, respectively, to A−, B, and C journals. As reported later in Exhibit 5, we use these weights to test differences in perceptions of journal tiers.

Exhibit 2 shows high consensus for high-quality journals and lower consensus for lower quality journals. For example, the proportion of our sample schools rating these elite journals as "A+" ranged from 79% (for *Review of Accounting Studies*) to 100% (for JAE, JAR, and TAR); only one program ranked any such journal below "A." The corresponding weighted average ratings (i.e., journal weights times the number of schools selecting the journal divided by total responses for each journal) range from 4.76 to 5.00. The high top 6 journals ratings conform to the findings in the prior literature. For example, Reinstein and Calderon (2006) report that the elite doctoral-granting schools, schools that have no doctoral degrees, and even schools whose faculties have not published in any elite journals, often rank journals as elite — although many respondents from lower ranked schools never read their contents (i.e., a halo effect).

The next nine journals in Exhibit 2 are ranked as excellent (A). The proportion of the sampled schools selecting the journal ranged from 50% (for *Journal of Business, Finance and Accounting*) to 76% (for *Journal of Accounting, Auditing and Finance*). The corresponding weighted averages are 3.65 and 4.16, respectively.

*Exhibit 2.* 38[a] Sampled Schools Journal Quality Based Primarily on Glover et al. (2012) and by Schools in the Sample.

| Glover et al. (2012) | Journal | Number of Schools That Ranked Each Journal (Percentage Represents the Most Frequent Ranking) | | | | | Total Answers | Weighted Average |
|---|---|---|---|---|---|---|---|---|
| | | A+ (5) | A (4) | A− (3) | B (2) | C (1) | | |
| Top 6 (A+) | Journal of Accounting and Economics | 37(100%) | 0 | 0 | 0 | 0 | 37 | 5.00 |
| | Journal of Accounting Research | 38(100%) | 0 | 0 | 0 | 0 | 38 | 5.00 |
| | The Accounting Review | 38(100%) | 0 | 0 | 0 | 0 | 38 | 5.00 |
| | Accounting, Organizations and Society | 27(84%) | 5 | 0 | 0 | 0 | 32 | 4.84 |
| | Contemporary Accounting Research | 35(92%) | 3 | 0 | 0 | 0 | 38 | 4.92 |
| | Review of Accounting Studies | 26(79%) | 6 | 1 | 0 | 0 | 33 | 4.76 |
| Next 9 (A) | Accounting Horizons | 6 | 14(61%) | 3 | 0 | 0 | 23 | 4.13 |
| | Auditing: A Journal of Practice & Theory | 7 | 17(68%) | 1 | 0 | 0 | 25 | 4.24 |
| | Behavioral Research in Accounting | 5 | 17(74%) | 1 | 1 | 0 | 23 | 4.17 |
| | Journal of Accounting and Public Policy | 5 | 18(75%) | 1 | 0 | 0 | 24 | 4.17 |

| | | | | | | | |
|---|---|---|---|---|---|---|---|
| Journal of Accounting, Auditing and Finance | 5 | 19(76%) | 1 | 0 | 0 | 25 | 4.16 |
| Journal of Accounting Literature | 2 | 14(67%) | 4 | 1 | 0 | 21 | 3.81 |
| Journal of Business, Finance and Accounting | 3 | 10(50%) | 4 | 3 | 0 | 20 | 3.65 |
| Journal of the American Taxation Association, The | 6 | 16(70%) | 1 | 0 | 0 | 23 | 4.22 |
| National Tax Journal | 3 | 10(67%) | 0 | 2 | 0 | 15 | 3.93 |
| Next 12 (A−) Abacus | 1 | 12(60%) | 6 | 1 | 0 | 20 | 3.65 |
| Accounting and Business Research | 1 | 7(44%) | 5 | 3 | 0 | 16 | 3.38 |
| Accounting and the Public Interest | 0 | 3 | 3 | 4(40%) | 0 | 10 | 2.90 |
| Advances in Accounting | 1 | 8(42%) | 6 | 4 | 0 | 19 | 3.32 |
| Advances in Taxation | 0 | 3 | 7(54%) | 2 | 1 | 13 | 2.92 |
| Issues in Accounting Education | 1 | 12(60%) | 6 | 1 | 0 | 20 | 3.65 |
| Journal of Accounting Education | 1 | 4 | 8(42%) | 6 | 0 | 19 | 3.00 |
| Journal of Information Systems | 2 | 13(72%) | 3 | 0 | 0 | 18 | 3.94 |
| Journal of Management Accounting Research | 4 | 15(71%) | 2 | 0 | 0 | 21 | 4.10 |

***Exhibit 2.*** *(Continued)*

| Glover et al. (2012) Journal | Number of Schools That Ranked Each Journal (Percentage Represents the Most Frequent Ranking) | | | | | Total Answers | Weighted Average |
|---|---|---|---|---|---|---|---|
| | A+ (5) | A (4) | A− (3) | B (2) | C (1) | | |
| *Research in Governmental and Nonprofit Accounting* | 1 | 2 | 6(46%) | 4 | 0 | 13 | 3.00 |
| *Research in Accounting Regulation* | 1 | 2 | 5(38%) | 5(38%) | 0 | 13 | 2.92 |
| *Review of Quantitative Finance and Accounting* | 0 | 5(45%) | 3 | 3 | 0 | 11 | 3.18 |

[a]The 38 sampled programs include 34 respondents; 3 from the Internet; WSU's own rankings which we relate to Glover et al.'s (2012) rankings.

The evidence on the next 120 journals (A– per Glover et al. 2012, plus two others deriving high composite scores – *Accounting and the Public Interest* and *Research in Accounting Regulation*) indicates high variation due to some shifting from "A–" to "A" for some of these journals since more of our sample gives an "A" ranking to these journals than an "A–." In fact, based on the proportion of the programs' rankings, seven of the 10 journals can be reclassified as excellent (A) journals because the sample journal lists gave higher proportion of journals to A than to A– (see journals in the "Next 10" category in Exhibit 2). A few of the 38 accounting programs even ranked these journals as A +.

We show in Exhibit 3 how our four types of programs ranked the top 27 journals. For example, when one examines the first two columns, four of the five Type I schools ranked JATA. All four of these schools ranked JATA as an "A" (excellent) journal.

Exhibit 4 lists the next 46 journals, which received lower rankings (B or C) mixed with a few A or A– (and occasional A +) rankings, but no recognizable pattern. Thus we present these journals in an alphabetical order in Exhibit 4 without any indication of journal rankings. These results indicate high variation among our sample's journal lists.

To examine journal rankings by category, we computed differences in means as shown in Exhibit 5. The scoring scheme to compute the average was A + (5), A (4), A– (3), B (2), and C (1). For example, the mean score of B journals is 2.87, arising from some of our study's schools ranking a B journal higher than B. The analysis reveals that comparisons of journal ranking categories differ significantly, except for B and C ranked journals. Differentiation beyond the top three categories (A +, A, A–) is not discernible. Thus, there appear to be generally accepted "bright lines" among the top three categories. Schools can tailor their listings from the wide variety of B or C classified journals to create their own sets of acceptable journals outside the top A +, A, and A– categories.

## INSIGHTS FROM OUR SAMPLED SCHOOLS

### *Ranking*

To help accounting programs develop their own criteria, we now highlight how WSU identified a broad list of potentially ranked journals, which we

**Exhibit 3.** Four Types of Schools Ranking Glover et al.'s Top 6, Next 9 and Next 12 Journals.

| Glover et al. (2012) | Journal | Type I Urban Non-Doctoral (5 Schools) | | Type II Non-Nationally Ranked, Non-Doctoral (5 Schools) | | Type III Non-Nationally Ranked, Doctoral (15 Schools) | | Type IV Nationally Ranked (13 Schools) | |
|---|---|---|---|---|---|---|---|---|---|
| | | # of schools ranking the journal | Most frequent ranking in this category (percentage) | # of schools ranking the journal | Most frequent ranking in this category (percentage) | # of schools ranking the journal | Most frequent ranking in this category (Percentage) | # of schools ranking the journal | Most frequent ranking in this category (percentage) |
| Top 6 (A+) | Journal of Accounting and Economics | 5 | A + (100%) | 5 | A + (100%) | 14 | A + (100%) | 13 | A + (100%) |
| | Journal of Accounting Research | 5 | A + (100%) | 5 | A + (100%) | 15 | A + (100%) | 13 | A + (100%) |
| | The Accounting Review | 5 | A + (100%) | 5 | A + (100%) | 15 | A + (100%) | 13 | A + (100%) |
| | Accounting, Organizations and Society | 5 | A + (100%) | 5 | A + (100%) | 11 | A + (79%) | 6 | A + (75%) |
| | Contemporary Accounting Research | 5 | A + (100%) | 5 | A + (100%) | 13 | A + (89%) | 12 | A + (92%) |
| | Review of Accounting Studies | 4 | A + (75%) | 5 | A + (100%) | 9 | A + (78%) | 9 | A + (90%) |
| Next 9 (A) | Accounting Horizons | 5 | A + (60%) | 5 | A (100%) | 11 | A 45% | 2 | A (100%) |
| | Auditing: A Journal of Practice & Theory | 5 | A (80%) | 5 | A (80%) | 11 | A + (45%) | 4 | A (100%) |
| | Behavioral Research in Accounting | 5 | A (80%) | 5 | A (80%) | 10 | A (55%) | 3 | A (100%) |
| | Journal of Accounting and Public Policy | 5 | A (80%) | 5 | A (60%) | 11 | A (72%) | 3 | A (100%) |
| | Journal of Accounting, Auditing and Finance | 5 | A (80%) | 5 | A (60%) | 11 | A (72%) | 4 | A (100%) |

| Journal | | | | | | | |
|---|---|---|---|---|---|---|---|
| Journal of Accounting Literature | 5 | A (60%) | 5 | A (80%) | 10 | A (67%) | 1 | A (100%) |
| Journal of Business, Finance and Accounting | 3 | B (67%) | 4 | A (100%) | 9 | A− (44%) | 4 | A (75%) |
| Journal of the American Taxation Association, The | 4 | A (100%) | 4 | A (75%) | 10 | A (60%) | 5 | A (60%) |
| National Tax Journal | 2 | A (50%) | 5 | A (60%) | 7 | A (71%) | 1 | A (100%) |
| Abacus | 5 | A (40%) | 5 | A (80%) | 8 | A (63%) | 2 | A (50%) |
| Accounting and Business Research | 3 | B (67%) | 4 | A (50%) | 7 | A (57%) | 2 | A (50%) |
| Accounting and the Public Interest | 2 | A− (50%) | 4 | B (50%) | 4 | B (75%) | 0 | N/A |
| Advances in Accounting | 5 | A (60%) | 5 | A− (60%) | 8 | A− (38%) | 1 | A− (100%) |
| Advances in Taxation | 3 | A− (33%) | 3 | A− (67%) | 6 | A− (50%) | 1 | A− (100%) |
| Issues in Accounting Education | 5 | A (60%) | 5 | A (80%) | 9 | A (56%) | 1 | A− (100%) |
| Journal of Accounting Education | 5 | A (40%) | 5 | A− (80%) | 7 | B (57%) | 2 | A− (50%) |
| Journal of Information Systems | 5 | A (80%) | 4 | A (100%) | 8 | A (63%) | 1 | A− (100%) |
| Journal of Management Accounting Research | 5 | A (80%) | 5 | A (80%) | 9 | A (67%) | 2 | A (50%) |
| Research in Governmental and Nonprofit Accounting | 3 | A+ (33%) | 3 | A− (100%) | 6 | B (50%) | 1 | A− (100%) |
| Research in Accounting Regulation | 4 | B (50%) | 5 | A− (80%) | 4 | B (75%) | 0 | N/A |
| Review of Quantitative Finance and Accounting | 2 | A (50%) | 2 | A (50%) | 5 | A (60%) | 2 | A− (50%) |

Next 12 (A−)

***Exhibit 4.***　Other Frequently Ranked Journals by the 38 Schools in the Sample.

*Academy of Accounting and Financial Studies Journal*

*Accounting and Finance*

*Accounting Education: An International Journal*

*The Accounting Educators' Journal*

*Accounting Forum*

*Accounting Historians Journal*

*Accounting, Auditing & Accountability Journal*

*Advances in Accounting Behavioral Research*

*Advances in Accounting Education: Teaching and Curriculum Innovations*

*Advances in Accounting Information Systems*

*Advances in International Accounting*

*Advances in Management Accounting*

*Advances in Public Interest Accounting*

*British Accounting Review, The*

*Critical Perspectives on Accounting*

*Current Issues in Auditing*

*European Accounting Review*

*Internal Auditing*

*Internal Auditor*

*International Journal of Accounting, The*

*International Journal of Accounting Information Systems*

*International Journal of Auditing*

*International Journal of Intelligent Systems in Accounting, Finance and Management*

*Journal of Accountancy*

*Journal of Accounting Ethics and Public Policy*

*Journal of Business Ethics*

*Journal of Cost Management*

*Journal of Emerging Technologies in Accounting*

*Journal of Forensic Accounting*

*Journal of International Accounting Research*

*Journal of International Accounting, Auditing and Taxation*

*Journal of International Financial Management & Accounting*

*Journal of Public Budgeting, Accounting & Financial Management*

*Journal of Taxation*

**Exhibit 4.** (*Continued*)

*Management Accounting Quarterly*

*Management Accounting Research*

*Management Accounting/Strategic Finance*

*Managerial Auditing [Research]*

*Ohio CPA Journal*

*Pacific Accounting Review*

*The CPA Journal*

*The Tax Adviser*

*The Tax Executive*

*Tax Notes*

*Taxes – The Tax Magazine*

*The ATA Journal of Legal Tax Research*

**Exhibit 5.** Differences in Mean Journal Rankings (*p*-values).

| Ranking | Weight | Mean Weight | SD | Difference in Mean Weight Score (*p*-Values from *t*-tests) | | | |
|---|---|---|---|---|---|---|---|
| | | | | Ranking | | | |
| | | | | A+ | A | A− | B |
| A+ | 5 | 4.92 | 0.10 | | | | |
| A | 4 | 4.05 | 0.21 | 0.87 | | | |
| | | | | 0.0000 | | | |
| A− | 3 | 3.33 | 0.42 | 1.59 | 0.72 | | |
| | | | | 0.0000 | 0.0001 | | |
| B | 2 | 2.87 | 0.42 | 2.05 | 1.18 | 0.46 | |
| | | | | 0.0000 | 0.0000 | 0.0036 | |
| C | 1 | 2.83 | 0.98 | 2.09 | 1.22 | 0.50 | 0.04 |
| | | | | 0.0000 | 0.0000 | 0.0018 | 0.6227 |

culled to meet the limited number of journals that we could use as the key basis to assess the research components for merit raises, P & T decisions, faculty workloads, spring/summer research grants, and sabbatical purposes.

WSU's recent decision to update its accounting program's journal list motivated this case study. An urban AACSB-accredited school, WSU offers undergraduate and master's, but not doctoral degrees in accounting. WSU's peer schools also have urban locations and missions, and do not offer doctoral degrees in accounting. While WSU's faculty named four aspirational schools, its Accounting Department Journal Vetting Committee wanted to examine other peer and aspirational schools' journal lists — those offering and not offering accounting doctoral degrees — plus nationally ranked accounting programs.

WSU's accounting and four non-accounting programs each ranked about 4–6 "A+" journals; 7–9 "A" journals; and 20–25 "B" journals, with tri-annual reexaminations based upon peer and aspirational schools rankings, journal rankings from the discipline's literature or citation studies. A+ journals usually appear on multiple aspirational schools' lists and on the *Financial Times* (FT) Top 45 list.[4] Other programs can similarly rank as many journals they see fit into each category (including ranking "C" journals).

## Journal Lists Modifications

Some programs use specific criteria to define journal rankings, for example, whether practicing accountants regularly read these journals (e.g., *Journal of Accountancy*, *The CPA Journal*, and *Strategic Finance*). Others limit their premier journals to the very top echelon of scholarly outlets, or state that publication in such journals would likely derive positive P & T recommendations (for research expectations) at peer research universities and at research universities with reputations to which they aspire. Walker et al. (2010) associate this lack of department-specific written scholarship standards or journal lists with faculty perceptions of vague P & T scholarship criteria. Greater emphasizing publications in elite accounting journals also often "harms" junior faculty in programs with no formal P & T guidelines. Programs often use such journal ranking criteria as "A+," "A," or "strong" categories to include journals that:

• Are highly respected and which many programs place in their top tiers — allowing some dispersion of views as to whether these outlets have attained premier status.

"A−" or "high-quality" categories include journals that:

- Peer programs would view positively for P & T decisions, but by themselves would not lead to P & T.

"B" or "quality" categories include journals that:

- Many (non-Top 75) programs would view as those below the high-quality list, but which still contained rigorous publication standards.

Lastly, lower-level journals (e.g., "C") include those that several programs consider as strong enough to "count."

Many of our 38 accounting programs allow certain flexibilities for their faculty in forming journal lists. For example, one program allows faculty to request placing a non-listed journal in a specific category after the article was accepted using program criteria (e.g., peer and aspirational school rankings and citation studies), plus the caliber of the journal's editorial board. Another program allowed such appeals to occur *before* the faculty member completed the journal article, which seems to be a presumably fairer policy.

## ADDITIONAL ANALYSIS

### *Examining Lower-Level Journals*

The 286 lower-level journals in appendix indicate a wide variety of acceptable journals below the A+, A, and A− tiers. This may be reflective of the variety of missions for our sampled schools as well as perhaps an outcome of the political process inherent in developing these lists. Publication pressure has also led to the rise of "predatory" journals, which send announcements to a wide array of faculty members asking them to submit their journals along with publication fees. Beall (2014) finds many such journals, which we compared to the journals in our appendix. Surprisingly, none of our 359 journals appeared in any of the 743 journals in Beall's (2014) list. Thus, our sampled accounting programs do not grant credit for faculty publications in vanity or predatory press journals.

## SELECTING PEER SCHOOLS

Former AACSB Chair Williams (2012) notes that just as the dictionary defines "peer" as something of the same rank, value, quality, or ability, the

AACSB requires peer schools to have similar characteristics in terms of mission, priorities, degree programs and orientation. WSU's deliberations found several criteria to define peer and aspirational schools, such as accreditation; school mission; degrees granted; student size; student type (e.g., undergraduate or graduate); faculty type (e.g., full- and part-time); faculty size; Carnegie Classification (e.g., Public or Private and High or Very High Research Activity); endowment size; and operating budget.

### Process of Selecting Journals

After obtaining broad lists of journal rankings from our participants (shown in Appendix), we used both Glover et al.'s (2012) journal break-down and our survey results as the primary basis to update WSU's journal list. We ignored journals that appeared on fewer than four of our examined programs' rankings in any category. We prioritized (in ascending order) all named aspirational schools, other peer and aspirational non-Top 75 programs that offered doctoral degrees in accounting, non-Top 75 programs that offered doctoral degrees in accounting, and Top 75 programs named. To maintain credibility, we sought to move approximately the same number of journals "up" on our list as we moved "down."

For example, the WSU Committee recommended adding *Review of Accounting Studies* to our "A+" list, since it appeared on the FT Top 45 list, the Glover et al. (2012) "Through Top 6" category, and 26 of our 33 schools who rated this journal ranked it as a top journal. Interestingly, the next highest numbers of such classifications were for *Auditing: A Journal of Practice & Theory* with five such top rankings and *Accounting Horizons* with four. We proposed upgrading the *Journal of Business, Finance and Accounting* to "A" from "B" and downgrading *Journal of Information Systems* (*JIS*) to "B" from "A," again due to our survey results and Glover et al.'s (2012) findings; for example, its 3.94 overall score in Appendix was lower than any other ranked "A" journal. This downgrading of some systems journals occurred with full support of the chair of the school-wide oversight committee who was a senior accounting systems faculty member. He did so after examining how our peer and aspirational schools ranked such journals.

The WSU committee also suggested removing *Advances in Accounting Information Systems* and *International Journal of Accounting Information Systems* from our "B" list, and adding the *European Accounting Review*, as well as three AAA journals (*Accounting and the Public Interest, Current*

*Issues in Auditing,* and *Journal of International Accounting Research*), plus four other well-ranked journals – *International Journal of Auditing, Advances in Accounting Behavioral Research, Research in Accounting Regulation,* and *Tax Notes*) based on other peer and aspirational school rankings.

Finally, we summarize in Exhibit 6 eight other important issues that arose in the WSU committee deliberations, whose resolution could help other programs develop their own journal ranking lists. WSU's Committee used this processes to develop its new suggested rankings with virtual unanimity and no rancor, and then passed its recommendations to the entire Accounting Department and to the Business School Committee and Dean, again with no objections received.

***Exhibit 6.*** Issues and Responses in WSU's Revised Journal List Criteria.

| Issue No. | Issue to Address in Developing Journal Rankings | WSU's Solution to this Issue |
|---|---|---|
| 1 | WSU wanting to ascertain the journal lists of the Top 75 accounting programs nationwide, that is, beyond its peer and aspirational schools. | To increase our national exposure, we examined these premier accounting programs' journal lists and help WSU objectively decide which faculty members should receive the large resources available to its top researchers. Such resources included hitting "A+" journals becoming a key criterion for promotion and tenure, receiving much lighter teaching loads than other faculty members, and getting a three-year $75,000 Dean's Research Grant (in lieu of teaching during the spring or summer semesters). |
| 2 | Ensuring committee members' decisions represent all accounting disciplines (e.g., tax, international accounting, MIS, and business ethics) rather than their own research areas. | WSU required that at least five other accounting programs ranked (or failed to rank) all potential journals to consider adding (or deleting) a journal to or from our lists. All committee members pledged to consider the journal lists of all colleagues (rather than merely one's own) in making these decisions. |
| 3 | Minimizing personal conflicts when making journal list decisions. | The WSU Committee often communicated by email, rather than in person, to decrease personal conflicts in its deliberations. |
| 4 | Minimizing tenured faculty "pressuring" untenured faculty to vote with them, especially in difficult decisions. | A non-tenured, research-active faculty member chaired the Committee, and required copying all incoming and outgoing e-mails to all committee members regarding this process. |

### Exhibit 6.    (Continued)

| Issue No. | Issue to Address in Developing Journal Rankings | WSU's Solution to this Issue |
|---|---|---|
| 5 | Limiting the number of journals that made the lists, besides merely counting the number of schools ranking such journals? | WSU required at least four of the five available Committee votes to add or delete journals from its prior lists. Besides the method described in Exhibit 2, WSU agreed to add only one journal, *Review of Accounting Studies* to its "A+ Watch List" of journals that will likely appear in future "A+" lists. WSU then repeated this process for its current "A" and "B" journal lists – without using Watch Lists. |
| 6 | Determining the number of journals to place in our final lists, since all other Departments have about 5–7 A+ journals, usually matching the *Financial Times* (FT) journal lists. | WSU also used this constraint, although fewer of its accounting faculty usually "hit" A+ journals than do faculty in other disciplines (cf., Swanson, 2004). |
| 7 | Counting *Journal of Business Ethics* (JBE) that is on the FT list, plus other non-accounting journals not appearing on the FT list. | All five business school Departments agreed to put JBE along with *Business Ethics Quarterly* on a general Journal list, but rate as an "A" journal. The "A+" general Journal list also included five other, elite Business journals: *American Business Law Review, Harvard Business Review, Journal of International Business Studies, Management Science,* and *MIT Sloan Management Review* |
| 8 | Balancing practitioner and academic components of journal lists | We ranked as B two practitioner journals (i.e., *The CPA Journal* and *Journal of Accountancy*) and gave "some" credit for other leading practitioner journals (e.g., *Management Accounting Quarterly, Strategic Finance,* and *The Internal Auditor.* |

# DISCUSSION AND CONCLUSIONS

Given other schools' journal ranking policies, we find no one method to fit all programs. After sampling 38 accounting programs we suggest that programs consider our method to develop their own lists, adapting it to their mission statements' current and future research productivity standards measures. Our data, related analyses, and reflection upon our experiences in updating our journal list provide information for schools developing or updating their own journal lists. Exhibit 7 summarizes WSU's research journal ranking procedures.

In addition to the factors we considered, a school may wish to consider the following factors. Programs can consider the trend or time elements as programs include newer journals or those that did not improve their quality for long periods of time. For P & T, annual evaluations and other similar purposes, programs should also consider other issues with using journal lists, stressing that journal lists should primarily reflect an accounting program's research mission. Herron and Hall (2004) found that the top 20 highest quality journals for sub-discipline areas have little in common with an overall top 20 journal listing − stressing that sub-discipline journal ratings may be more useful for some decisions than a single overall ranking list. Since strong research can appear in weak journals, and vice versa, committee members could assess publication quality by both consulting journal lists and carefully reading the journal articles under consideration − especially for critical decisions such as P & T decisions. In light of a program's

***Exhibit 7.*** Summary of Steps Needed to Derive a Program's Journal Listing.

1. Have the departmental faculty agree on the need to develop such lists, for example, spurred by AACSB accreditation requirements or to increase the perceived objectivity of assessing research.

2. The business school and Dean should concur on the key parameters of this listing (e.g., maximum number of "A" journals to count; how to consider unranked journals).

3. Elect a faculty committee to represent various accounting areas (e.g., financial accounting, AIS, and taxation).

4. Develop Journal List Committee criteria (e.g., printed journal ranking studies and peer and aspirational schools rankings) to justify initial journal rankings and "movements" in rankings.

5. Set standards for including or excluding certain journals (e.g., require a majority to renew a journal from a prior list, but a two-thirds vote to remove or add a journal to the list).

6. Have all tenured/tenure-track faculty vote to accept, add or delete journals to these lists.

7. Check that all "standard-sized" business school departments (e.g., Accounting and Finance) use about the same numbers of journals in all journal categories (e.g., premier, strong, and good journals) − recognizing that much smaller (e.g., Logistics) and much larger (e.g., Economics) can use fewer or greater numbers of journals than do "standard-sized" faculty departments.

8. Develop department and school committees to periodically update such lists (e.g., every five years) and to assess the quality of journals not appearing on such lists (e.g., premier science or anthropology journals).

research mission, no single method should serve as a *sole surrogate* to assess research quality.

Programs should also recognize some pitfalls of using journal lists, including ranking journals unknown to most of their colleagues, or allowing deans and P & T committees to use these lists to prevent otherwise high-quality faculty from receiving P & T. Also, such lists should consider the inherent quality of the areas that faculty members research (e.g., tax, auditing, and systems) and the differences between empirical and practitioner research relative to the schools' teaching and research missions (e.g., importance of empirical research).

Our study has several limitations that signal a need for future investigation. First, we believe that departmental colleagues reading their colleagues' published papers provide higher validity in assessing publication quality than relying solely on journal lists. We also note, however, that many programs lack qualified reviewers with sufficient available time or expertise to assess a colleague's publication quality. Reference to the journal assessments of many sources such as Glover et al. (2012) and peer, aspirational, and nationally ranked schools can provide guidance to assess their colleague's research quality with more credibility.

Second, support for journal lists is not universal. For example, Willmott (2011) stresses that journal lists often stifle diversity, constrict scholarly innovation, and impair the overall research culture. Richardson (2008) echoes that counting too few journals to measure research quality often creates barriers to entry based on nationality, research method, or type/location of doctoral training. But most accounting programs in our sample noted the importance of journal rankings, while other programs permitted some flexibility in using such lists. For example, one accounting doctoral-granting program stated that P & T candidates should achieve a "sufficient" record of scholarly publications, which they could achieve via alternative combinations of scholarship. Another doctoral program generally required its untenured faculty to have 6−8 publications in A+ and A journals, with at least one A+ publication.

Other programs listed some qualitative factors that supplement journal rankings, such as: (1) the number of co-authors; (2) lead author designation; (3) existence of multi-disciplinary work; (4) research awards or other formal recognition; (5) type of research (academic, applied, or pedagogical); (6) frequency of citation or other impact indicators; and (7) presentations at conferences or workshops at other high-level universities.

Third, some of the sampled journal lists were generated earlier than others, and several respondents indicated that they soon plan to revisit their journal list rankings. Moreover, as stated at the bottom of Appendix while some programs use Glover et al. (2012), others use other methods. For example, Danielson and Heck (2010) used several studies to assess journal quality, including the *Financial Times* (FT) listing of the Top 40/45 Journals and the Australian Business Deans' Council (ABDC) Journal Lists. Nonetheless, inconsistency arises in how accounting programs rank lower level and non-accounting journals. For example, some highly ranked schools included some highly ranked finance (e.g., *Journal of Finance*) or ethics (e.g., *Journal of Business Ethics*) journals, but most accounting programs ranked only accounting journals. Also, some schools with relatively weak (strong) tax, international or MIS departments ranked such sub-disciplines very low (high).

Fourth, while highly ranked programs generally ranked few, mostly A +, journals, Hasselback et al. (2011) find that such programs often promoted or tenured faculty using a much wider spectrum of journals than they had indicated, a statement supported by our study. These points indicate that accounting programs contemplating new journal lists or revising old ones should be cognizant of informal journal evaluation processes in their own university. Also, random sampling for a future research study may be more appropriate than the convenience sampling we used in this study. Finally, based on our results, we believe that other pitfalls to using journal lists include (1) letting one clique of faculty dominate this process; and (2) keeping all faculty apprised of our tentative results and processes (e.g., types/names of schools surveyed and asking for input of other schools to survey), so that no surprises arise.

# SUMMARY

In summary, using journal lists can:

- More objectively assess colleagues' research productivity and strength, in order to assist with P & T and hiring decisions for experienced faculty members;
- Support the validity of allocation of school and university resources or to otherwise assess the quality of university programs, for example, for AACSB purposes; and
- Assess more objectively the faculty's research strength, for example, in deciding whether to add master's or doctoral programs and to hire experienced faculty members.

We developed our methodology from experience in constructing WSU's journal list — but it does not represent a one-size-fits-all approach. For example, while WSU only considered journals that at least five other programs used and limited the total number of A+, A, and B journals ranked, other programs can use higher or lower "counting" thresholds. Programs can apply our methodology, or develop/revise their own journal lists based on their own needs and circumstances. After all, who knows their own research needs better than they do?

## NOTES

1. WSU is a member of the Great Cities University Coalition (formerly the Urban 13), which includes programs such as the University of Missouri at St. Louis, the University of Illinois at Chicago, and the University of Louisville.
2. The fact that 37 of the 40 surveyed schools had such lists indicates that lists are a growing trend.
3. WSU deemed four of these 16 accounting doctoral-granting programs as "aspirational schools," whose research standards falls between Glover et al.'s (2012) top 75 schools and other PhD-granting schools.
4. "Notes" in A+/A journals will count as A+/A papers if they go through the standard peer-review process; however, such categorizations exclude book reviews, guest editorials, errata, short papers criticizing published papers at the editor's discretion, authors' responses to readers' comments, interpretations and research ideas, and other items not going through standard peer-review processes.

## ACKNOWLEDGMENTS

We thank Mohammad Abdolmohammadi (Bentley University), Natalie Churyk (Northern Illinois University), Melvin Houston (Attorney at Law), Marty Leibowitz (Yeshiva University), Brigitte Muehlmann (Babson College), Jim Rebele (Robert Morris University), Arline Savage (University of Alabama-Birmingham), Dave Stout (Youngstown State University), Leah Woodall (Google), Greg Trompeter (University of Central Florida), and Omar Zeben (Graduate Research Assistant, Wayne State University) for their excellent comments on an earlier draft of this chapter.

# REFERENCES

Association to Advance Collegiate Schools of Business (AACSB). (2013). *Accreditation guidelines*. Retrieved from http://www.aacsb.edu/en/accreditation/standards/2013-business/strategic-management-and-innovation/standard1/. Accessed on July 19, 2015.

Attaway, A. N., Baxendale, S. J., Foster, B. P., & Karcher, J. N. (2008). Reassessing accounting faculty scholarly expectations: Journal classification by author affiliation. *Academy of Educational Leadership Journal, 12*(3), 71–86.

Ballas, A., & Theoharakis, V. (2003). Exploring diversity in accounting through faculty journal perceptions. *Contemporary Accounting Research, 20*, 619–644.

Beall, J. (2014, January 2). *List of predatory publishers*. Retrieved from http://scholarlyoa.com/2014/01/02/list-of-predatory-publishers-2014/. Accessed on July 19, 2015.

Behn, B. K., Ezzell, W. F., Murphy, L. A., Rayburn, J. D., Stith, M. T., & Strawser, J. R. (2012). The Pathways Commission on accounting higher education: Charting a national strategy for the next generation of accountants. *Issues in Accounting Education, 27*(3), 595–600.

Bonner, S., Hesford, J., Van der Stede, W., & Young, S. (2006). The most influential journals in academic accounting. *Accounting, Organizations and Society, 31*, 663–685.

Brown, L. D. (2003). Ranking journals using social science research network downloads. *Review of Quantitative Finance and Accounting, 20*, 291–307.

Brown, L. D., & Gardner, J. C. (1985). Applying citation analysis to evaluate the research contributions of accounting faculty and doctoral programs. *The Accounting Review, 60*(2), 262–277.

Brown, L. D., & Laksmana, I. (2004). Ranking accounting PhD programs and faculties using social science research network downloads. *Review of Quantitative Finance and Accounting, 22*, 249–266.

Campbell, D. R., & Morgan, R. G. (1987). Publication activity of promoted accounting faculty. *Issues in Accounting Education, 2*(1), 28–43.

Chan, K. C., Chen, C. R., & Cheng, L. T. (2007). Global ranking of accounting programmes and the elite effect in accounting research. *Accounting & Finance, 47*(2), 187–220.

Chan, K. C., Seow, G. S., & Tam, K. (2009). Ranking accounting journals using dissertation citation analysis: A research note. *Accounting, Organizations and Society, 34*(6), 875–885.

Chow, C. W., Haddad, K., Singh, G., & Wu, A. (2007). On using journal rank to proxy for an article's contribution or value. *Issues in Accounting Education, 22*(3), 411–427.

Coyne, J. G., Summers, S. L., Williams, B., & Wood, D. A. (2010). Accounting program research rankings by topical area and methodology. *Issues in Accounting Education, 25*(4), 631–654.

Danielson, M. G., & Heck, J. L. (2010). Giving credit where credit is due: Summary analysis of the most prolific authors in 15 high-impact accounting journals. *Advances in Accounting, 26*(2), 195–206.

Everett, T. O., Klamm, B., & Stoltzfus, R. (2004). Developing benchmarks for evaluating publication records at doctoral programs in accounting. *Journal of Accounting Education, 22*(3), 229–252.

Glover, S. M., Prawitt, D. F., Summers, S. L., & Wood, D. A. (2012). Publication benchmarking data based on faculty promoted at the top 75 U.S. accounting research institutions. *Issues in Accounting Education, 27*(3), 647–670.

Glover, S. M., Prawitt, D., & Wood, D. A. (2006). Publication records of faculty promoted at the top 75 accounting research programs. *Issues in Accounting Education, 21*(3), 195–218.

Hasselback, J. R., & Reinstein, A. (2011). What happened to the class of year 2000: Examining their research records and current employment. *Advances in Accounting*, *27*(2), 318–324.

Hasselback, J. R., Reinstein, A., & Abdolmohammadi, M. (2012). Benchmarking the research productivity of accounting doctorates. *Issues in Accounting Education*, *27*(4), 943–978.

Hasselback, J. R., Reinstein, A., & Reckers, P. M. J. (2011). A longitudinal study of the research productivity of graduates of accounting doctoral programs. *Advances in Accounting*, *27*(1), 10–16.

Hasselback, J. R., Reinstein, A., & Schwan, E. S. (2000). Benchmarks for evaluating the research productivity of accounting faculty. *Journal of Accounting Education*, *18*, 79–97.

Hasselback, J. R., Reinstein, A., & Schwan, E. S. (2003). Prolific authors of accounting literature. *Advances in Accounting*, *20*, 95–125.

Herron, T. L., & Hall, T. W. (2004). Faculty perceptions of journals: Quality and publishing feasibility. *Journal of Accounting Education*, *22*(3), 2004.

Lewis, B. (2008). Judging the journals. *BizEd.*, November–December, pp. 42–45.

Moore, L. (2015). Exploring the role of symbolic legitimation in voluntary journal list adoption. *Accounting Education: An International Journal*, *24*(3), 256–273.

Moya, S., Prior, D., & Rodríguez-Pérez, G. (2015). Performance based incentives and the behavior of accounting academics: Responding to changes. *Accounting Education: An International Journal*, *24*(3), 208–232.

Parker, L. (2011). University corporatisation: Driving redefinition. *Critical Perspectives on Accounting*, *22*(4), 434–450.

Reinstein, A., & Calderon, T. G. (2006). Examining accounting departments' rankings of accounting journals. *Critical Perspectives on Accounting*, *17*(4), 457–490.

Richardson, A. J. (2008). Strategies in the development of accounting history as an academic discipline. *Accounting History*, *13*(3), 247–280.

Sangster, A. (2015). You cannot judge a book by its cover: The problems with journal rankings. *Accounting Education: An International Journal*, *24*(3), 175–186.

Street, D. L., Baril, C. P., & Benke, R. L., Jr. (1993). Research, teaching, and service in promotion and tenure decisions of accounting faculty. *Journal of Accounting Education*, *11*(1), 43–60.

Swanson, E. P. (2004). Publishing in the majors: A comparison of accounting, finance, management, and marketing. *Contemporary Accounting Research*, *21*(1), 223–255.

Trieschmann, J. S., Dennis, A. R., Northcraft, G. B., & Niemi, A. W. (2000). Serving multiple constituencies in the business school: MBA program versus research performance. *Academy of Management Journal*, *43*(6), 1130–1141.

Walker, K. B., Fleishman, G. M., & Stephenson, T. (2010). The incidence of documented standards for research in departments of accounting at U.S. institutions. *Journal of Accounting Education*, *28*(2), 43–52.

Williams, J. (2012, January). *AACSB Newsline*. The value of peer review, E-Newsline. Retrieved from http://enewsline.aacsb.edu/chair/value-of-peer-review.asp. Accessed on July 19, 2015.

Willmott, H. C. (2011). Journal list fetishism and the perversion of scholarship: Reactivity and the ABS List. *Organization*, *18*(4), 429–442.

# APPENDIX: ANALYSIS OF KEY SCHOOLS JOURNAL RANKINGS

| | Glover et al. (2012) | WSU | Urban Programs | | | | | | | | | Non-Nationally Ranked Schools *NOT* Offering Accounting Doctoral Degrees | | | | | | | | | |
|---|---|---|---|---|---|---|---|---|---|---|---|---|---|---|---|---|---|---|---|---|---|
| | | | U1 | U2 | U3 | U4 | A+ | A | A− | B | C | NNRND1 | NNRND2 | NNRND3 | NNRND4 | NNRND5 | A+ | A | A− | B | C |
| **A + /Elite** | | | | | | | | | | | | | | | | | | | | | |
| (Based Primarily Glover et al.'s Rankings) | | | | | | | | | | | | | | | | | | | | | |
| Journal of Accounting and Economics | A+ | A+ | A+ | A+ | A+ | A+ | 5 | 0 | 0 | 0 | 0 | A+ | A+ | A+ | A+ | A+ | 5 | 0 | 0 | 0 | 0 |
| Journal of Accounting Research | A+ | A+ | A+ | A+ | A+ | A+ | 5 | 0 | 0 | 0 | 0 | A+ | A+ | A+ | A+ | A+ | 5 | 0 | 0 | 0 | 0 |
| The Accounting Review | A+ | A+ | A+ | A+ | A+ | A+ | 5 | 0 | 0 | 0 | 0 | A+ | A+ | A+ | A+ | A+ | 5 | 0 | 0 | 0 | 0 |
| Accounting, Organizations and Society | A+ | A+ | A+ | A+ | A+ | A+ | 5 | 0 | 0 | 0 | 0 | A+ | A+ | A+ | A+ | A+ | 5 | 0 | 0 | 0 | 0 |
| Contemporary Accounting Research | A+ | A+ | A+ | A+ | A+ | A+ | 5 | 0 | 0 | 0 | 0 | A+ | A+ | A+ | A+ | A+ | 5 | 0 | 0 | 0 | 0 |
| Review of Accounting Studies | A+ | A | | A+ | A+ | A+ | 3 | 1 | 0 | 0 | 0 | A+ | A+ | A+ | A+ | A+ | 5 | 0 | 0 | 0 | 0 |
| **Total number of journals ranked** | 6 | 6 | 5 | 6 | 6 | 6 | | | | | | 6 | 6 | 6 | 6 | 6 | | | | | |

## A/Excellent/Category 1-A/High Quality/Premier
(Based Primarily Glover et al.'s Rankings)

| | | | | | | | | | | | | | | | | | | | | | | |
|---|---|---|---|---|---|---|---|---|---|---|---|---|---|---|---|---|---|---|---|---|---|---|
| Accounting Horizons | A | A | A+ | A | A+ | A+ | 3 | 2 | 0 | 0 | 0 | A | A | A | A | A | A | 0 | 5 | 0 | 0 | 0 |
| Auditing: A Journal of Practice & Theory | A | A | A+ | A | A | A | 1 | 4 | 0 | 0 | 0 | A | A | A+ | A | A+ | A | 1 | 4 | 0 | 0 | 0 |
| Behavioral Research in Accounting | A | A | A+ | A | A | A | 1 | 4 | 0 | 0 | 0 | A | A | A+ | A | A+ | A | 1 | 4 | 0 | 0 | 0 |
| Journal of Accounting and Public Policy | A | A | A+ | A | A | A | 1 | 4 | 0 | 0 | 0 | A+ | A+ | A+ | A | A+ | A | 2 | 3 | 0 | 0 | 0 |
| Journal of Accounting, Auditing & Finance | A | A | A+ | A | A | A | 1 | 4 | 0 | 0 | 0 | A+ | A+ | A+ | A | A+ | A | 2 | 3 | 0 | 0 | 0 |
| Journal of Accounting Literature | A | B | A+ | A | A | A | 1 | 3 | 0 | 1 | 0 | A | A | A | A | A | A− | 0 | 4 | 1 | 0 | 0 |
| Journal of Business, Finance and Accounting | A | B | A+ | | | B | 1 | 0 | 0 | 2 | 0 | A | A | A | A | A | A | 0 | 4 | 0 | 0 | 0 |
| Journal of the American Taxation Association | A | A | | A | A | A | 0 | 4 | 0 | 0 | 0 | A | A | A+ | A | A+ | A | 1 | 3 | 0 | 0 | 0 |
| National Tax Journal | A | B | | A | A | A | 0 | 1 | 0 | 1 | 0 | B | A | A+ | A | A | A | 1 | 3 | 0 | 1 | 0 |
| **Total number of journals ranked** | 9 | 9 | 7 | 8 | 7 | 8 | | | | | | 9 | 9 | 9 | 9 | 9 | 9 | | | | | |

## Non-Nationally Ranked Schools Offering Accounting Doctoral Degrees

| | NNRD1 | NNRD2 | NNRD3 | NNRD4 | NNRD5 | NNRD6 | NNRD7 | NNRD8[a] | NNRD9 | NNRD10[b] | NNRD11[c] |
|---|---|---|---|---|---|---|---|---|---|---|---|
| **A+/Elite** | | | | | | | | | | | |
| (Based Primarily Glover et al.'s Rankings) | | | | | | | | | | | |
| *Journal of Accounting and Economics* | A+ | A+ | A+ | A+ | A+ | A+ | | A+ | A+ | A+ | A+ |
| *Journal of Accounting Research* | A+ | A+ | A+ | A+ | A+ | A+ | A+ | A+ | A+ | A+ | A+ |
| *The Accounting Review* | A+ | A+ | A+ | A+ | A+ | A+ | A+ | A+ | A+ | A+ | A+ |
| *Accounting, Organizations and Society* | A+ | A | | A+ | A+ | A+ | A+ | A+ | A+ | A+ | A+ |
| *Contemporary Accounting Research* | A+ | A | A+ | A+ | A+ | A+ | A+ | A+ | A+ | A+ | A+ |
| *Review of Accounting Studies* | A+ | A | A+ | A− | A | A+ | | A+ | A+ | A+ | A+ |
| **Total number of journals ranked** | 6 | 6 | 5 | 6 | 6 | 6 | 4 | 6 | 6 | 6 | 6 |
| **A/Excellent/Category 1-A/High Quality/Premier** | | | | | | | | | | | |
| (Based Primarily Glover et al.'s Rankings) | | | | | | | | | | | |
| *Accounting Horizons* | A+ | A− | | A− | A | A+ | A | A+ | A | A | |
| *Auditing: A Journal of Practice & Theory* | A+ | A | | A | A | A+ | A+ | A+ | A | A+ | |
| *Behavioral Research in Accounting* | A+ | A | | A | A | A+ | A | A+ | A− | A | |
| *Journal of Accounting and Public Policy* | A+ | A | | A | A | A | A | A+ | A | A | |
| *Journal of Accounting, Auditing & Finance* | A | A | | A | A | A+ | | A+ | A | A | |
| *Journal of Accounting Literature* | A | A− | | A− | A | A | A | A+ | A− | A | |
| *Journal of Business, Finance and Accounting* | A+ | A− | | A− | A | A− | A | A+ | A− | | |
| *Journal of the American Taxation Association* | A+ | A | | A | A | A+ | A | A+ | A | | |
| *National Tax Journal* | A | | | A | A | A+ | A | A+ | A | | |
| **Total number of journals ranked** | 9 | 8 | 0 | 9 | 9 | 9 | 8 | 9 | 9 | 6 | 0 |

| | Non-Nationally Ranked Schools Offering Accounting Doctoral Degrees | | | | A+ | A | A− | B | C |
|---|---|---|---|---|---|---|---|---|---|
| | NNRD12[d] | NNRD13[d] | NNRD14[d] | NNRD15[d] | | | | | |
| **A+/Elite** | | | | | | | | | |
| (Based Primarily Glover et al.'s Rankings) | | | | | | | | | |
| *Journal of Accounting and Economics* | A+ | A+ | A+ | A+ | 14 | 0 | 0 | 0 | 0 |
| *Journal of Accounting Research* | A+ | A+ | A+ | A+ | 15 | 0 | 0 | 0 | 0 |
| *The Accounting Review* | A+ | A+ | A+ | A+ | 15 | 0 | 0 | 0 | 0 |
| *Accounting, Organizations and Society* | A+ | A | A | A+ | 11 | 3 | 0 | 0 | 0 |
| *Contemporary Accounting Research* | A+ | A | A+ | A+ | 13 | 2 | 0 | 0 | 0 |
| *Review of Accounting Studies* | A+ | A | A | A+ | 9 | 4 | 1 | 0 | 0 |
| **Total number of journals ranked** | 6 | 6 | 6 | 6 | | | | | |
| **A/Excellent/Category 1-A/High Quality/Premier** | | | | | | | | | |
| (Based Primarily Glover et al.'s Rankings) | | | | | | | | | |
| *Accounting Horizons* | A | A− | | | 3 | 5 | 3 | 0 | 0 |
| *Auditing: A Journal of Practice & Theory* | A | A− | | | 5 | 5 | 1 | 0 | 0 |
| *Behavioral Research in Accounting* | A | | | | 3 | 6 | 1 | 0 | 0 |
| *Journal of Accounting and Public Policy* | A | A− | | | 2 | 8 | 1 | 0 | 0 |
| *Journal of Accounting, Auditing & Finance* | A | A− | A | | 2 | 8 | 1 | 0 | 0 |
| *Journal of Accounting Literature* | A | | | | 1 | 6 | 3 | 0 | 0 |
| *Journal of Business, Finance and Accounting* | A | | | | 2 | 3 | 4 | 0 | 0 |
| *Journal of the American Taxation Association* | A | A− | | | 3 | 6 | 1 | 0 | 0 |
| *National Tax Journal* | | | | | 2 | 5 | 0 | 0 | 0 |
| **Total number of journals ranked** | 8 | 5 | 1 | 0 | | | | | |

|  | | | | | | | Nationally Ranked Schools | | | | | | | | | | | |
| --- | --- | --- | --- | --- | --- | --- | --- | --- | --- | --- | --- | --- | --- | --- | --- | --- | --- | --- |
|  | NR1 | NR2 | NR3 | NR4 | NR5 | NR6 | NR7 | NR8 | NR94 | NR10 | NR11 | NR12 | NR13 | A+ | A | A− | B | C |
| **A+/Elite** | | | | | | | | | | | | | | | | | | |
| (Based Primarily Glover et al.'s Rankings) | | | | | | | | | | | | | | | | | | |
| *Journal of Accounting and Economics* | A+ | A+ | A+ | A+ | A+ | A+ | A+ | A+ | A+ | A+ | A+ | A+ | A+ | 13 | 0 | 0 | 0 | 0 |
| *Journal of Accounting Research* | A+ | A+ | A+ | A+ | A+ | A+ | A+ | A+ | A+ | A+ | A+ | A+ | A+ | 13 | 0 | 0 | 0 | 0 |
| *The Accounting Review* | A+ | A+ | A+ | A+ | A+ | A+ | A+ | A+ | A+ | A+ | A+ | A+ | A+ | 13 | 0 | 0 | 0 | 0 |
| *Accounting, Organizations and Society* | A+ | | A+ | | A | A | | A+ | A+ | | A+ | | A+ | 6 | 2 | 0 | 0 | 0 |
| *Contemporary Accounting Research* | A+ | A+ | A+ | A+ | A+ | A+ | A+ | A+ | A+ | A | A+ | A+ | A+ | 12 | 1 | 0 | 0 | 0 |
| *Review of Accounting Studies* | A+ | A+ | A+ | A+ | A+ | A+ | A+ | | A+ | | | A+ | A | 9 | 1 | 0 | 0 | 0 |
| *Total number of journals ranked* | 6 | 5 | 6 | 5 | 6 | 6 | 5 | 5 | 6 | 4 | 5 | 5 | 6 | | | | | |
| **A/Excellent/Category 1-A/High Quality/Premier** | | | | | | | | | | | | | | | | | | |
| (Based Primarily Glover et al.'s Rankings) | | | | | | | | | | | | | | | | | | |
| *Accounting Horizons* | | | | | A | | | | A | | | | | 0 | 2 | 0 | 0 | 0 |
| *Auditing: A Journal of Practice & Theory* | | | | | A | A | | | A | | | | A | 0 | 4 | 0 | 0 | 0 |
| *Behavioral Research in Accounting* | | | | | A | | | | A | | | | A | 0 | 3 | 0 | 0 | 0 |
| *Journal of Accounting and Public Policy* | | | | | A | | | | A | | | | A | 0 | 3 | 0 | 0 | 0 |
| *Journal of Accounting, Auditing & Finance* | | | | | A | | | | A | A | | | A | 0 | 4 | 0 | 0 | 0 |
| *Journal of Accounting Literature* | | | | | | | | | A | | | | | 0 | 1 | 0 | 0 | 0 |
| *Journal of Business, Finance and Accounting* | | | | | A | | | | A | B | | | A | 0 | 3 | 0 | 1 | 0 |
| *Journal of the American Taxation Association* | | | | | A | | | | A | A | | A+ | A+ | 2 | 3 | 0 | 0 | 0 |
| *National Tax Journal* | | | | | | | | | A | | | | | 0 | 1 | 0 | 0 | 0 |
| **Total number of journals ranked** | 0 | 0 | 0 | 0 | 7 | 1 | 0 | | 9 | 3 | 0 | 1 | 6 | | | | | |

|  | Grand Total of All Rankings | | | | | No. of Rankings | Weighted Average |
|---|---|---|---|---|---|---|---|
|  | A+ | A | A− | B | C |  |  |
| **A+/Elite** | | | | | | | |
| (Based Primarily Glover et al.'s Rankings) | | | | | | | |
| *Journal of Accounting and Economics* | 37 | 0 | 0 | 0 | 0 | 37 | 5.00 |
| *Journal of Accounting Research* | 38 | 0 | 0 | 0 | 0 | 38 | 5.00 |
| *The Accounting Review* | 38 | 0 | 0 | 0 | 0 | 38 | 5.00 |
| *Accounting, Organizations and Society* | 27 | 5 | 0 | 0 | 0 | 32 | 4.84 |
| *Contemporary Accounting Research* | 35 | 3 | 0 | 0 | 0 | 38 | 4.92 |
| *Review of Accounting Studies* | 26 | 6 | 1 | 0 | 0 | 33 | 4.76 |
| **A/Excellent/Category 1-A/High Quality/Premier** | | | | | | | |
| (Based Primarily Glover et al.'s Rankings) | | | | | | | |
| *Accounting Horizons* | 6 | 14 | 3 | 0 | 0 | 23 | 4.13 |
| *Auditing: A Journal of Practice & Theory* | 7 | 17 | 1 | 0 | 0 | 25 | 4.24 |
| *Behavioral Research in Accounting* | 5 | 17 | 1 | 0 | 0 | 23 | 4.17 |
| *Journal of Accounting and Public Policy* | 5 | 18 | 1 | 0 | 0 | 24 | 4.17 |
| *Journal of Accounting, Auditing & Finance* | 5 | 19 | 1 | 0 | 0 | 25 | 4.16 |
| *Journal of Accounting Literature* | 2 | 14 | 4 | 1 | 0 | 21 | 3.81 |
| *Journal of Business, Finance and Accounting* | 3 | 10 | 4 | 3 | 0 | 20 | 3.65 |
| *Journal of the American Taxation Association* | 6 | 16 | 1 | 0 | 0 | 23 | 4.22 |
| *National Tax Journal* | 3 | 10 | 0 | 2 | 0 | 15 | 3.93 |

## A–/Top 25/Category 1/Quality

(Based Primarily Glover et al.'s Rankings)

| | Glover et al. (2012) | WSU | Urban Programs | | | | | | | | | Non-Nationally Ranked Schools *NOT* Offering Accounting Doctoral Degrees | | | | | | | | | |
|---|---|---|---|---|---|---|---|---|---|---|---|---|---|---|---|---|---|---|---|---|---|
| | | | U1 | U2 | U3 | U4 | A+ | A | A– | B | C | NNRND1 | NNRND2 | NNRND3 | NNRND4 | NNRND5 | A+ | A | A– | B | C |
| *Abacus* | A– | B | A+ | A– | A | A | 1 | 2 | 1 | 1 | 0 | A– | A | A | A | A | 0 | 4 | 1 | 0 | 0 |
| *Accounting and Business Research* | A– | B | A+ | | B | | 1 | 0 | 0 | 2 | 0 | A– | A | A– | A | | 0 | 2 | 2 | 0 | 0 |
| *Accounting and the Public Interest* | | | | A– | | B | 0 | 0 | 1 | 1 | 0 | A– | A– | A | | A | 0 | 2 | 2 | 0 | 0 |
| *Advances in Accounting* | A– | B | A+ | A | A | A | 1 | 3 | 0 | 1 | 0 | A– | A | A | A– | A | 0 | 3 | 2 | 0 | 0 |
| *Advances in Taxation* | A– | | A– | C | | B | 0 | 0 | 1 | 1 | 1 | A– | | A | A– | | 0 | 1 | 2 | 0 | 0 |
| *Issues in Accounting Education* | A– | B | A+ | A | A | A | 1 | 3 | 0 | 1 | 0 | A– | A | A | A | A | 0 | 4 | 1 | 0 | 0 |
| *Journal of Accounting Education* | A– | B | A+ | A– | A | A | 1 | 2 | 1 | 1 | 0 | A– | A– | A– | A– | A | 0 | 1 | 4 | 0 | 0 |
| *Journal of Information Systems* | A– | A | A+ | A | A | A | 1 | 4 | 0 | 0 | 0 | A | | A | A | A | 0 | 4 | 0 | 0 | 0 |
| *Journal of Management Accounting Research* | A– | A | A+ | A | A | A | 1 | 4 | 0 | 0 | 0 | A | A | A+ | A | A | 1 | 4 | 0 | 0 | 0 |
| *Research in Governmental and Nonprofit Accounting* | A– | | A+ | A– | | B | 1 | 0 | 1 | 1 | 0 | A– | A– | A– | | | 0 | 0 | 3 | 0 | 0 |
| *Research in Accounting Regulation* | | | A+ | A | B | B | 1 | 1 | 0 | 2 | 0 | A– | A– | A– | A– | A | 0 | 1 | 4 | 0 | 0 |
| *Review of Quantitative Finance and Accounting* | A– | B | | | | A | 0 | 1 | 0 | 1 | 0 | A– | | | | A | 0 | 1 | 1 | 0 | 0 |
| **Total number of journals ranked** | 10 | 8 | 10 | 10 | 8 | 11 | | | | | | 12 | 9 | 11 | 9 | 9 | | | | | |

| | Non-Nationally Ranked Schools Offering Accounting Doctoral Degrees | | | | | | | | | | |
|---|---|---|---|---|---|---|---|---|---|---|---|
| | NNRD1 | NNRD2 | NNRD3 | NNRD4 | NNRD5 | NNRD6 | NNRD7 | NNRD8[a] | NNRD9 | NNRD10[b] | NNRD11[c] |
| **A−/Top 25/Category I/Quality** (Based Primarily Glover et al.'s Rankings) | | | | | | | | | | | |
| *Abacus* | A | A− | | A− | A | A | | | A− | A | |
| *Accounting and Business Research* | A | A− | | B | A | A | | | A− | A | |
| *Accounting and the Public Interest* | | | | A | | B | | | B | B | |
| *Advances in Accounting* | A | B | | B | A− | A− | | | A− | B | |
| *Advances in Taxation* | A | A− | | B | A− | A | A | | A− | | |
| *Issues in Accounting Education* | A | A− | | A− | A− | A | A | | A− | A | |
| *Journal of Accounting Education* | A | B | | B | A− | A− | | | B | B | |
| *Journal of Information Systems* | A+ | A− | | A | A | A | A | | A− | | |
| *Journal of Management Accounting Research* | A+ | A | | A | A+ | A+ | A | | | A | |
| *Research in Governmental and Nonprofit Accounting* | A | A− | | B | | A | | | B | B | |
| *Research in Accounting Regulation* | | | | B | | B | | | A− | B | |
| *Review of Quantitative Finance and Accounting* | A | A− | | | A | A | | | B | | |
| **Total number of journals ranked** | 10 | 10 | 0 | 11 | 9 | 12 | 4 | | 11 | 9 | 0 |

| A−/Top 25/Category 1/Quality (Based Primarily Glover et al.'s Rankings) | NNRD12[d] | NNRD13[d] | NNRD14[d] | NNRD15[d] | A+ | A | A− | B | C |
|---|---|---|---|---|---|---|---|---|---|
| Abacus | A | | | | 0 | 5 | 3 | 0 | 0 |
| Accounting and Business Research | | | | | 0 | 4 | 2 | 1 | 0 |
| Accounting and the Public Interest | | | | | 0 | 1 | 0 | 3 | 0 |
| Advances in Accounting | | | | | 0 | 2 | 3 | 3 | 0 |
| Advances in Taxation | | | | | 0 | 2 | 3 | 1 | 0 |
| Issues in Accounting Education | A | | | | 0 | 5 | 4 | 0 | 0 |
| Journal of Accounting Education | | | | | 0 | 1 | 2 | 4 | 0 |
| Journal of Information Systems | A | | | | 1 | 5 | 2 | 0 | 0 |
| Journal of Management Accounting Research | A | A− | | | 2 | 6 | 1 | 0 | 0 |
| Research in Governmental and Nonprofit Accounting | | | | | 0 | 2 | 1 | 3 | 0 |
| Research in Accounting Regulation | | | | | 0 | 0 | 1 | 3 | 0 |
| Review of Quantitative Finance and Accounting | | | | | 0 | 3 | 1 | 1 | 0 |
| **Total number of journals ranked** | 4 | 1 | 0 | 0 | | | | | |

## Nationally Ranked Schools

### A-/Top 25/Category I/Quality
(Based Primarily Glover et al.'s Rankings)

| | NR1 | NR2 | NR3 | NR4 | NR5 | NR6 | NR7 | NR8 | NR9[c] | NR10 | NR11 | NR12 | NR13 | A+ | A | A- | B | C |
|---|---|---|---|---|---|---|---|---|---|---|---|---|---|---|---|---|---|---|
| *Abacus* | | | | | | | | | A- | | | | A | 0 | 1 | 1 | 0 | 0 |
| *Accounting and Business Research* | | | | | | | | | A- | | | | A | 0 | 1 | 1 | 0 | 0 |
| *Accounting and the Public Interest* | | | | | | | | | | | | | | 0 | 0 | 0 | 0 | 0 |
| *Advances in Accounting* | | | | | | | | | A- | | | | | 0 | 0 | 1 | 0 | 0 |
| *Advances in Taxation* | | | | | | | | | A- | | | | | 0 | 0 | 1 | 0 | 0 |
| *Issues in Accounting Education* | | | | | | | | | A- | | | | | 0 | 0 | 1 | 0 | 0 |
| *Journal of Accounting Education* | | | | | | | | | A- | B | | | | 0 | 0 | 1 | 1 | 0 |
| *Journal of Information Systems* | | | | | | | | | A- | | | | | 0 | 0 | 1 | 0 | 0 |
| *Journal of Management Accounting Research* | | | | | A | | | | A- | | | | | 0 | 1 | 1 | 0 | 0 |
| *Research in Governmental and Nonprofit Accounting* | | | | | | | | | A- | | | | | 0 | 0 | 1 | 0 | 0 |
| *Research in Accounting Regulation* | | | | | | | | | | | | | | 0 | 0 | 0 | 0 | 0 |
| *Review of Quantitative Finance and Accounting* | | | | | | | | | A- | B | | | | 0 | 0 | 1 | 1 | 0 |
| **Total number of journals ranked** | 0 | 0 | 0 | 0 | 1 | 0 | 0 | 0 | 10 | 2 | 0 | 0 | 2 | | | | | |

### A-/Top 25/Category I/Quality
(Based Primarily Glover et al.'s Rankings)

| | Grand Total of All Rankings | | | | | No. of Rankings | Weighted Average |
|---|---|---|---|---|---|---|---|
| | A+ | A | A- | B | C | | |
| *Abacus* | 1 | 12 | 6 | 1 | 0 | 20 | 3.65 |
| *Accounting and Business Research* | 1 | 7 | 5 | 3 | 0 | 16 | 3.38 |

| | Grand Total of All Rankings | | | | | No. of Rankings | Weighted Average |
|---|---|---|---|---|---|---|---|
| | A+ | A | A− | B | C | | |
| Accounting and the Public Interest | 0 | 3 | 3 | 4 | 0 | 10 | 2.90 |
| Advances in Accounting | 1 | 8 | 6 | 4 | 0 | 19 | 3.32 |
| Advances in Taxation | 0 | 3 | 7 | 2 | 1 | 13 | 2.92 |
| Issues in Accounting Education | 1 | 12 | 6 | 1 | 0 | 20 | 3.65 |
| Journal of Accounting Education | 1 | 4 | 8 | 6 | 0 | 19 | 3.00 |
| Journal of Information Systems | 2 | 13 | 3 | 0 | 0 | 18 | 3.94 |
| Journal of Management Accounting Research | 4 | 15 | 2 | 0 | 0 | 21 | 4.10 |
| Research in Governmental and Nonprofit Accounting | 1 | 2 | 6 | 4 | 0 | 13 | 3.00 |
| Research in Accounting Regulation | 1 | 2 | 5 | 5 | 0 | 13 | 2.92 |
| Review of Quantitative Finance and Accounting | 0 | 5 | 3 | 3 | 0 | 11 | 3.18 |

| Other Journals Receiving Five or More University Rankings[f] | Grand Total of All Rankings | | | | | No. of Rankings | Weighted Average |
|---|---|---|---|---|---|---|---|
| | A+ | A | A− | B | C | | |
| Academy of Accounting and Financial Studies Journal | 0 | 1 | 0 | 2 | 1 | 4 | 2.25 |
| Accounting and Finance | 0 | 3 | 3 | 2 | 1 | 9 | 2.89 |
| Accounting Education: An International Journal | 0 | 2 | 2 | 3 | 1 | 8 | 2.63 |
| The Accounting Educators' Journal | 1 | 0 | 3 | 4 | 1 | 9 | 2.56 |
| Accounting Forum | 0 | 1 | 2 | 1 | 0 | 4 | 3.00 |
| Accounting Historians Journal | 0 | 1 | 6 | 2 | 1 | 10 | 2.70 |
| Accounting, Auditing & Accountability Journal | 1 | 6 | 2 | 3 | 1 | 13 | 3.23 |

| Other Journals Receiving *Five or More* University Rankings[f] | Grand Total of All Rankings | | | | | No. of Rankings | Weighted Average |
|---|---|---|---|---|---|---|---|
| *Advances in Accounting Behavioral Research* | 0 | 1 | 2 | 4 | 1 | 8 | 2.38 |
| *Advances in Accounting Education* | 0 | 0 | 3 | 2 | 1 | 6 | 2.33 |
| *Advances in Accounting Information Systems* | 1 | 0 | 3 | 3 | 0 | 7 | 2.86 |
| *Advances in International Accounting* | 1 | 0 | 4 | 5 | 1 | 11 | 2.55 |
| *Advances in Management Accounting* | 1 | 2 | 4 | 4 | 0 | 11 | 3.00 |
| *Advances in Public Interest Accounting* | 1 | 1 | 4 | 5 | 0 | 11 | 2.82 |
| *British Accounting Review* | 0 | 3 | 3 | 3 | 0 | 9 | 3.00 |
| *Critical Perspectives on Accounting* | 0 | 8 | 4 | 3 | 1 | 16 | 3.19 |
| *Current Issues in Auditing* | 0 | 2 | 0 | 4 | 0 | 6 | 2.67 |
| *European Accounting Review* | 0 | 4 | 3 | 3 | 0 | 10 | 3.10 |
| *Internal Auditing* | 0 | 1 | 1 | 4 | 2 | 8 | 2.13 |
| *Internal Auditor* | 0 | 1 | 3 | 6 | 0 | 10 | 2.50 |
| *International Journal of Accounting* | 1 | 7 | 4 | 2 | 0 | 14 | 3.50 |
| *International Journal of Accounting Information Systems* | 1 | 6 | 3 | 0 | 0 | 10 | 3.80 |
| *International Journal of Auditing* | 0 | 0 | 2 | 2 | 0 | 4 | 2.50 |
| *International Journal of Intelligent Systems in Accounting, Finance and Management* | 0 | 2 | 1 | 3 | 0 | 6 | 2.83 |
| *Journal of Accountancy* | 1 | 3 | 5 | 4 | 1 | 14 | 2.93 |
| *Journal of Accounting Ethics and Public Policy* | 0 | 3 | 4 | 0 | 0 | 7 | 3.43 |
| *Journal of Business Ethics* | 0 | 4 | 1 | 0 | 0 | 5 | 3.80 |
| *Journal of Cost Management* | 1 | 3 | 3 | 3 | 0 | 10 | 3.20 |
| *Journal of Emerging Technologies in Accounting* | 0 | 3 | 1 | 3 | 0 | 7 | 3.00 |
| *Journal of Forensic Accounting* | 0 | 1 | 2 | 5 | 0 | 8 | 2.50 |
| *Journal of International Accounting Research* | 0 | 3 | 4 | 2 | 0 | 9 | 3.11 |

## Other Journals Receiving *Five or More* University Rankings[f]

| | Grand Total of All Rankings | | | | | No. of Rankings | Weighted Average |
|---|---|---|---|---|---|---|---|
| Journal of International Accounting, Auditing and Taxation | 1 | 3 | 5 | 3 | 0 | 12 | 3.17 |
| Journal of International Financial Management & Accounting | 0 | 4 | 0 | 1 | 0 | 5 | 3.60 |
| Journal of Public Budgeting, Accounting and Financial Management | 0 | 1 | 1 | 0 | 0 | 2 | 3.50 |
| Journal of Taxation | 0 | 2 | 2 | 4 | 0 | 8 | 2.75 |
| Management Accounting Quarterly | 0 | 0 | 2 | 2 | 1 | 5 | 2.20 |
| Management Accounting Research | 0 | 6 | 4 | 2 | 0 | 12 | 3.33 |
| Management Accounting/Strategic Finance | 1 | 2 | 5 | 2 | 1 | 11 | 3.00 |
| Managerial Auditing [Research] | 0 | 1 | 3 | 6 | 0 | 10 | 2.50 |
| Ohio CPA Journal (Now called Catalyst) | 0 | 2 | 1 | 2 | 1 | 6 | 2.67 |
| Pacific Accounting Review | 0 | 2 | 2 | 1 | 0 | 4 | 3.25 |
| The CPA Journal | 1 | 3 | 4 | 6 | 0 | 14 | 2.93 |
| The Tax Adviser | 0 | 1 | 3 | 3 | 0 | 7 | 2.71 |
| The Tax Executive | 0 | 0 | 2 | 2 | 1 | 5 | 2.20 |
| Tax Notes | 1 | 0 | 3 | 3 | 1 | 8 | 2.63 |
| Taxes – The Tax Magazine | 0 | 0 | 3 | 5 | 0 | 8 | 2.38 |
| The ATA Journal of Legal Tax Research | 0 | 3 | 2 | 3 | 0 | 8 | 3.00 |

## Other Journals Receiving *Fewer than Five* University Rankings[f]

| | Grand Total of All Rankings | | | | | No. of Rankings | Weighted Average |
|---|---|---|---|---|---|---|---|
| Academy of Management Journal | 0 | 1 | 0 | 0 | 0 | 1 | 4.00 |
| Academy of Management Review | 0 | 1 | 0 | 0 | 0 | 1 | 4.00 |
| Accountancy | 0 | 0 | 0 | 2 | 1 | 3 | 1.67 |
| Accounting, Accountability and Performance Journal | 0 | 0 | 0 | 1 | 1 | 2 | 1.50 |

| Other Journals Receiving *Fewer than Five* University Rankings[f] | Grand Total of All Rankings | | | | | No. of Rankings | Weighted Average |
|---|---|---|---|---|---|---|---|
| *Accounting and Business* | 0 | 0 | 0 | 1 | 0 | 1 | 2.00 |
| *Accounting and Finance Research* | 0 | 0 | 1 | 0 | 1 | 2 | 2.00 |
| *Accounting and Financial Management Journal* | 0 | 0 | 0 | 1 | 0 | 1 | 2.00 |
| *Accounting & Taxation* | 0 | 0 | 0 | 0 | 1 | 1 | 1.00 |
| *Accounting Enquiries* | 0 | 0 | 1 | 0 | 0 | 1 | 3.00 |
| *Accounting History* | 0 | 0 | 0 | 1 | 1 | 2 | 1.50 |
| *Accounting in Europe* | 0 | 0 | 0 | 1 | 0 | 1 | 2.00 |
| *Accounting Instructors' Report* | 0 | 0 | 0 | 2 | 0 | 2 | 2.00 |
| *Accounting, Management and Information Technologies* | 0 | 0 | 1 | 2 | 0 | 3 | 2.33 |
| *Accounting Perspectives* | 0 | 0 | 2 | 1 | 0 | 3 | 2.67 |
| *Accounting Research Journal* | 0 | 0 | 2 | 0 | 0 | 2 | 3.00 |
| *Accounting Technology* | 0 | 0 | 0 | 2 | 0 | 2 | 2.00 |
| *Accounting Today* | 0 | 0 | 0 | 2 | 0 | 2 | 2.00 |
| *Administrative Science Quarterly* | 0 | 1 | 1 | 0 | 0 | 2 | 3.50 |
| *Advances in Environmental Accounting and Management* | 0 | 0 | 0 | 2 | 0 | 2 | 2.00 |
| *Advances in Quantitative Analysis of Finance & Accounting* | 0 | 2 | 2 | 0 | 0 | 4 | 3.50 |
| *Akron Tax Journal* | 0 | 0 | 1 | 0 | 0 | 1 | 3.00 |
| *Alternative Perspectives on Finance and Accounting* | 0 | 0 | 0 | 1 | 1 | 2 | 1.50 |
| *Asian Journal of Accounting and Governance* | 0 | 0 | 0 | 0 | 1 | 1 | 1.00 |
| *Asian Journal of Business and Accounting* | 0 | 0 | 0 | 0 | 1 | 1 | 1.00 |
| *Asian Journal of Finance & Accounting* | 0 | 0 | 0 | 0 | 1 | 1 | 1.00 |
| *Asian Review of Accounting* | 0 | 0 | 0 | 0 | 1 | 1 | 1.00 |

| Other Journals Receiving *Fewer than Five University Rankings*[f] | Grand Total of All Rankings | | | | | No. of Rankings | Weighted Average |
|---|---|---|---|---|---|---|---|
| *Asia-Pacific Journal of Accounting* | 0 | 0 | 0 | 1 | 1 | 2 | 1.50 |
| *Asia-Pacific Journal of Accounting and Economics* | 0 | 0 | 0 | 1 | 0 | 1 | 2.00 |
| *Asia-Pacific Management Accounting Journal* | 0 | 0 | 0 | 1 | 0 | 1 | 2.00 |
| *Australian Accounting Review* | 0 | 0 | 0 | 1 | 0 | 1 | 2.00 |
| *Australian CPA* (formerly *The Australian Accountant*) | 0 | 0 | 0 | 1 | 0 | 1 | 2.00 |
| *The Australian Journal of Accounting Education* | 0 | 0 | 0 | 0 | 1 | 1 | 1.00 |
| *Australian Journal of Management* | 0 | 0 | 0 | 0 | 1 | 1 | 1.00 |
| *Australasian Accounting, Business and Finance Journal* | 0 | 0 | 0 | 0 | 1 | 1 | 1.00 |
| *Australasian Journal of Business and Behavioural Sciences* | 0 | 0 | 0 | 1 | 0 | 1 | 2.00 |
| *Behaviour & Information Technology* | 0 | 0 | 1 | 1 | 0 | 2 | 2.50 |
| *Business and Professional Ethics Journal* | 0 | 1 | 1 | 0 | 0 | 2 | 3.50 |
| *Business and Society* | 0 | 0 | 1 | 1 | 0 | 2 | 2.50 |
| *Business Ethics Quarterly* | 0 | 1 | 0 | 0 | 1 | 2 | 2.50 |
| *Business Horizons* | 0 | 0 | 1 | 0 | 0 | 1 | 3.00 |
| *CA Magazine* | 0 | 0 | 0 | 1 | 1 | 2 | 1.50 |
| *California CPA Quarterly, The* (formally *Outlook*) | 0 | 0 | 0 | 3 | 0 | 3 | 2.00 |
| *Canadian Tax Journal* | 0 | 0 | 0 | 1 | 0 | 1 | 2.00 |
| *Central Business Review* | 0 | 0 | 1 | 0 | 0 | 1 | 3.00 |
| *China Journal of Accounting Research* | 0 | 0 | 0 | 0 | 1 | 1 | 1.00 |
| *CMA: The Management Accounting Magazine* | 0 | 0 | 0 | 2 | 1 | 3 | 1.67 |
| *College Teaching* | 0 | 0 | 1 | 0 | 0 | 1 | 3.00 |
| *Communications of the Association for Information Systems* | 0 | 0 | 1 | 0 | 0 | 1 | 3.00 |

| Other Journals Receiving *Fewer than Five* University Rankings[f] | Grand Total of All Rankings | | | | | No. of Rankings | Weighted Average |
|---|---|---|---|---|---|---|---|
| *Computers & Operations Research* | 0 | 0 | 1 | 0 | 0 | 1 | 3.00 |
| *Controllers Quarterly* | 0 | 0 | 0 | 1 | 0 | 1 | 2.00 |
| *The Cooperative Accountant* | 0 | 0 | 0 | 1 | 0 | 1 | 2.00 |
| *Corporate Accounting/Financial Manager* | 1 | 0 | 0 | 0 | 0 | 1 | 5.00 |
| *Corporate Controller* | 0 | 0 | 0 | 1 | 0 | 1 | 2.00 |
| *Corporate Finance Review* | 0 | 0 | 0 | 1 | 0 | 1 | 2.00 |
| *Corporate Governance: An International Review* | 0 | 0 | 0 | 1 | 0 | 1 | 2.00 |
| *Corporate Ownership and Control* | 0 | 0 | 0 | 1 | 0 | 1 | 2.00 |
| *Corporate Taxation* | 0 | 1 | 1 | 1 | 0 | 3 | 3.00 |
| *CPA Statement* | 0 | 0 | 0 | 1 | 0 | 1 | 2.00 |
| *Decision Science* | 0 | 2 | 0 | 0 | 0 | 2 | 4.00 |
| *Decision Support Systems* | 0 | 0 | 2 | 0 | 0 | 2 | 3.00 |
| *Disclosures (Virginia Society of CPAs)* | 0 | 0 | 0 | 1 | 0 | 1 | 2.00 |
| *eJournal of Tax Research* | 0 | 0 | 1 | 0 | 0 | 1 | 3.00 |
| *Estate Planning* | 0 | 0 | 1 | 2 | 0 | 3 | 2.33 |
| *The Estate, Gifts and Trusts Journal* | 0 | 0 | 0 | 1 | 1 | 2 | 1.50 |
| *European Journal of Information Systems* | 0 | 0 | 1 | 0 | 0 | 1 | 3.00 |
| *European Journal of Operational Research* | 0 | 0 | 1 | 0 | 0 | 1 | 3.00 |
| *The Exempt Organization Tax Review* | 0 | 0 | 1 | 0 | 0 | 1 | 3.00 |
| *Financial Accountability & Management* | 0 | 2 | 0 | 0 | 0 | 2 | 4.00 |
| *Financial Analysts Journal* | 0 | 1 | 2 | 0 | 0 | 3 | 3.33 |
| *Financial Executive/FE Magazine* | 0 | 0 | 0 | 1 | 0 | 1 | 2.00 |

| Other Journals Receiving *Fewer than Five University Rankings*[f] | Grand Total of All Rankings | | | | | No. of Rankings | Weighted Average |
|---|---|---|---|---|---|---|---|
| *Financial Management* | 0 | 1 | 2 | 0 | 0 | 3 | 3.33 |
| *Financial Reporting, Regulation and Governance* | 0 | 0 | 0 | 0 | 1 | 1 | 1.00 |
| *Florida Tax Review* | 0 | 1 | 0 | 0 | 0 | 1 | 4.00 |
| *Foundation and Trends in Accounting* | 0 | 1 | 0 | 0 | 0 | 1 | 4.00 |
| *Games and Economic Behavior* | 0 | 1 | 0 | 0 | 0 | 1 | 4.00 |
| *Georgia Journal of Accounting* | 1 | 0 | 0 | 0 | 0 | 1 | 5.00 |
| *Global Perspectives on Accounting Education* | 0 | 0 | 1 | 1 | 1 | 3 | 2.00 |
| *Government Accountants Journal* | 0 | 0 | 0 | 2 | 2 | 4 | 1.50 |
| *Harvard Business Review* | 0 | 0 | 1 | 0 | 1 | 2 | 2.00 |
| *Health Affairs* | 0 | 1 | 0 | 0 | 0 | 1 | 4.00 |
| *Health Economics* | 0 | 1 | 0 | 0 | 1 | 2 | 2.50 |
| *Health Services Research* | 0 | 1 | 0 | 0 | 0 | 1 | 4.00 |
| *Healthcare Financial Management* | 0 | 0 | 0 | 1 | 1 | 2 | 1.50 |
| *Heckerling Institute on Estate Planning* | 0 | 0 | 1 | 0 | 1 | 2 | 2.00 |
| *Hospital and Health Services Administration* | 0 | 0 | 1 | 1 | 0 | 2 | 2.50 |
| *Human Performance* | 0 | 0 | 1 | 1 | 0 | 2 | 2.50 |
| *Human Relations* | 0 | 0 | 1 | 1 | 0 | 2 | 2.50 |
| *Human Resource Management* | 0 | 0 | 1 | 0 | 0 | 1 | 3.00 |
| *Human Resource Management Review* | 0 | 0 | 1 | 0 | 1 | 2 | 2.00 |
| *Houston Business & Tax Law Journal* | 0 | 0 | 1 | 0 | 1 | 2 | 2.00 |
| *IMA Educational Case Journal* | 0 | 0 | 0 | 1 | 1 | 2 | 1.50 |
| *Indonesian Management and Accounting Research* | 0 | 0 | 0 | 0 | 1 | 1 | 1.00 |

| Other Journals Receiving *Fewer than Five* University Rankings[c] | Grand Total of All Rankings | | | | | No. of Rankings | Weighted Average |
|---|---|---|---|---|---|---|---|
| *Industrial and Labor Relations Review* (or **ILR Review**) | 0 | 0 | 1 | 0 | 1 | 2 | 2.00 |
| *Information and Management* | 0 | 1 | 1 | 0 | 0 | 2 | 3.50 |
| *Information and Organization* | 0 | 0 | 1 | 0 | 1 | 2 | 2.00 |
| *Information Systems Control Journal* | 0 | 0 | 0 | 1 | 0 | 1 | 2.00 |
| *Information Systems Journal* | 0 | 0 | 1 | 0 | 0 | 1 | 3.00 |
| *Information Systems Research* | 0 | 0 | 2 | 0 | 0 | 2 | 5.00 |
| *INFORMS Journal on Computing* | 1 | 0 | 0 | 0 | 0 | 1 | 3.00 |
| *Insurance: Mathematics and Economics* | 0 | 0 | 1 | 0 | 0 | 1 | 3.00 |
| *Intelligent System in Accounting, Finance and Management* | 0 | 0 | 0 | 1 | 0 | 1 | 2.00 |
| *International Journal of Accounting and Information Management* | 0 | 0 | 1 | 0 | 0 | 1 | 3.00 |
| *International Journal of Accounting, Auditing and Performance Evaluation* | 0 | 1 | 0 | 0 | 0 | 1 | 4.00 |
| *International Journal of Finance Research* | 0 | 0 | 1 | 0 | 0 | 1 | 3.00 |
| *International Journal of Government Auditing* | 0 | 1 | 0 | 0 | 0 | 1 | 4.00 |
| *International Journal of Human-Computer Studies* | 0 | 0 | 1 | 0 | 0 | 1 | 3.00 |
| *International Journal of Industrial Organization* | 0 | 0 | 1 | 0 | 0 | 1 | 3.00 |
| *International Journal of Managerial Finance* | 0 | 0 | 1 | 0 | 0 | 1 | 3.00 |
| *International Journal of Production Economics* | 0 | 0 | 1 | 0 | 0 | 1 | 3.00 |
| *International Journal of Research in Marketing* | 0 | 0 | 1 | 0 | 0 | 1 | 3.00 |
| *International Tax Journal* | 0 | 1 | 0 | 0 | 3 | 4 | 1.75 |
| *Journal of 21st Century Accounting* | 0 | 0 | 0 | 1 | 0 | 1 | 2.00 |
| *Journal of the Academy of Marketing Science* | 0 | 0 | 1 | 0 | 0 | 1 | 3.00 |
| *Journal of Accountability and Management* | 0 | 1 | 0 | 0 | 0 | 1 | 4.00 |

| Other Journals Receiving *Fewer than Five* University Rankings[f] | Grand Total of All Rankings | | | | | No. of Rankings | Weighted Average |
|---|---|---|---|---|---|---|---|
| *Journal of Accounting & Business Research* | 0 | 0 | 1 | 1 | 0 | 2 | 2.50 |
| *Journal of Accounting and Computers* | 0 | 1 | 0 | 1 | 1 | 3 | 2.33 |
| *Journal of Accounting and Finance Research* | 0 | 0 | 1 | 1 | 0 | 2 | 2.50 |
| *Journal of Accounting and Management Information Systems* | 0 | 0 | 0 | 0 | 1 | 1 | 1.00 |
| *Journal of Accounting & Organizational Change* | 0 | 0 | 0 | 2 | 0 | 2 | 2.00 |
| *Journal of Accounting Case Research* | 0 | 1 | 0 | 0 | 0 | 1 | 4.00 |
| *Journal of Accounting, Auditing and Taxation* | 0 | 0 | 1 | 0 | 1 | 2 | 2.00 |
| *Journal of Accounting, Finance and Economics* | 0 | 0 | 1 | 0 | 0 | 1 | 3.00 |
| *Journal of Applied Accounting Research* | 0 | 0 | 1 | 0 | 0 | 1 | 3.00 |
| *Journal of Applied Business Research* | 0 | 0 | 2 | 0 | 0 | 2 | 3.00 |
| *Journal of Applied Psychology* | 1 | 1 | 0 | 0 | 0 | 2 | 4.50 |
| *Journal of Bank Cost & Management Accounting* | 0 | 1 | 0 | 0 | 0 | 1 | 4.00 |
| *Journal of Banking & Finance* | 0 | 0 | 1 | 0 | 0 | 1 | 3.00 |
| *Journal of Behavioral Finance* | 0 | 0 | 1 | 0 | 0 | 1 | 3.00 |
| *Journal of Budgeting and Financial Management* | 0 | 0 | 0 | 1 | 0 | 1 | 2.00 |
| *Journal of Business & Economics Research* | 0 | 0 | 1 | 0 | 0 | 1 | 3.00 |
| *Journal of Business* | 0 | 1 | 0 | 0 | 0 | 1 | 4.00 |
| *Journal of Business Venturing* | 0 | 0 | 1 | 0 | 0 | 1 | 3.00 |
| *Journal of College Teaching & Learning* | 0 | 0 | 1 | 0 | 0 | 1 | 3.00 |
| *Journal of Computer Information Systems* | 0 | 1 | 0 | 0 | 0 | 1 | 4.00 |
| *Journal of Consumer Psychology* | 0 | 0 | 1 | 0 | 0 | 1 | 3.00 |
| *Journal of Consumer Research* | 1 | 0 | 0 | 0 | 0 | 1 | 5.00 |

| Other Journals Receiving *Fewer than Five* University Rankings[f] | Grand Total of All Rankings | | | | | No. of Rankings | Weighted Average |
|---|---|---|---|---|---|---|---|
| *Journal of Contemporary Accounting and Economics* | 0 | 0 | 1 | 0 | 0 | 1 | 3.00 |
| *Journal of Corporate Accounting and Finance* | 0 | 0 | 2 | 1 | 0 | 3 | 2.67 |
| *Journal of Corporate Finance* | 0 | 1 | 1 | 0 | 0 | 2 | 3.50 |
| *Journal of Corporate Taxation* | 0 | 0 | 0 | 3 | 1 | 4 | 1.75 |
| *Journal of Cost Analysis* | 1 | 0 | 0 | 1 | 2 | 4 | 2.25 |
| *Journal of Cost Analysis and Parametrics* | 0 | 0 | 1 | 0 | 1 | 2 | 2.00 |
| *Journal of Econometrics* | 0 | 1 | 0 | 0 | 0 | 1 | 4.00 |
| *Journal of Economic Theory* | 0 | 1 | 0 | 0 | 0 | 1 | 4.00 |
| *Journal of Education for Business* | 0 | 1 | 0 | 0 | 0 | 1 | 4.00 |
| *Global Journal of Emerging Market Economies* | 0 | 1 | 0 | 0 | 1 | 2 | 2.50 |
| *Journal of Empirical Legal Studies* | 0 | 1 | 0 | 0 | 0 | 1 | 3.00 |
| *Journal of Finance* | 2 | 0 | 0 | 0 | 0 | 2 | 5.00 |
| *Journal of Finance, Information Technology and Accounting* | 0 | 1 | 0 | 0 | 0 | 1 | 4.00 |
| *Journal of Financial and Quantitative Analysis* | 1 | 1 | 0 | 0 | 0 | 2 | 4.50 |
| *Journal of Financial Economics* | 2 | 0 | 0 | 0 | 0 | 2 | 5.00 |
| *Journal of Financial Intermediation* | 0 | 0 | 1 | 0 | 0 | 1 | 3.00 |
| *Journal of Financial Markets* | 0 | 0 | 1 | 0 | 0 | 1 | 3.00 |
| *Journal of Financial Services Professionals* | 0 | 0 | 0 | 1 | 0 | 1 | 2.00 |
| *Journal of Forensic Accounting: Auditing, Fraud & Risk issue* | 0 | 0 | 0 | 0 | 1 | 1 | 1.00 |
| *Journal of Government Financial Management* | 0 | 0 | 1 | 0 | 0 | 1 | 3.00 |
| *Journal of Governmental & Nonprofit Accounting* | 0 | 1 | 0 | 1 | 2 | 4 | 2.00 |
| *Journal of Health Economics* | 0 | 1 | 0 | 0 | 1 | 2 | 2.50 |

| Other Journals Receiving *Fewer than Five* University Rankings[f] | Grand Total of All Rankings | | | | | No. of Rankings | Weighted Average |
|---|---|---|---|---|---|---|---|
| *Journal of Human Resource Costing & Accounting* | 0 | 0 | 0 | 0 | 1 | 1 | 1.00 |
| *Journal of Human Resources* | 0 | 0 | 1 | 0 | 0 | 1 | 3.00 |
| *Journal of Information Technology* | 0 | 0 | 1 | 0 | 0 | 1 | 3.00 |
| *Journal of International Business* | 0 | 1 | 1 | 0 | 0 | 2 | 3.50 |
| *Journal of International Financial Management & Accounting* | 0 | 1 | 2 | 1 | 0 | 4 | 3.00 |
| *Journal of International Money and Finance* | 0 | 0 | 1 | 0 | 0 | 1 | 3.00 |
| *Journal of International Money and Finance* | 0 | 0 | 1 | 1 | 0 | 2 | 2.50 |
| *Journal of International Taxation* | 0 | 0 | 0 | 1 | 0 | 1 | 2.00 |
| *Journal of Islamic Accounting and Business Research* | 0 | 0 | 0 | 0 | 1 | 1 | 1.00 |
| *Journal of Labor Economics* | 0 | 0 | 1 | 0 | 0 | 1 | 3.00 |
| *Journal of Law and Economics* | 0 | 0 | 1 | 0 | 0 | 1 | 3.00 |
| *Journal of Learning in Higher Education* | 0 | 0 | 1 | 0 | 0 | 1 | 3.00 |
| *Journal of Management* | 0 | 1 | 0 | 0 | 0 | 1 | 4.00 |
| *Journal of Management Information Systems* | 0 | 2 | 0 | 0 | 0 | 2 | 4.00 |
| *Journal of Management Studies* | 0 | 0 | 1 | 0 | 1 | 2 | 2.00 |
| *Journal of Managerial Issues* | 0 | 0 | 1 | 0 | 0 | 1 | 3.00 |
| *Journal of Marketing* | 1 | 0 | 1 | 0 | 0 | 2 | 4.00 |
| *Journal of Marketing Research* | 1 | 0 | 0 | 0 | 0 | 1 | 5.00 |
| *Journal of Monetary Economics* | 0 | 1 | 0 | 0 | 0 | 1 | 4.00 |
| *Journal of Money, Credit and Banking* | 0 | 1 | 0 | 0 | 0 | 1 | 4.00 |
| *Journal of Multinational Financial Management* | 0 | 1 | 0 | 0 | 0 | 1 | 4.00 |
| *Journal of Occupational and Organizational Psychology* | 0 | 0 | 1 | 0 | 0 | 1 | 3.00 |

| Other Journals Receiving *Fewer than Five* University Rankings[f] | Grand Total of All Rankings | | | | | No. of Rankings | Weighted Average |
|---|---|---|---|---|---|---|---|
| Journal of the Operational Research Society | 0 | 0 | 1 | 0 | 0 | 1 | 3.00 |
| Journal of Operations Management | 0 | 1 | 0 | 0 | 0 | 1 | 4.00 |
| Journal of Organizational Behavior | 0 | 1 | 0 | 0 | 0 | 1 | 4.00 |
| Journal of Partnership Taxation | 0 | 0 | 0 | 2 | 1 | 3 | 1.67 |
| Journal of Passthrough Entities | 0 | 0 | 1 | 0 | 0 | 1 | 3.00 |
| Journal of Pension Planning & Compliance | 0 | 0 | 1 | 0 | 0 | 1 | 3.00 |
| Journal of Performance Management | 0 | 0 | 1 | 0 | 0 | 1 | 3.00 |
| Journal of Product Innovation Management | 0 | 0 | 1 | 0 | 0 | 1 | 3.00 |
| Journal of Public Economics | 0 | 2 | 0 | 0 | 0 | 2 | 4.00 |
| Journal of Retailing | 0 | 0 | 1 | 0 | 0 | 1 | 3.00 |
| Journal of Retirement Planning | 0 | 0 | 1 | 0 | 0 | 1 | 3.00 |
| Journal of Risk and Insurance | 1 | 0 | 0 | 0 | 0 | 1 | 5.00 |
| Journal of Risk and Uncertainty | 0 | 1 | 0 | 0 | 0 | 1 | 4.00 |
| Journal of Small Business Management | 0 | 1 | 0 | 0 | 0 | 1 | 4.00 |
| Journal of State Taxation | 0 | 0 | 2 | 0 | 1 | 3 | 2.33 |
| Journal of Strategic Performance Measurement | 0 | 0 | 0 | 1 | 0 | 1 | 2.00 |
| Journal of Systems Management | 0 | 1 | 1 | 0 | 0 | 2 | 3.00 |
| Journal of Tax Practice and Procedure | 0 | 0 | 1 | 0 | 0 | 1 | 3.00 |
| Journal of Taxation of Investments | 0 | 0 | 1 | 1 | 0 | 2 | 2.50 |
| Journal of Taxation of Corporate Transactions | 0 | 0 | 1 | 0 | 0 | 1 | 3.00 |
| Journal of Taxation of Financial Products | 0 | 0 | 1 | 0 | 0 | 1 | 3.00 |
| Journal of the Asia Pacific Centre for Environmental Accountability | 0 | 0 | 0 | 0 | 1 | 1 | 1.00 |

| Other Journals Receiving *Fewer than Five* University Rankings[f] | Grand Total of All Rankings | | | | | No. of Rankings | Weighted Average |
|---|---|---|---|---|---|---|---|
| *Journal of the Association of Information Systems* | 1 | 0 | 1 | 0 | 1 | 3 | 3.00 |
| *Journal of Urban Economics* | 0 | 0 | 1 | 0 | 0 | 1 | 3.00 |
| *Leadership Quarterly* | 0 | 0 | 1 | 0 | 0 | 1 | 3.00 |
| *Long Range Planning* | 0 | 0 | 1 | 0 | 0 | 1 | 3.00 |
| *The Management Accountant* | 0 | 1 | 0 | 0 | 1 | 2 | 2.50 |
| *Management Accounting Research* | 0 | 1 | 0 | 1 | 0 | 2 | 3.00 |
| *Management Science* | 2 | 0 | 0 | 0 | 0 | 2 | 5.00 |
| *Manufacturing & Service Operations Management* | 0 | 0 | 1 | 0 | 0 | 1 | 3.00 |
| *Marketing Science* | 1 | 0 | 0 | 0 | 1 | 2 | 3.50 |
| *Massachusetts CPA Review* | 0 | 1 | 0 | 2 | 0 | 3 | 2.67 |
| *Meditari Accountancy Research* | 0 | 1 | 0 | 0 | 0 | 1 | 1.00 |
| *Mid-American Journal of Business* | 0 | 1 | 0 | 0 | 0 | 1 | 4.00 |
| *MIS Quarterly* | 2 | 1 | 0 | 0 | 0 | 3 | 4.67 |
| *National Public Accountant* | 0 | 1 | 0 | 2 | 2 | 5 | 2.00 |
| *New Accountant* | 0 | 1 | 0 | 3 | 1 | 5 | 2.20 |
| *New Directions in Public Administration Research* | 0 | 1 | 0 | 0 | 0 | 1 | 4.00 |
| *North American Actuarial Journal* | 0 | 1 | 0 | 0 | 0 | 1 | 3.00 |
| *Oil and Gas Tax Quarterly* | 0 | 0 | 1 | 0 | 0 | 1 | 4.00 |
| *Omega* | 0 | 0 | 1 | 0 | 0 | 1 | 3.00 |
| *On Balance (formerly Wisconsin CPA)* | 0 | 1 | 0 | 2 | 0 | 3 | 2.67 |
| *Operations Research* | 1 | 0 | 0 | 0 | 0 | 1 | 5.00 |
| *Organizational Research Methods* | 0 | 0 | 1 | 0 | 0 | 1 | 3.00 |

| Other Journals Receiving *Fewer than Five* University Rankings[f] | Grand Total of All Rankings | | | | | No. of Rankings | Weighted Average |
|---|---|---|---|---|---|---|---|
| *Organization Studies* | 0 | 0 | 1 | 0 | 0 | 1 | 3.00 |
| *Organizational Behavior and Human Decision Processes* | 1 | 1 | 0 | 0 | 0 | 2 | 4.50 |
| *Pennsylvania CPA Journal* | 0 | 1 | 0 | 1 | 0 | 2 | 3.00 |
| *Personnel Psychology* | 1 | 0 | 0 | 0 | 0 | 1 | 5.00 |
| *Pittsburgh Tax Review* | 0 | 0 | 1 | 0 | 0 | 1 | 3.00 |
| *Practical Accountant* | 0 | 1 | 1 | 1 | 1 | 4 | 2.50 |
| *Practical Tax Strategies* (Taxation for Accountants) | 0 | 0 | 2 | 0 | 2 | 4 | 2.00 |
| *Practicing CPA* | 0 | 1 | 0 | 2 | 0 | 3 | 2.67 |
| *Production and Operations Management* | 0 | 1 | 0 | 0 | 0 | 1 | 4.00 |
| *Public Administrative Review* | 0 | 1 | 0 | 0 | 0 | 1 | 4.00 |
| *Public Budgeting & Finance* | 0 | 3 | 0 | 0 | 1 | 4 | 3.25 |
| *Public Finance and Accountancy* | 0 | 0 | 2 | 0 | 0 | 2 | 3.00 |
| *Public Finance/Finances Publiques* | 0 | 1 | 0 | 0 | 0 | 1 | 4.00 |
| *Public Finance Review* | 0 | 0 | 1 | 0 | 0 | 1 | 3.00 |
| *Qualitative Research in Accounting & Management* | 0 | 0 | 0 | 1 | 0 | 1 | 2.00 |
| *RAND Journal of Economics* | 0 | 0 | 1 | 0 | 0 | 1 | 3.00 |
| *Real Estate Economics* | 0 | 0 | 1 | 0 | 0 | 1 | 3.00 |
| *Real Estate Taxation* | 0 | 0 | 1 | 0 | 0 | 1 | 3.00 |
| *Research on Accounting Ethics* | 0 | 1 | 0 | 2 | 1 | 4 | 2.25 |
| *Research in Third World Accounting* | 0 | 1 | 0 | 0 | 0 | 1 | 4.00 |
| *Research on Professional Responsibility and Ethics in Accounting* | 0 | 1 | 3 | 0 | 0 | 4 | 3.25 |
| *Research Policy* | 0 | 0 | 1 | 0 | 0 | 1 | 3.00 |

| Other Journals Receiving *Fewer than Five University Rankings*[f] | Grand Total of All Rankings | | | | | No. of Rankings | Weighted Average |
|---|---|---|---|---|---|---|---|
| *Review of Accounting and Finance* | 0 | 0 | 2 | 1 | 0 | 3 | 2.67 |
| *Review of Business (or Accounting) Information Systems* | 0 | 0 | 2 | 0 | 0 | 2 | 3.00 |
| *Review of Economic Dynamics* | 0 | 0 | 1 | 0 | 0 | 1 | 3.00 |
| *Review of Economics and Statistics* | 0 | 1 | 0 | 0 | 0 | 1 | 4.00 |
| *Review of Finance* | 0 | 0 | 1 | 0 | 0 | 1 | 3.00 |
| *Review of Financial Studies* | 1 | 1 | 0 | 0 | 0 | 2 | 4.50 |
| *Review of Taxation of Individuals* | 0 | 0 | 0 | 0 | 1 | 1 | 1.00 |
| *Small Business Controller* | 0 | 1 | 0 | 0 | 0 | 1 | 4.00 |
| *State Tax Notes* | 0 | 0 | 1 | 2 | 0 | 3 | 2.33 |
| *State Tax Review* | 0 | 0 | 0 | 2 | 0 | 2 | 2.00 |
| *Strategic Management Journal* | 1 | 0 | 0 | 0 | 0 | 1 | 5.00 |
| *Studies in Accounting and Finance* | 0 | 1 | 0 | 0 | 1 | 2 | 2.50 |
| *Studies in Managerial and Financial Accounting* | 0 | 0 | 0 | 1 | 0 | 1 | 2.00 |
| *TaxFacts News* | 0 | 0 | 0 | 1 | 0 | 1 | 2.00 |
| *Tax Ideas* | 0 | 0 | 0 | 1 | 1 | 2 | 1.50 |
| *Tax Law Review* | 0 | 1 | 0 | 0 | 0 | 1 | 4.00 |
| *Tax Lawyer* | 0 | 1 | 1 | 1 | 0 | 3 | 3.00 |
| *Tax Management International Journal* | 0 | 0 | 1 | 0 | 0 | 1 | 3.00 |
| *Tax Management Memorandum* | 0 | 0 | 1 | 0 | 0 | 1 | 3.00 |
| *Tax Notes International* | 0 | 0 | 1 | 0 | 0 | 1 | 3.00 |
| *Taxation for Accountants* | 0 | 0 | 0 | 2 | 1 | 3 | 1.67 |
| *Taxation for Lawyers* | 0 | 0 | 0 | 1 | 0 | 1 | 2.00 |

| Other Journals Receiving *Fewer than Five* University Rankings[f] | Grand Total of All Rankings | | | | | No. of Rankings | Weighted Average |
|---|---|---|---|---|---|---|---|
| *Taxation of Exempts* | 0 | 0 | 1 | 1 | 0 | 2 | 2.50 |
| *Tennessee CPA* | 0 | 1 | 0 | 0 | 0 | 1 | 4.00 |
| *The Accountant* | 0 | 0 | 0 | 1 | 0 | 1 | 2.00 |
| *The Asset* | 0 | 0 | 0 | 1 | 0 | 1 | 2.00 |
| *Today's CPA* | 0 | 1 | 0 | 1 | 0 | 2 | 3.00 |
| *Transportation Science* | 0 | 1 | 0 | 0 | 0 | 1 | 4.00 |
| *Trusts & Estates* | 0 | 1 | 0 | 2 | 0 | 3 | 2.67 |
| *Virginia Accountant Quarterly* | 0 | 1 | 0 | 0 | 0 | 1 | 4.00 |
| *Virginia Tax Review* | 0 | 1 | 0 | 0 | 0 | 1 | 4.00 |
| *The Woman CPA* | 0 | 0 | 0 | 1 | 0 | 1 | 2.00 |

[a]Journal List based upon Danielson and Heck (2010).
[b]Journal List based upon Australian Business Deans Council.
[c]Journal List based upon *Financial Times Top 45 Journals*.
[d]These are Wayne State's University's (WSU) four named "Aspirational Schools," whose research quality is deemed somewhere between the top 75 schools per Glover et al. (2012) and other PhD-granting accounting schools.
[e]Journal Lists based upon Glover et al. (2012) *Issues in Accounting Education* study.
[f]The details of this summary are available upon request from either coauthor.

# SPECIAL SECTION ON ACCOUNTING ETHICS COURSES

# DESIGNING A THEME-BASED ETHICS COURSE IN ACCOUNTING

Cynthia Blanthorne

## ABSTRACT

*Accounting educators and practitioners believe that ethics instruction should be incorporated into the accounting curriculum. Methods of incorporation include integrating ethics into existing accounting courses or offering a stand-alone ethics course. There are, however, obstacles to meaningful implementation. The purpose of this chapter is to discuss how the two featured chapters in this special section provide examples of two intriguing accounting ethics courses. This chapter outlines the "who" (i.e., who should teach ethics), "what," and "how" of teaching ethics gleaned from prior literature to lay the foundation for the current chapters and future research. Ultimately, the chapter summarizes "best practice" articles about designing a theme-based ethics course in accounting. Each course: (1) is taught by accounting faculty (i.e., who); (2) includes topics and material likely to resonate with students (i.e., what); (3) is a unique stand-alone course structured in a meaningful manner (i.e., how). Faculty and administrators should find this chapter helpful as it provides*

Advances in Accounting Education: Teaching and Curriculum Innovations, Volume 20, 135–140
ISSN: 1085-4622/doi:10.1108/S1085-462220170000020006

*materials and guidance that speak directly to the obstacles of ethics course implementation.*

**Keywords:** Ethics in accounting; accounting education; accounting curriculum

Accounting educators and practitioners are in agreement that ethical instruction is important and that there should be an increased emphasis on ethics in accounting curricula (Abdolmohammadi & Reinstein, 2012; Blanthorne, Kovar, & Fisher, 2007; Rezaee, Szendi, Elmore, & Zhang, 2012). The National Association of State Boards of Accountancy requires a three-hour course in accounting or business ethics, or the integration equivalent (NASBA, 2008). In terms of state-regulated professional licensure, increased emphasis is evidenced by the expansion of state requirements for a mandatory: (1) ethics component of the state CPA exam; (2) ethics course for initial CPA licensure; and/or (3) ethics CPE for license renewal.

Following the NASBA requirements, models of how to incorporate ethics in accounting curricula include integration and/or offering a stand-alone ethics course.[1] The primary impediments to ethics instruction are limited materials, faculty time, knowledge and ability to incorporate ethics as well as curricular space limitations. This special section of AIAE includes two very different and intriguing models of successful ethics accounting course implementation that speak directly to these impediments. Each provides materials and guidance to improve faculty knowledge and ability to facilitate implementation of a meaningful ethics accounting course.

## BRIEF SUMMARY OF PRIOR DISCUSSION

This introduction to *Advances in Accounting Education*'s special section — Designing a Theme-Based Ethics Course in Accounting — is organized in a journalistic manner. That is, by answering the "who, what, why, and how" questions about ethics instruction (e.g., who should teach ethics) to ultimately describe how the papers in the special section contribute to the topic.

To motivate *any* discussion on ethical training in the accounting curriculum the most basic question is:

### Should Accounting Students Receive Ethics Training?

The answer is a resounding˙yes! Virtually all prior ethics education literature either specifically states or is premised upon the belief that ethics is of value and should be incorporated into the accounting student experience. Ninety-five percent of faculty surveyed by Blanthorne et al. (2007) thought that accounting students should receive ethical training. In addition, faculty and practitioners agree that ethical development is crucial to the profession and that trust, in the profession, needs to be reestablished due to public scandals (Blanthorne et al., 2007; Rezaee et al., 2012).

### Why Aren't We Doing It (More)?

The sentiment from accounting faculty and practitioners is that there should be an increased emphasis on ethics in the accounting curriculum. In terms of impediments, however, faculty report a lack of time and extant teaching materials. In addition, faculty are hesitant to teach ethics due to perceived limited ability or knowledge about how and what to teach. Finally, there is the pragmatic issue of the lack of space in the curriculum (Blanthorne et al., 2007; Massey & Van Hise, 2009).

### Who Should Teach Ethics?

Faculty believe that the instruction of ethics content to accounting students should be provided by accounting faculty, either individually or in teams with nonaccounting faculty (Blanthorne et al., 2007).

### What Should Be Taught?

Content and skills required for success on the uniform CPA Examination focus on professional guidance in the areas of Audit and Regulation, such as the AICPA Code of Professional Conduct (AICPA, 2013, 2016). Similarly, professional CPE requirements focus on the technical application of code(s) rather than on the professional development of accountants.

Accounting faculty and practitioners, however, envision a focus on more robust topics with the potential to resonate with students (Abdolmohammadi & Reinstein, 2012; Blanthorne et al., 2007). Examples of these types of topics include ethical issues faced by the profession and contemplation and understanding of professional and moral obligations.

## *How Should Ethics Be Taught?*

While interested parties continue to debate whether ethics should be taught in a stand-alone ethics course or integrated throughout the curriculum, both approaches have unique merits. Interestingly, practitioners more strongly believe that a stand-alone course is warranted as compared to academicians (Rezaee et al., 2012). Faculty preference for integration is likely tied to the impediments noted earlier. As stated by Armstrong (1993), framing the debate as an either/or proposition creates an unnecessary false dichotomy. Meaningful ethics tutelage is the common goal. Therefore, with an acknowledgment that integrating ethics throughout the curriculum is an acceptable approach, this special section of AIAE concentrates on designing an ethics accounting course.

# CONTRIBUTION OF THE SPECIAL SECTION CHAPTERS

The two chapters featured in this special section communicate "best practices" based on lengthy (i.e., years of) course development. The chapters provide two very different and intriguing examples of creative ways for accounting faculty to teach an ethics course. Consistent with the "what should be taught" opinion of faculty and practitioners, each chapter describes a thought-provoking ethics course likely to resonate with students.

In the first chapter, Kelly (2017) presents ethics training in a leadership context, thereby intertwining leadership and ethics in a complimentary manner. He provides a detailed description of the course specifics (readings, assignments, etc.) which includes the integration of ethics and leadership on a week-by-week basis. Notably, accounting ethics courses, with detailed course guidance, are also described in the fairly recent prior literature by Massey and Van Hise (2009) and Langmead and Sedaghat (2007).

In a vastly different approach, the focus of the second chapter is described as a course on "how to live life" (Shaub, 2017). Fundamental to this course is a systematic reasoning process to emphasize long-term thinking, accountability, and the impact of ethics-related decisions on others. The goal is develop students' wisdom so that young accounting professionals are less susceptible to fallacies of thinking that can undermine careers and personal lives. Prior literature by Mintz (2006) outlines a course that is similar in that it applies to student thought processes. Students apply reflective thinking, based on virtue theory, to evaluate conflicts faced by professionals.

These ethics course chapters address various impediments identified in the discussion of ethics education in accounting. Each manuscript provides teaching materials and guidance to improve knowledge and ability for successful course implementation. The work and, perhaps more importantly to colleagues, the sharing of their materials and experiences should facilitate efficient implementation by peers. While not specifically addressed in the chapters of this special section, limited curricula space is addressed by Massey and Van Hise (2009).

The mention of ethics courses from prior literature is not meant to minimize the contributions by Kelly (2017) and Shaub (2017). While the chapters may be related in limited ways, they are vastly different in most respects. Accounting ethics education lacks any agreed-upon topics or course material. Quite the contrary, there is tremendous discussion and debate about what should be taught. Therefore, each ethics course described in the special section, as well as the others noted, provides a *unique* contribution to the literature.

The continued dissemination of meaningful ethical course design or incorporation of ethics instruction in the accounting curriculum is valuable, enhancing our knowledge and ability to teach ethics. Because each course is unique, the opportunity for future research is vast as is the potential for results that are impactful.

## NOTE

1. In this discussion, the term "ethics course" refers to the myriad of different types of courses of ethical training and instruction (e.g., professional conduct, social responsibility).

140                                                            CYNTHIA BLANTHORNE

# REFERENCES

Abdolmohammadi, M. J., & Reinstein, A. (2012). Practicing accountants' views of the content of accounting ethics courses and course effects on attitudes and behavior. *Advances in Accounting Education: Teaching and Curriculum Innovations, 13,* 213–236.

AICPA. (2013). *Content and skill specifications for the uniform CPA examination.* New York, NY: American Institute of Certified Public Accountants, Inc.

AICPA. (2016). *Uniform CPA examination blueprints.* New York, NY: American Institute of Certified Public Accountants, Inc.

Armstrong, M. B. (1993). Ethics and professionalism in accounting education: A sample course. *Journal of Accounting Education, 11,* 77–92.

Blanthorne, C., Kovar, S. E., & Fisher, D. G. (2007). Accounting educators' opinions about ethics in the curriculum: An extensive view. *Issues in Accounting Education, 22*(3), 355–390.

Kelly, P. T. (2017). Integrating leadership topics into an accounting ethics course − Preparing students for a challenging profession. In T. J. Rupert & B. B. Kern (Eds.), *Advances in Accounting Education: Teaching and Curriculum Innovations* (Vol. 20, pp. 141–180). Advances in Accounting Education: Teaching and Curriculum Innovations. Bingley, UK: Emerald Group Publishing Limited.

Langmead, J. M., & Sedaghat, A. M. (2007). Integrating professionalism in the business school curriculum: The development of a course of the financial reporting crisis on the professionalism and ethical framework of corporate controllership and financial officers. *Advances in Accounting Education: Teaching and Curriculum Innovations, 7,* 135–158.

Massey, D. W., & Van Hise, J. (2009). Walking the walk: Integrating lessons from multiple perspectives in the development of an accounting ethics course. *Issues in Accounting Education, 24*(4), 481–510.

Mintz, S. M. (2006). Accounting ethics education: Integrating reflective learning and virtue ethics. *Journal of Accounting Education, 24*(2–3), 97–117.

NASBA. (2008). *Model education rules.* Retrieved from https://nasba.org/blog/2008/05/01/nonworking-linkmay-2008-model-education-rules-approved/. Accessed on July 2016.

Rezaee, Z., Szendi, J., Elmore, R. E., & Zhang, R. (2012). Corporate governance and ethics education: Viewpoints from accounting academicians and practitioners. *Advances in Accounting Education: Teaching and Curriculum Innovations, 13,* 127–158.

Shaub, M. K. (2017). A wisdom-based accounting ethics course. In T. J. Rupert & B. B. Kern (Eds.), *Advances in Accounting Education: Teaching and Curriculum Innovations* (Vol. 20, pp. 181–216). Advances in Accounting Education: Teaching and Curriculum Innovations. Bingley, UK: Emerald Group Publishing Limited.

# INTEGRATING LEADERSHIP TOPICS INTO AN ACCOUNTING ETHICS COURSE – PREPARING STUDENTS FOR A CHALLENGING PROFESSION

Patrick T. Kelly

## ABSTRACT

*This chapter examines the integration of leadership topics into an accounting ethics course. Literature review, course review, student feedback. Both practitioners and educators have called for broader education of accounting students in general, and student learning of leadership and interpersonal skills in particular, to prepare students who are entering the profession. I have used the leadership topics and activities discussed in this chapter in a stand-alone ethics course in a graduate business program, but they could also be integrated into an undergraduate course. I provide details regarding course content and delivery, including a weekly schedule of accounting ethics and leadership readings, short cases, and leadership/ethics case research topics.*

Advances in Accounting Education: Teaching and Curriculum Innovations, Volume 20, 141–180
Copyright © 2017 by Emerald Publishing Limited
ISSN: 1085-4622/doi:10.1108/S1085-462220170000020007

*Many of the leadership and ethics subjects in the course are expected to be addressed in the accounting workplace — exploring these topics helps better prepare students to confront future challenges. Although both practitioners and educators have called for broader education of accounting students in general, and student learning of leadership and interpersonal skills in particular, little progress has been made in this area. This chapter contributes to this area by highlighting the value of integrating leadership topics into an accounting ethics course.*

**Keywords:** Accounting ethics education; teaching accounting ethics; leadership and accounting ethics

Accounting ethics instruction has received a great amount of attention since the turn of the century. The failure of Enron, the demise of Andersen, the KPMG tax shelter scandal, and the 2008 financial crisis all caused additional scrutiny of the accounting profession. The resulting increased focus on accounting ethics has led to an examination of the ethical education provided to accounting students and calls for increased ethics coverage in colleges (Haas, 2005; Mintz, 2007; NASBA, 2005, 2007). Some states, including Texas, California, Illinois, Maryland, and West Virginia, require ethics courses for those who will be a licensed CPA in their states (Mastracchio, Jimenez-Angueira, & Toth, 2015). Many educators believe that accounting students need ethics education; Blanthorne, Kovar, and Fisher (2007) found that almost all surveyed accounting faculty felt that accounting students should receive ethics training and most thought that accounting faculty should be teaching ethics. However, research does not provide a clear view as to whether ethics should be taught as a separate ethics course or integrated across the accounting curriculum (Blanthorne et al., 2007; Hurtt & Thomas, 2008). And while there appears to be some agreement as to "how" ethics should be taught to accounting students (Blanthorne et al., 2007), there are a variety of views on the different topics that should be taught (Blanthorne et al., 2007; Hurtt & Thomas, 2008).

Accounting educator efforts to address ethics are occurring at a time when students are entering their classrooms with an increasingly diverse set of personal values which may not be consistent with those expected of those in the profession. Stephens, Vance, and Pettegrew (2012) provide a bleak picture of student values, reporting results from a 2008 Josephson Institute "Report Card on the Ethics of American Youth" that addressed student ethical actions relating to lying (82% lied to a parent about something significant), cheating (64% cheated on an exam at least once in high school), and theft (30% stole something from a store). They also reported:

> ... over 92% of those surveyed said they were satisfied with their personal ethics and character, which strongly suggests that today's youth has a view of ethics that is far different from what the accounting profession needs to turn the ethical corner. (Stephens et al., 2012, p. 18)

These results are comparable with those from the 2010 Josephson Institute Survey, with similar high rates of lying, cheating, and theft (Josephson Institute, 2011).

Stephens et al. (2012) acknowledged that the values of those entering colleges are not up to the ethical demands of the accounting profession, but recognized the need for the high ethical standards demanded by the profession and the challenge facing the profession in recruiting individuals with high ethical standards. They rightly indicate "the profession must attract a core of individuals with a passion for becoming leaders who are honest, trustworthy, and of high personal integrity" (Stephens et al., 2012, p. 18). These concepts are well recognized in the profession and have been for decades (see the below discussion of The Bedford Committee, 1986; Albrecht & Sack, 2000; the Accounting Education Change Commission, 1990; The Treadway Commission, 1987; and the AICPA Core Competency Framework, 2000).

While much accounting ethics instruction, whether integrated throughout the accounting curriculum or in a separate course, addresses topics of honesty and integrity, many programs do not address topics of leadership in general, or moral leadership in particular. For example, Hurtt and Thomas (2008) identify 28 different topics to be covered in an ethics course. Leadership is not among them, although some concepts such as moral exemplars, making correct choices under pressure, justice, caring, and compassion could be expected to touch on the topic of leadership. However, accounting educators are realizing the importance of leadership skills for those entering the accounting profession. For example, Bloch, Brewer, and Stout (2012) cite practitioner surveys indicating the importance of leadership skills, but note the absence of leadership topics in accounting curricula, along with a lack of instructional resources available to accounting faculty. They developed a three-week leadership module to be used in an undergraduate cost accounting course, but also indicate that this module could be used in other upper level accounting courses (Bloch et al., 2012). Their leadership module is organized around two important leadership concepts: "(1) defining a vision and motivating others" and "(2) establishing a culture of organizational integrity" (Bloch et al., 2012, p. 530).

It is not surprising that Bloch et al. (2012) include the concept of integrity in their leadership module. Leadership provides a useful context when learning about accounting ethical topics and can greatly enhance the study of accounting ethics. Accounting professionals rarely make ethical decisions "in a vacuum," but rather while serving in a supervisory position or as a member of a team. Understanding leadership subjects such as motivation, power, values, and organizational culture can assist individuals who will invariably be called upon to make ethical decisions. In addition, the development of leadership skills such as self-confidence, critical thinking ability, and the ability to communicate effectively can contribute to the processes of moral motivation and moral character identified by Rest, Narvaez, Bebeau, and Thoma (1999) that impact ethical behavior. Furthermore, addressing leadership topics can be quite valuable to those students about to enter the profession, given the high level demands associated with the today's accounting workplace and the responsibility placed on junior people at a relatively early stage in their careers.

The next section of this chapter provides background on accounting ethics courses and instruction, with a focus on course content and calls for inclusion of various leadership topics. This is followed by a section describing course structure and how I incorporate the leadership topics into a stand-alone accounting ethics course taught in a graduate business program, along with specifics on various aspects of the course, including the reflection journal, case assignments, and the accounting leader and ethics research project. That is followed by a section on student feedback. I conclude with a discussion of the advantages associated with integrating leadership topics into an accounting ethics course and opportunities for additional research in this area.

# BACKGROUND ON ACCOUNTING ETHICS COURSES AND THE CASE FOR INCORPORATING COVERAGE OF LEADERSHIP

While accounting ethics education and topics for course content have received increased focus in recent years, this trend is not new and attention was being paid to these topics well over 20 years ago. In many cases recommendations on course content included both traditional ethics topics (integrity, independence) and the inclusion of many subjects that are related to leadership and would serve to broaden the education base for students. For example, in 1986 the American Accounting Association Committee on the Future Structure, Content, and Scope of Accounting Education (the Bedford Committee) noted the importance of educators emphasizing required knowledge and ethical standards. However, it also included the need to provide a broad education and encourage the development of personal characteristics that include empathy, understanding cultural and intellectual differences, creative thinking, professional commitment, and leadership (The Bedford Committee, 1986). In 1987 the Report of the National Commission on Fraudulent Financial Reporting (The Treadway Commission) endorsed liberal arts study to serve as a foundation for additional study in accounting and business. The Commission noted that accounting programs had not provided enough emphasis on ethics and values and recommended an ethics across the accounting curriculum approach. It also recommended increased coverage of topics across the business curricula, including the ethical tone at the top of organizations, how management sets goals and motivates people to achieve those goals, and pressures that can result in fraudulent financial reporting (The Treadway Commission, 1987). In 1990 the Accounting Education Change Commission (AECC) identified the professional orientation needed by accounting graduates entering the profession, which encompassed qualities including ethics, value-based judgments, integrity, objectivity, and concern for the public interest. The AECC also identified capabilities needed by accounting graduates. Personal capacities and attitudes included motivation, persistence, and leadership, while interpersonal skills included working with others, leading them, and resolving conflict (Accounting Education Change Commission, 1990).

A decade later, but before the Enron and Andersen failures, Albrecht and Sack (2000) identified a number of perceived problems with accounting education, including not properly addressing issues of values, ethics, and integrity. They also recommended more time and effort on skills that contribute to student success, including written and oral communications, interpersonal skills, teamwork, leadership, and professional demeanor (Albrecht & Sack, 2000). Also in 2000, the AICPA's *Core Competency Framework for Entry into the Accounting Profession* identified a Professional Demeanor Personal Competency, which included objectivity, integrity and ethical behavior. Leadership was also identified as a personal competency and included elements such as motivating others to achieve excellence, facilitating the development of consensus, and gaining the support of others to achieve results (AICPA Core Competency Framework, 2000).

Accounting educators also recognized the need to improve accounting ethics education well before Enron, Andersen and the other well publicized failures after 2001. For example, in response to the Bedford Committee and Treadway Commission reports identified above, Loeb (1988) discussed the need for and goals associated with accounting ethics education. Possible goals included developing the abilities to deal with ethical dilemmas and the uncertainties of the profession, along with a sense of moral obligation or responsibility (Loeb, 1988). Armstrong (1993) also supported additional ethics instruction and recommended a "sandwich approach" to teach ethics to accounting students (a general ethics course that could be taught in the philosophy department, followed by ethics case studies in accounting courses, and then an Ethics and Professionalism (E&P) capstone course to complete the ethics education). The E&P course relies on three theoretical foundations: ethical theories from philosophy, theories of moral development, and sociology theories that inform professions. The sociology base helps students address the role of the profession in society, professional duties, and personal responsibility as a professional (Armstrong, 1993).

Since the Enron and Andersen failures in 2001, accounting ethics has received increased attention from educators. Jennings (2004) identified voids in business and accounting ethics education programs that contributed to notable business failures from 1999 to 2002. She recommended seminal works to help accountants resolve ethical dilemmas, including the following: *Ethical Leadership and the Psychology of Decision Making* by Messick and Bazerman, *Behavioral Study of Obedience* by Milgram, and *Effects of Group Pressure on the Modification and Distortion of Judgment* by Asch. Jennings noted that these works help explain some of the business and accounting failures while serving to develop accounting student ethical values (Jennings, 2004). Thomas (2004) noted the increased emphasis for accounting ethics education and provided an inventory of teaching materials. This included textbooks, notable cases, and resources for various topics related to accounting ethics (e.g., integrity and professionalism, corporate governance, independence, and financial accounting/auditing/fraud) (Thomas, 2004). Waddock (2005) noted the roles that accountants played in the financial failures and called on accounting educators to provide a more broad-based education for accountants that results in them being "mindful."

> The accounting profession seems to have failed to acknowledge that accounting is fundamentally an ethical, rather than a technical, discourse. Accountability inescapably assumes the fulfilling of some dutiful requirements. If we want accountants who are capable of acting with integrity and understanding the broader system in which they work, we must teach them to be mindful — aware of their belief systems, conscious of consequences, and capable of thinking broadly about the impact of their actions and decisions. (Waddock, 2005, p. 147)

Waddock went on to identify various leadership-oriented skills that will develop integrity and integrated thinking, including:

- Individual and institutional integrity, responsibility, accountability, and transparency …

- The importance of self-efficacy, voice, and confidence

- The ability to speak one's own mind while being sensitive to the perspectives of others

- The ability to reflect on the implications of actions, decisions, attitudes, and behaviors

- The ability to understand the consequences of actions, and, when needed, to take corrective action or change course (Waddock, 2005, p. 148).

As previously mentioned, Blanthorne et al. (2007) surveyed accounting educators on a variety of ethics topics. Almost all (95%) responded that accounting ethics should be taught and that accounting faculty should serve as the teachers. A subsequent survey by Miller and Becker (2011) found that 78% of surveyed accounting faculty responded that ethics should be taught, a notable decrease when compared to Blanthorne et al. (2007). In terms of ethics integration, Blanthorne et al. (2007) found that almost all accounting educators (98.1%) recommended integration of ethics topics across the accounting curriculum and 80.7% said that ethics should be presented in every accounting course. Miller and Becker (2011) subsequently found that integration efforts may be lacking and consisted of "… an ad hoc list of topics that is implemented as a collection of topics rather than as a synchronized set of topics that build student knowledge" (Miller & Becker, 2011, p. 7).

Regarding whether or not accounting ethics should be taught as a separate course, Blanthorne et al. (2007) reported a relatively small percentage of those surveyed (22.6%) felt there should be a separate course in the accounting program. However, Bean and Bernardi (2007) argued for a stand-alone accounting ethics course, noting the past accounting scandals and the importance of ethics to the accounting profession. Furthermore, in the aftermath of Enron, Andersen, and other notable failures, several different states now require ethics classes for accounting students (Mastracchio et al., 2015). State regulatory requirements may limit flexibility in providing a fully integrated leadership-oriented ethics course and instructors should review topic requirements for their respective states.

Hurtt and Thomas (2008) reported on educator experiences associated with the Texas ethics requirement that began in 2005. They used a triangulated approach in this study, obtaining approved syllabi from the Texas State Board of Public Accountancy, surveying accounting ethics instructors, and interviewing Texas Board members and staff. In examining the syllabi, they found that 53% of the accounting ethics courses were taught in accounting departments, 44% were taught in other business departments, and the remaining courses were taught outside the business school in philosophy departments (Hurtt & Thomas, 2008). Hurtt and Thomas also asked instructors to rank the topics covered by importance using a 1 (Unnecessary to Cover) to 10 (Mandatory) scale. Instructors reported five topics with a mean score that exceeded 9: Integrity, Honesty, Ethical Reasoning, Making correct choices under pressure, and Independence. Other topics regarded as important and related to leadership topics included objectivity, impartiality, moral exemplars, and discretion (Hurtt & Thomas, 2008).

Accounting educators have addressed a variety of other topics relating to accounting ethics courses and their content. Blanthorne et al. (2007) reported that surveyed faculty noted that in addition to ethical issues faced by the profession, ethical decision-making processes/models, and professional guidance, the pursuit of personal excellence and understanding professional moral obligations should also be emphasized. Bean and Bernardi (2007) recommended specific topics for such a course that relate to both ethics and leadership. These include ethical theories, codes of ethics, tone at the top, auditor independence, and whistle-blowing. Massey and Van Hise (2009) also provided insights on the design of an accounting ethics course. Many of their course content recommendations were similar to those of Bean and Bernardi (2007), including classical ethical theories, codes of professional ethics, characteristics of a professional, ethical decision making, whistle-blowing, corporate governance and ethical issues associated with different aspects of accounting, such as audit practice ethics, tax ethics, and consulting practice ethics (Massey & Van Hise, 2009). In a subsequent paper Van Hise and Massey (2010) explain how and why the Ignation Pedagogical Paradigm (IPP) can be a suitable framework for use in an accounting ethics course. They use five components of the IPP (context, experience, reflection, action, and evaluation) to provide recommendations on course content and process, including professionals' decision process, use of positive and negative accounting exemplars, codes of conduct, and written reflections (Van Hise & Massey, 2010). More recently, Kidwell, Fisher, Braun, and Swanson (2013) used Bloom's taxonomy to develop learning objectives in six essential content areas: codes of conduct, corporate governance, the accounting profession, moral development, classical ethics theories, and decision models.

## COURSE STRUCTURE

As noted earlier, Stephens et al. (2012) stressed the need for ethical leaders to join the accounting profession. Yet despite calls from both practitioners and educators to address various leadership topics, in most cases these subjects are not specifically addressed in accounting ethics courses. I have found a synergistic fit in incorporating leadership concepts in an accounting ethics course over a number of semesters and students appear to appreciate the complementary relationship between these subjects.

This section will describe how leadership topics are integrated into one stand-alone graduate accounting ethics course offered at a college in the northeastern United States. Similar to the approach described in Massey and Van Hise (2009), the education program at this institution has introduced an accounting ethics course in its graduate program and this course is one of two courses that fulfills the ethics requirement for the program. In a typical semester this course has one weekly 3-hour meeting, which permits both active learning techniques and an in-depth discussion of course content.

In approaching the design of this accounting ethics course, Rest's Four Component Model proves instructive (Rest, 1994; Rest et al., 1999). He identified four processes that determine ethical behavior. These are described below.

1. Moral *Sensitivity* (interpreting the situation, role taking how various actions would affect the parties concerned, imagining cause-effect chains of events, and being aware that there is a moral problem when it exists)

2. Moral *Judgment* (judging which action would be most justifiable in a moral sense…)

3. Moral *Motivation* (the degree of commitment to taking a moral course of action, valuing moral values over other values, and taking personal responsibility for moral outcomes)

4. Moral *Character* (persisting in a moral task, having courage, overcoming fatigue and temptations, and implementing subroutines that serve a moral goal (Rest et al., 1999, p. 60)

After consideration of Rest's Four Component Model, I developed the following course objectives. At the end of this course, it is expected that students will:

- Develop an understanding of professional ethical standards that apply to business and professional contexts, specifically accounting contexts (relates to the development of moral awareness);
- Recognize ethical issues and dilemmas in business contexts, specifically accounting contexts and offer values-based decisions (relates to the development of moral awareness and moral reasoning ability);
- Understand major ethical theories and how they apply when resolving ethical dilemmas in business and accounting situations (relates to the development of moral reasoning ability);
- Explain and justify values-based decisions in response to ethical situations (relates to the development of moral motivation and moral character);
- Gain an understanding of moral leadership and the actions that they as leaders can take to foster ethical decisions and an ethical organizational climate (relates to the development of moral motivation and moral character).

Both Blanthorne et al. (2007) and Massey and Van Hise (2009) discuss the importance of different teaching methods for accounting ethics courses. For this course, I employ many of the methods identified by Blanthorne et al. (2007). These include case analyses, vignettes, articles and other readings, ethical debates, ethical questions from textbooks, and student maintenance of a reflection journal. There is minimal lecturing by the instructor, but rather student group case presentations on a weekly basis, focused discussions on weekly ethics and leadership readings, as well as a leader/ethical case research paper and presentation. Graham, Kelly, Massey, and Van Hise (2013) recommend these multiple teaching strategies to meet accounting ethics students' different learning styles.

I also cover in this course many of the important subjects addressed in accounting ethics courses highlighted by educators (Bean & Bernardi, 2007; Blanthorne et al., 2007; Hurtt & Thomas, 2008; Massey & Van Hise, 2009). These include professional ethical standards (AICPA Code of Conduct, IMA Code of Conduct, Sarbanes-Oxley Act), a review of classical ethical theories, moral reasoning ability, ethics cases (personal conduct, revenue recognition, audit, corporate governance), moral exemplars, whistleblowing, and fraud prevention. In addition, I also address various leadership topics, including leadership traits, personality preferences, tone at the top, followership, organizational culture, motivation, power, and various leadership theories, including servant leadership, transformational leadership, transactional leadership, and situational leadership. Fig. 1 provides an overview of the leadership lessons for this course.

Two textbooks are recommended for this course. The first is *Ethical Obligations and Decision Making in Accounting — Text and Cases* (Fourth Edition, McGraw-Hill Irwin) by Mintz and Morris (2017), which replaced the Third Edition Mintz and Morris (2014) text that I used in previous semesters of this course. To facilitate instructor usage in future accounting ethics courses, I have updated this chapter to reflect topics and cases included in the Fourth Edition of Mintz and Morris (2017).

The second recommended textbook is *The Leader's Companion (TLC) — Insights on Leadership Through the Ages* (Free Press) edited by Wren (1995). This book has 64 articles, many dealing with classic leadership topics. The diverse set of articles provides a wide variety of different ways to address leadership in an accounting ethics course. While there are other textbooks such as *Business Leadership — A Jossey Bass Reader* (2003) that could be used in this course with supplemental articles such as Kelley (1988), the wide range of topics included in Wren (1995) has facilitated leadership integration in this course.

Both Mintz and Morris (2017) and Wren (1995) provide a complementary mix of concepts and cases appropriate for an accounting ethics course. Table 1 provides the weekly schedule of ethics and leadership topics for a typical 15-week semester. This schedule provides flexibility in addressing both the ethics and leadership subjects throughout the course. Student group presentations of the Mintz and Morris ethics cases (each case is read by all students prior to the respective class) begin in Week 3 and continue through Week 10, leading up to individual student presentations of their leader/ethical case research papers. In addition, each week there is a discussion of ethical concepts from the readings in the Mintz and Morris textbook, along with a discussion of leadership topics from the Wren textbook. A course management system (e.g., SAKAI, Blackboard) facilitates posting of weekly assignments, articles for students to read, and drop boxes for weekly student submissions of their case solutions, reflection journals, and assigned questions.

Instructor evaluations of the reflection journals, assigned questions, group case presentations, and class participation determine student course grades. These four components, along with a peer evaluation of group members, comprise 50% of a student's grade. I base the remaining 50% on the Leader/Ethical Case Research Assignment paper and class presentation.

PATRICK T. KELLY

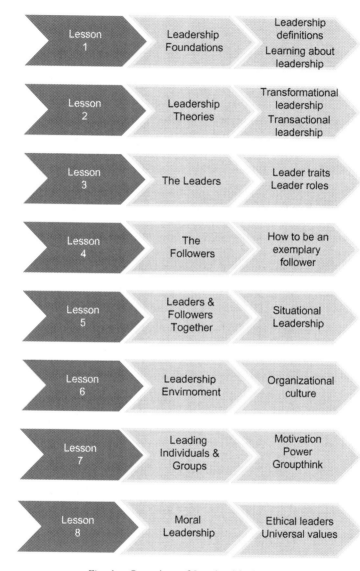

*Fig. 1.* Overview of Leadership Lessons.

*Table 1.* Ethics and Leadership Topics — Weekly Schedule.

| Week | Ethics Topic | Mintz and Morris (2017) Chapter | Leadership Topic | Wren (1995) Part |
|------|-------------|--------------------------------|------------------|------------------|
| 1. | Intro./Course Administration | None | n/a | None |
| 2. | Ethics and Professional Judgment in Accounting | 4 | Leadership Foundations | Part I |
| 3. | Ethical Reasoning: Implications for Accounting | 1 | Leadership Foundations | Part II |
| 4. | Cognitive Processes and Ethical Decision Making | 2 | Leadership Theories | Parts III & IV (Chapters 18–21) |
| 5. | Organizational Ethics and Corporate Governance | 3 | The Leaders | Part IV (Chapter 22) Part V |
| 6. | Fraud in Financial Statements and Auditor Responsibilities | 5 | The Followers | Part VI |
| 7. | Legal, Regulatory, and Professional Obligations of Auditor | 6 | Leaders and Followers Together | Part VII |
| 8. | Earnings Management | 7 | The Leadership Environment and Organizational Culture | Part VIII |
| 9. | Ethical Leadership and Decision-Making in Accounting | 8 | Leading Individuals and Groups | Part IX & X |
| 10. | Ethical Leadership and Decision-Making in Accounting | None | Moral Leadership | Part XI & XIII |
| 11–15. | Leader/Case Research Presentations | None | | None |

In the following sections, I provide a description of the various topics and assignments used in the course. To ease instructor adoption of these materials in an accounting ethics course, I provide a detailed weekly schedule for course topics and activities in Appendix A.

### Weekly Schedule Incorporating Leadership Topics

This section describes the leadership topics that are addressed throughout this course (Table 1). Leadership Lesson 1 deals with leadership foundations. We explore these foundational concepts in Weeks 2 and 3 to provide a context from which to address subsequent leadership topics in the course. In Week 2 students read Wren's (1995) "The Crisis of Leadership" and there is initial discussion of general leadership topics (state of leadership in our country/organizations, and whether leaders are "born" or "made"). In Week 3 there is an examination of different definitions of leadership and processes of learning about leadership.

The class addresses Leadership Theories, Leadership Lesson 2, in Week 4. Students read Part III "Historical Views of Leadership" and Part IV "Modern Views of Leadership," Chapters 18–21. Topics include transformational and transactional leadership, the relationship between leadership and ethics, and tasks associated with leadership. During this class, discussion centers on how transformational leaders raise others to "higher levels of motivation and morality." Students usually agree that while it may be easier to function as transactional leaders in the workplace, they would rather work for and aspire to be transformational leaders, who they regard as more effective.

Leadership Lesson 3 is included in Week 5 with the examination of traits and personal factors, and students read Part IV, Chapter 22, and Part V "The Leader" of the Wren (1995) textbook. Leadership traits discussed include leadership drive, leadership motivation, honesty and integrity, self-confidence, cognitive ability, and knowledge of the business. This discussion provides another opportunity to reinforce the importance of leaders being honest and persons of integrity and the significance of establishing trust as a leader.

We also discuss personality preferences in this course beginning in Week 5. If available, the Myers-Briggs Type Indicator (MBTI) is used for students to learn about their personality preferences and how they interact with others in the workplace. Instructors can frequently obtain the MBTI from the College or University Career Center or Counseling Center. There is frequently not enough time for the MBTI review during the Week 5 Class, so we usually address it in the "Catch-Up" session in Weeks 10 or 11. During that session, students receive their MBTI results and learn about the differences in personality preferences.

In Week 6 we explore the concept of followership, as students read Part VI "The Followers" of the Wren (1995) textbook for Leadership Lesson 4. In this class, students realize and appreciate the relationship between followership and ethical behavior. Students typically conclude that frequently followers who behave like "sheep" may be more prone to act unethically due to pressure from their boss or other superiors. The "exemplary followers" who critically think about situations are more likely to make the correct ethical decision. Students also learn about their followership roles as new hires at accounting firms and other organizations, including the responsibility to develop their expertise and judgment as accounting professionals.

For Week 7, students read Part VII "Leaders and Followers Together" for Leadership Lesson 5. The main leadership concept examined is situational leadership, with specific focus on how it applies to accounting firms. For example, when students begin their careers as new accountants and auditors, they can expect to receive specific instructions and close supervision. This situation will change as their "follower readiness" develops over time and eventually tasks will be delegated to them as more seasoned professionals. Discussion also focuses on the need to clearly communicate expectations, to effectively train and develop individuals, and to properly evaluate performance. Students can usually relate to the importance of these concepts based on past experiences during internships or other work situations.

For Leadership Lesson 6 in Week 8 students read Part VIII "The Leadership Environment" of the Wren (1995) textbook and "Leadership and Organizational Culture: Lessons Learned from Arthur Andersen" (Kelly & Earley, 2009). Organizational culture is the main leadership topic addressed and students learn about the importance of an ethical culture in an organization. We also pay specific attention to how leader actions impact the ethical culture of an organization, thereby addressing the last course objective (gain an understanding of moral leadership and the actions they as leaders can take to foster ethical decisions and an ethical organizational climate). Such leader actions include role-modeling behaviors, allocation of rewards and status, and reactions to critical incidents.

In Week 9, Leadership Lesson 7 focuses on Part IX "Leading Individuals" and Part X "Leading Groups" of the Wren (1995) textbook.

Leadership topics include motivation (Maslow, Herzberg) and bases of power, including French and Raven's five bases of power, and groupthink. Students gain insight into the motivation associated with ethical and unethical behavior, along with the power bases that can potentially impact moral decisions. Students also learn about the potential for groupthink in an accounting firm due to pressure, self-censorship, and "mindguards," in cases when a partner or another senior executive expresses a particular point of view on a subject.

We address Leadership Lesson 8 in Week 10. Students read Part XI "Skills of a Leader" and Part XIII "Practicing Moral Leadership" of the Wren (1995) textbook, along with "Ethical Leaders in Accounting" by Kelly and Earley (2011). Topics include essential leadership competencies, moral leadership, individual moral development, and universal human values and help address the final course objective (gain an understanding of moral leadership and the actions that they as leaders can take to foster ethical decisions). The Kelly and Earley's (2011) paper reinforces the idea that in many cases accounting professionals have acted ethically when presented with challenging circumstances. The ethical leaders provide examples of conduct to aspire to for students entering the accounting profession. Finally, the fourth edition of Mintz and Morris (2017) includes a new final chapter "Ethical Leadership and Decision-Making in Accounting." This provides a valuable opportunity to reinforce the moral leadership concepts from the Wren (1995) textbook and revisit leadership topics such as transformational leadership, servant leadership, followership, and organizational culture (Mintz & Morris, 2017).

### Reflection Journal

As noted, prior research has advocated for the use of reflection journals in an accounting ethics course (Graham et al., 2013; Van Hise & Massey, 2010). Reflection journals in this course facilitate the examination of both leadership and ethics topics. Appendix B contains a complete list of recommended reflection questions for the semester based on Wren (1995) and Mintz and Morris (2017). I provide selective leadership reflections questions for Weeks 2, 8, 9, and 11−15 in Exhibit 1 and address topics such as the relationship between ethics and leadership, organizational culture, bases of social power, and groupthink.

The use of reflection journals provides a number of advantages in this course. From a practical standpoint, having students do the reflection

***Exhibit 1.*** Sample of Reflection Journal Leadership Questions – Based on Reading from Wren (1995).

*Week 2 Questions* – Based on Readings in Part 1:

1. In our society today, is there a "crisis of leadership"? Provide an example to support your position.
2. Are leaders "born" or "made" (or can leadership be taught)?
3. Does servant leadership apply to accounting ethics?

*Week 8 Questions* – Based on Readings in Part 8, along with *Leadership and Organization Culture: Lessons Learned from Arthur Andersen* by Kelly and Earley (2009).

1. Given the actions by leaders at Arthur Andersen, was the demise of the firm to be expected? Do you agree that Andersen should have been indicted?
2. What are the implications of Andersen's demise for other large accounting firms?
3. Other than the leaders who we will examine in our research papers, name a leader who influenced the culture of his or her organization (positively or negatively) and describe the impact.

Please read Part 8. After reading Chapter 38, please write a paragraph that describes the organizational culture for the student body at our College.

*Week 9 Questions* – Based on Readings in Parts 9 and 10:

1. For Chapter 44: Do you agree or disagree with Herzberg's Two-Factor Theory? Provide an example to support your position.
2. For Chapter 45: See the discussion of five bases of social power. Name a leadership position that you have held during your lifetime. What Power Base(s) contributed to your success in this position?
3. For Chapter 47: Assess the potential for groupthink in a large accounting or other business firm. How can it be prevented?

*Weeks 11–15 Journal* – No specific reflection journal questions assigned – students maintain journals based on what they learn from the Leader/Ethical Case Research Assignment class presentations. This tends to promote active learning and facilitates students making connections with prior course material.

journals before class ensures they have read the assigned material, thought critically about concepts, and are normally comfortable in contributing to a productive class discussion. This is particularly true for the course leadership concepts, because students may not have studied these concepts in prior courses and usually have not considered these subjects in an accounting context.

Students can also gain valuable learning and insight during this reflection process as they analyze both positive and negative leadership and ethical actions. For example, the final leadership journal entry provides an opportunity for this learning as students reflect on what they have learned from the leader/ethical case research presentations. Students learn both from the ethical actions taken by role models as well as from the mistakes made by those in leadership positions. They frequently apply this learning to their future roles and challenges as accounting professionals.

### Case Assignments

Case analyses have been widely recommended for accounting ethics courses (Armstrong, 1993; Graham et al., 2013) and group case analyses are an important component of this course. The various ethics cases covered in this course help address both the second course objective (recognize ethical issues and dilemmas and offer values-based decisions) and the fourth course objective (explain and justify values-based decisions in response to ethical situations).

I assign groups alphabetically during the Week 1 introductory class. Either four (for smaller classes of 20–24) or eight (for larger classes of 25 or larger) groups usually work best for case presentations. Beginning in Week 3, the assigned groups present cases to the class using the following format:

1. *Facts* of the case. Who are the people involved? What is the case about? What are the relevant facts?
2. What are the *ethical issues*/dilemma(s)?
3. What *decision* should be made? What accounting or other information applies to this case? What are the possible outcomes and implications?
4. What ethical *theory* applies to this case?
5. Provide answers to the textbook case questions.

Case presentations are facilitated by the use of the Mintz and Morris textbook, which usually has 10 cases at the end of each chapter. The number of cases presented each week varies by subject and ranges from four to seven, depending on the topic. Exhibit 2 includes recommended case assignments for Chapters 4, 1, and 2, based on the fourth edition of Mintz and Morris (2017). For shorter cases, more than one case may be assigned to a particular group.

I require all students to familiarize themselves with the assigned cases prior to their weekly presentations. This helps promote questions and

**Exhibit 2.**  Recommended Weekly Cases for Select Weeks — Based on Cases from *Ethical Obligations and Decision Making in Accounting* by Mintz and Morris (2017).

---

*Week 3 Group Cases* — Based on Chapter 4 "Ethics and Professional Judgment in Accounting.":

Group 1: Case 4-1: Professional judgments in auditing

Group 2: Case 4-2: AICPA code of conduct — Auditor confidentiality obligations

Group 3: Case 4-3: Rules of revenue recognition

Group 4: Case 4-9: Ethical obligations in addressing fraud

*Week 4 Group Cases* — Based on Chapter 1 "Ethical Reasoning: Implications for Accountants" Cases in Readings in M&M:

Group 5: Case 1-1: College cheating scandal

    Case 1-5: Acceptance/reneging on an accounting job offer

Group 6: Case 1-2: Personal relationships in the accounting workplace

    Case 1-7: Eating time at an accounting firm

Group 7: Case 1-4: Audit documentation

    Case 1-6: Capitalization versus expensing

Group 8: Case 1-10: Addressing improper conduct by fellow employees

*Week 5 Group Cases* — Based on Chapter 2 "Cognitive Processes and Ethical Decision Making in Accounting" Cases in Readings in M&M:

Group 1: Case 2-1: Audit team member obligations

Group 2: Case 2-3: Responding to client pressure to act unethically

Group 3: Case 2-4: Admitting a budgeting mistake

Group 4: Case 2-8: Client classification of marketable securities

---

dialogue during the case presentations. All students in each group have a speaking role in that week's presentation and I assign them a group grade.

### Accounting Leader and Ethics Research Project

The Accounting Leader and Ethics Research Project is a key component of this course. This provides an opportunity for students to apply what they have learned in the course by analyzing a leader's actions involving an ethics case. Exhibit 3 includes the Leader/Ethical Case Research Assignment. Students rely on what they have learned in the course, including moral philosophy, ethical standards, leadership concepts, and ethical decision making in analyzing a leader's actions.

***Exhibit 3.***  Leader/Ethical Case Research Assignment.

---

*Accounting Leader and Ethics Case Research Project.* This course will provide you with an opportunity to study an accounting ethics case and leader of interest to you. You will select a case and a leader of your choice, once receiving approval by me.

In approaching both the leader and the case you should identify them and provide some background (individual background, company history), along with identification of the ethical issue. In analyzing the case and/or actions by a leader, rely on what you have learned in the course, which could include:

1. Rest's Four Component Model of morality (pp. 69–72 of M&M)
2. The ethical decision making model (pp. 77–79 of M&M)
3. Modern moral philosophies (pp. 24–33 of M&M)
4. Guidance for accountants and business professionals (AICPA Code of Conduct, PCAOB Standards, Sarbanes-Oxley Law)
5. Leadership concepts from Wren (1995) (Transformational leadership, Transactional leadership, Servant leadership, Leadership traits, Followership, Culture, Power, Groupthink)

Using the above concepts, along with others in the course, analyze the actions by those involved with your ethics case and leader. As appropriate, this may include the following: What did they do? Was it successful? Why or why not? What theories apply to the case or leader actions?

*Format\*.* Papers must be written according to the MLA Style guide. Ideas and concepts that are not your original thought must be properly cited to source material. Papers must be prepared using Word and must be checked for spelling and grammar. Papers must be well constructed, and include a bibliography, and defined introduction and conclusion sections. The length of your paper should not exceed 15 pages.

*Class Presentation.* Beginning on April 7, students will present their papers to the others in the class. Students usually use PPT for this presentation. This should provide a summary of your case study and leader. Your PPT Presentation will be evaluated by me and your grade will become part of your grade for this assignment.

*Due Date\*:* Papers are due in class one week after your Class Presentation. The paper must be submitted to me in two forms, electronically to the appropriate SAKAI Drop Box and in paper form in person in class. The research paper file must be in the following format: Yourlastname Yourfirstname researchname.

---

\*Format and Due Date instructions are used in a variety of school of Business research assignments.

Students select their leader/ethical case research topic during Week 5. Students have discretion in who they select; however, because each student presents in class, no students may select the same leader/ethical case. Exhibit 4 provides a sample list of the past semester topics. The individuals identified include both people who have made ethical mistakes (David Duncan, Rita Crundwell, Bernard Ebbers, Dennis Koslowsky, Andrew

**Exhibit 4.**   Some Leader/Ethical Case Research Assignment Topics.

Arthur Andersen – Arthur Andersen LLP

Eddie Antar – Crazy Eddie

David Bagley – HSBC Holdings

Vishnu Bhagat – Reebok India

Joseph Berardino – Arthur Andersen LLP

Abraham Briloff – Accounting Professor, Baruch College, CUNY

Dean Buntrock – Waste Management

Charles Conaway – Kmart

Cynthia Cooper – WorldCom

Rita Crundwell – Comptroller and Treasurer, Dixon, Illinois

William Donaldson – Securities and Exchange Commission (SEC) Chair

David Duncan – Arthur Andersen LLP

Albert Dunlap – Sunbeam

Bernard Ebbers – WorldCom

Andrew Fastow – Enron

Timothy Flynn – KPMG

Richard Fuld – Lehman Brothers

David Kotz – SEC Inspector General

Dennis Kozlowski – Tyco

Kenneth Lay – Enron

Matthew Lee – Lehman Brothers

Arthur Levitt – Securities and Exchange Commission (SEC) Chair

Michael Lynch – Autonomy/HP

Bernard Madoff – Madoff Investment Securities, LLC

Harry Markopolos – Rampart Investment Management

Eli Mason – Mason and Company

William McDonough – PCAOB Chair

Barry Minkow – ZZZZ Best

Mickey Monas – Phar-Mor

Mark Morze – ZZZZ Best

Subhinder Singh Prem – Reebok India

Franklin Raines – Fannie Mae

John Rigas – Adelphi Communications

Joseph St. Denis – AIG

Richard Scrushy – Health South

| Exhibit 4. (Continued) |
| --- |
| Jeffrey Skilling – Enron |
| Leonard Spacek – Arthur Andersen LLP |
| Allen Stanford – Stanford Financial Group |
| Calisto Tanzi – Parmalat |
| David Walker – U.S. Comptroller General |
| Sherron Watkins – Enron |
| Frank Wilson – IRS Agent |

Fastow) and moral exemplars who have made the correct ethical decisions under some challenging circumstances (Arthur Andersen, Timothy Flynn, Cynthia Cooper, Joseph St. Denis). Beginning in either Week 11 or 12, students present their ethics cases and leader profiles, reinforcing concepts of moral exemplars and unethical actions taken by different leaders. Students maintain their reflection journals on what they learn from these presentations, which tends to keep students engaged and helps them make connections with prior course material.

## IMPLEMENTATION GUIDANCE

The details provided in this chapter can assist faculty who may be interested in integrating leadership topics into an accounting ethics course. While in the past accounting faculty may have been reluctant to teach a separate accounting ethics course, more states are requiring ethics courses for those entering the accounting profession. My experience is that integrating leadership topics in an accounting ethics course is an interesting and effective way to approach this topic for both the instructor and students. I provide Learning Objectives for this course in the Course Structure Section of this chapter, which also provides specific information on the weekly schedule of leadership topics, reflection journals, case assignments, and the accounting leader and ethics research project. In addition, Appendix A provides a weekly schedule for course topics and activities that can be easily adapted for an accounting ethics course, particularly if an instructor is planning to use the Mintz and Morris (2017) textbook.

Instructors may be most concerned about how to address the leadership topics in the course. There are a number of factors that facilitate this process. First, the Wren textbook is easy to understand, even for faculty without a background in leadership. This textbook should work well for both undergraduate and graduate courses. Second, Appendix B provides both leadership and ethics questions for the reflection journal and permits focal points for engaging class discussions. Third, the two leadership papers by Kelly and Earley recommended for the course, "Leadership and Organizational Culture: Lessons Learned from Arthur Andersen" and "Ethical Leaders in Accounting" are valuable supplements that have been used successfully in past semesters of this course. Finally, the Leader/ Ethical Case Research Assignment provided in Exhibit 3 and the Assignment Topics included in Exhibit 4 facilitate student semester research projects that when presented to the class provide a valuable opportunity to reinforce course concepts. While there is an instructor investment during the first semester teaching this course to gain familiarity with the readings, learn about the cases, etc., this initial investment pays dividends in future semesters of the course.

This course represents a significant amount of work for the students, with both ethics and leadership readings, reflection journal questions, group case analyses, and the leader and ethics research project. One of the ways that has proven successful in encouraging students to fully apply themselves in this course is to point out that leadership and ethical issues will provide some of the most significant challenges during their careers and how they respond to these challenges will ultimately help determine their future success or failure. I stress that there are far too many instances of people making incorrect decisions in ethical situations and putting in the time and effort to reflect on leadership and ethics topics represents an investment in their future. Students seem to appreciate these points and usually put forth the effort needed to succeed in this course.

There is a fair amount of flexibility in delivering this course to different class sizes. In past semesters the course has been taught both in a traditional 15-week semester and in an accelerated five-day class format. Class sizes for this course have ranged from 11 to 42 students. One of the advantages of having a larger class is that students hear about a greater number of leader/ethics cases during class presentations. However, given the high amount of instructor involvement and delivery of feedback associated with this course (weekly reflection journals, weekly case presentations, a research paper and presentations), I recommend an upper limit of 45–50 students for a course taught in this format.

While the leadership topics identified in this chapter are particularly well suited for integration in an accounting ethics course, it is also possible to adapt or selectively use them in other accounting courses. These might include an Introduction to the Profession course, an Internship course, or an Accounting Capstone or Policy course. This is accomplished by using the Wren (1995) textbook and the questions for the reflection journal outlined in Appendix B. For example, a faculty member teaching an Introduction to the Profession or an Internship course may want to address the topic of followership. This is addressed by using the Kelley "In Praise of Followers" article (Kelley, 1988) along with that topic guidance and journal entry contained in this chapter. A faculty member teaching an Accounting Policy course may include organizational culture as a topic and use the Wren (1995) readings, along with Kelly and Earley (2009) and the questions from Week 8's reflection journal. Using this approach can make other accounting courses more relevant and interesting for students.

# STUDENT FEEDBACK

Students seem to appreciate the variety of topics and activities addressed in this accounting ethics course. During the many semesters I have taught this course I have found that students consistently make the investment to be well prepared for weekly group case presentations and leadership discussions. The reflection journal entries provide opportunities for students to think about how they would react to different situations and how they will function as accounting professionals. Students also usually put forth a substantial amount of effort for their Leadership/Ethics Case Research Assignments, which as noted, they present to the class. This provides a valuable opportunity to learn about a wide range of leaders and cases from others in the class.

Student feedback on the content, instructional approach and methods described in this chapter has been uniformly positive. In past semesters the course was evaluated as an "Excellent Course" using the IDEA Diagnostic Report, with an average rating of 4.7 on a 5.0 scale. Typical student comments are provided below:

- I really enjoyed this class. It is very applicable to my career as a public accountant and I will take a great deal of profession specific experience and information to work with me ...
- From a non-accounting major, he developed my interest in accounting and brought real life situations to life.
- Great class ... Loved the real-life examples − definitely has made me want to act more ethically by taking this course.

Table 2 provides student feedback from the 2014 and 2015 spring semesters of this course. Student feedback was generally favorable in these and other

***Table 2.***  Student Feedback — 2014 and 2015 Spring Semesters of
Accounting Ethics.

|  |  | 2014 Mean Score | 2015 Mean Score |
|---|---|---|---|
| 1. | The AICPA Code of Conduct and Sarbanes-Oxley Law were helpful to my understanding of accounting professional standards. | 4.46 | 4.55 |
| 2. | Weekly team briefings of ethics cases facilitated my understanding of the course concepts. | 4.46 | 4.45 |
| 3. | The ethics cases examined each week were too complex to be useful for class discussion. | 1.72 | 1.66 |
| 4. | Review of ethical theories facilitated case and leader research assignments. | 4.11 | 4.32 |
| 5. | Examination of business ethics cases (Ford Pinto, J&J Tylenol, Union Carbide Bhopal India) reinforced course concepts. | 4.50 | 4.55 |
| 6. | The ethics case and leader research assignments enabled application of the course material. | 4.54 | 4.42 |
| 7. | The leader and case research assignment did not increase my understanding of course concepts. | 1.82 | 1.71 |
| 8. | Examination of audit responsibilities and accounting fraud (including the fraud triangle) reinforced course concepts. | 4.43 | 4.39 |
| 9. | Examination of leadership theories (e.g., transactional leadership, transformational leadership) reinforced course concepts. | 4.42 | 4.45 |
| 10. | Examination of followership reinforced course concepts. | 4.18 | 4.29 |
| 11. | Examination of situational leadership reinforced course concepts. | 4.36 | 4.21 |
| 12. | Examination of organizational culture reinforced course concepts. | 4.43 | 4.39 |
| 13. | Examination of the concepts contained in the paper "Leadership and Organizational Culture: Lessons Learned from Arthur Andersen" reinforced course concepts. | 4.25 | 4.29 |
| 14. | Examination of the different bases of power reinforced course concepts. | 3.89 | 4.29 |
| 15. | Examination of groupthink reinforced course concepts. | 3.93 | 4.21 |
| 16. | Use of the Myers-Briggs Type Indicator (MBTI) reinforced course concepts. | 4.07 | 4.34 |
| 17. | Myers-Briggs Type Indicator (MBTI) in-class exercises were not helpful in explaining the MBTI personality dimensions. | 1.93 | 1.66 |

Student feedback was obtained using the following five point scale:

1. Strongly disagree
2. Disagree
3. Agree nor disagree
4. Disagree
5. Strongly agree

semesters. Students appeared to be most positive about the leader and ethics case research assignments, weekly ethics cases, accounting professional standards, the examination of leadership theories, and the examination of organizational culture.

# CONCLUSION

This chapter examines integrating leadership topics into an accounting ethics course. Both practitioners and educators have called for broader education of accounting students in general and student learning about leadership is one way to accomplish this goal. The accounting ethics course examined is a stand-alone graduate course that meets the ethics requirement in a graduate business program. I provide details on the topics addressed and I present a weekly schedule to provide the reader with the approaches taken to address both course content and delivery.

There are a number of advantages to such a course that integrates leadership and ethics topics. This course represents a positive response to calls for increased leadership education made by both accounting practitioners and educators. It can help reinforce ethical behavior by addressing both moral motivation and moral character as identified by Rest (1994). During this course students examine both the actions of moral exemplars who have demonstrated positive actions relating to ethical leadership, as well as those who made mistakes and did not behave ethically. Reflecting on the actions of accounting leaders as they address ethical issues invariably results in students considering what they would do in similar circumstances. In addition, students are also provided the opportunity to consider the view held by some that successful leadership includes an ethical dimension (Rhode, 2006). The complementary nature of ethical and leadership topics studied in this course provides a natural fit for students examining these concepts.

The opportunity to reflect on these and other ethical issues is somewhat unique in accounting programs. In many cases, accounting students are so busy in content-oriented courses (intermediate accounting, advanced accounting, cost accounting, and tax), that they are not provided opportunities to contemplate many of the topics addressed in this course, including their roles and responsibilities as a member of a profession, abilities as a team member, moral motivation, and values. Such self-assessment and learning is particularly important as students enter an increasingly demanding profession. Since the accounting profession has been receiving additional scrutiny from a number of stakeholders, including the PCAOB, those doing accounting work and conducting audits appear to be consistently working under demanding circumstances that includes increased accountability.

Another advantage of integrating leadership into an accounting ethics course is that it better prepares young professionals to serve in supervisory and leadership roles. Accounting professionals are given a great deal of responsibility at early stages in their careers as they provide direction and guidance to others. In some cases, supervising new associates may occur as early as six months to one year after entering the profession. Topics covered in this course, such as communicating expectations, monitoring performance, providing feedback, and mentoring others can make a positive impact on the performance of both the new employee and the team doing the work.

One limitation of this chapter is that it describes a stand-alone course used in a graduate program at an institution in the northeastern United States. Graduate students generally possessed the intellect, work ethic, and maturity to benefit from this course. While it is expected that undergraduate students would similarly benefit from such a course, this course has yet to be taught to undergraduates.

There are many opportunities for additional research in this area. Accounting ethics courses are evolving (Massey & Van Hise, 2009; Van Hise & Massey, 2010) and research will inform accounting educators of the most effective means to promote student learning of the ethics and leadership subjects addressed in this chapter. Additional research on moral reasoning ability, the development of student values, and leadership skills for those entering the accounting profession will help accounting educators to promote student learning in these areas. Further assessment of the accounting ethics and leadership teaching methods, including those described in this chapter, will permit their refinement to increase student learning. Finally, given the demanding nature of the accounting profession, research on student learning and competencies that result in successful entry into the profession would be valuable for both educators and practitioners.

## ACKNOWLEDGMENTS

I thank Cynthia Blanthorne, Cassandra Rohland, Steven Perreault, Jon Heller, Robert Costello, other members of the Providence College Accountancy Department, and participants at the AAA Northeast Regional Meeting, the AAA Ethics Symposium, and the AAA Annual

Meeting for their comments on previous drafts of this chapter. I also appreciate the assistance from the editor, Tim Rupert, and comments from two anonymous reviewers.

# REFERENCES

Accounting Education Change Commission. (1990). Position statement no. one: Objectives of education for accountants. *Issues in Accounting Education, 5*(2), 307–312.

Albrecht, W. S., & Sack, R. J. (2000). *Accounting education: Charting the course through a perilous future* (Vol. 16). Accounting Education Series. Sarasota, FL: American Accounting Association.

American Institute of Certified Public Accountants (AICPA). (2000). *Core competency framework for entry into the accounting profession – An online resource for curriculum change.* Retrieved from http://www.aicpa.org/interestareas/accountingeducation/resources/pages/corecompetency.aspx

Armstrong, M. B. (1993). Ethics and professionalism in accounting education: A sample course. *Journal of Accounting Education, 11*, 77–92.

Bean, D. F., & Bernardi, R. A. (2007). A proposed structure for an accounting ethics course. *Journal of Business Ethics Education, 4*, 27–54.

Blanthorne, C., Kovar, S., & Fisher, D. (2007). Accounting educators' opinions about ethics in the curriculum: An extensive view. *Issues in Accounting Education, 22*(3), 355–390.

Bloch, J., Brewer, P. C., & Stout, D. E. (2012). Responding to the leadership needs of the accounting profession: A module for developing a leadership mindset in accounting students. *Issues in Accounting Education, 27*(2), 525–554.

*Business Leadership – A Jossey-Bass Reader.* (2003). San Francisco: Wiley.

Graham, C. M., Kelly, P. T., Massey, D. W., & Van Hise, J. (2013). One size does not fit all – Different strategies for teaching accounting ethics. *Research on Professional Responsibility and Ethics in Accounting, 17*, 139–157.

Haas, A. (2005). Now is the time for ethics in education. *The CPA Journal, 75*(6), 66–68.

Hurtt, R. K., & Thomas, C. W. (2008). Implementing a required ethics class for students in accounting: The Texas experience. *Issues in Accounting Education, 21*(1), 31–51.

Jennings, M. M. (2004). Incorporating ethics and professionalism into accounting education and research: A discussion of the voids and advocacy for training in seminal works in business ethics. *Issues in Accounting Education, 19*(1), 7–26.

Josephson Institute Press Release. (2011). *What would honest Abe Lincoln say?* Retrieved from http://charactercounts.org/programs/reportcard/2010/installment02_report-card_honesty-integrity.html

Kelley, R. E. (1988). In praise of followers. *Harvard Business Review, 66*, 142–148.

Kelly, P. T., & Earley, C. E. (2009). Leadership and organizational culture: Lessons learned from Arthur Andersen. *Accounting and the Public Interest, 9*, 129–147.

Kelly, P. T., & Earley, C. E. (2011). Ethical leaders in accounting. *Advances in Accounting Education: Teaching and Curriculum Innovations, 12*, 53–76.

Kidwell, L. A., Fisher, D. G., Braun, R. L., & Swanson, D. L. (2013). Developing learning objectives for accounting ethics using Bloom's Taxonomy. *Accounting Education: An International Journal, 22*(1), 44–65.

Loeb, S. E. (1988). Teaching students accounting ethics: Some crucial issues. *Issues in Accounting Education, 3*, 316–329.

Massey, D. W., & Van Hise, J. (2009). Walking the walk: Integrating lessons from multiple perspectives in the development of an accounting ethics course. *Issues in Accounting Education, 24*(4), 481–510.

Mastracchio, N. J., Jr., Jimenez-Angueira, C., & Toth, I. (2015). The state of ethics in business and the accounting profession. *The CPA Journal, 85*(3), 48–52.

Miller, W. F., & Becker, D. A. (2011). Ethics in the accounting curriculum: What is really being covered? *American Journal of Business Education, 4*(10), 1–9.

Mintz, S. (2006). Accounting ethics education: Integrating reflective learning and virtue ethics. *Journal of Accounting Education, 24*, 97–117.

Mintz, S. (2007). Loeb's contribution to accounting ethics education and research. *Research on Professional Responsibility and Ethics in Accounting, 11*, 31–46.

Mintz, S., & Morris, R. (2014). *Ethical obligations and decision making in accounting* (3rd ed.). New York, NY: McGraw-Hill/Irwin.

Mintz, S., & Morris, R. (2017). *Ethical obligations and decision making in accounting* (4th ed.). New York, NY: McGraw-Hill/Irwin.

National Association of State Boards of Accountancy (NASBA). (2005). *Education committee task force framework, "UAA education rules 2005 exposure draft"*. Nashville, TN.

National Association of State Boards of Accountancy (NASBA). (2007). *"Rules 5–1 and 5–2 exposure draft"*. Nashville, TN.

Rest, J. (1994). Background: Theory and research. In J. Rest & D. Narvaez (Eds.), *Moral development in the professions: Psychology and applied ethics*. Hillsdale, NJ: Lawrence Erlbaum Associates.

Rest, J. R., Narvaez, D., Bebeau, M. J., & Thoma, S. J. (1999). *Postconventional moral thinking: A Neo-Kohlbergian approach*. Mahwah, NJ: Lawrence Erlbaum Associates.

Rhode, D. L. (Ed.). (2006). *Moral leadership*. San Francisco, CA: Wiley.

Stephens, W., Vance, C., & Pettegrew, L. (2012). Embracing ethics and morality – An analytic essay for the accounting profession. *The CPA Journal, 82*(1), 16–21.

The Bedford Committee (American Accounting Association Committee on the Future Structure, Content, and Scope of Accounting Education). (1986). Future accounting education: Preparing for the expanding profession. *Issues in Accounting Education, 1*, 168–195.

The Treadway Commission (National Commission on Fraudulent Financial Reporting). (1987). Report of the National Commission on Fraudulent Financial Reporting, October, pp. 1–187.

Thomas, C. W. (2004). An inventory of support materials for teaching ethics in the post-Enron era. *Issues in Accounting Education, 19*(1), 27–52.

Van Hise, J., & Massey, D. M. (2010). Applying the ignatian pedagogical paradigm to the creation of an accounting ethics course. *Journal of Business Ethics, 96*, 453–465.

Waddock, S. (2005). Hollow men and women at the helm ... Hollow accounting ethics? *Issues in Accounting Education, 20*(2), 145–150.

Wren, J. T. (1995). *The leader's companion – Insights on leadership through the ages*. New York, NY: The Free Press.

# APPENDIX A: WEEKLY SCHEDULE FOR COURSE TOPICS AND ACTIVITIES

A detailed weekly schedule for course topics and activities is provided below. Group cases on weekly topics are presented during the class immediately after the topic is discussed.

### Week 1 — Introduction/Course Administration

The first class meeting provides for course introduction, syllabus review, formation of student working groups, explanation of case analyses and the outline of reflection journal procedures. Either four (for smaller classes of 20–24) or eight (for larger classes of 25 or larger) groups usually work best for case presentations.

### Week 2 — Ethics and Professional Judgment in Accounting/Leadership Foundations

Professional standards and expectations for accounting professionals (the first course objective) are the focus of this session. Students read Chapter 4 of Mintz and Morris (2017) "Ethics and Professional Judgment in Accounting" and review the AICPA Code of Conduct and the Sarbanes-Oxley Act, which are posted on the course SAKAI site. Students participate in a debate on the necessity of the Sarbanes-Oxley Act given the AICPA Code of Conduct. During this debate students often find that while the Sarbanes-Oxley Act contained many provisions that were not previously addressed (PCAOB establishment and responsibilities, assessment of internal controls, certification of financial reports, and the increased use of criminal penalties), the AICPA Code of Conduct did provide specific provisions to guide the conduct of accountants and auditors (independence, integrity, due care, and objectivity).

Leadership Lesson 1 (Fig. 1) is also started during this class, with students reading Part I of the Wren (1995) textbook "The Crisis of Leadership." This is the first week that students submit the reflection journal entry. The reflection journal questions as well as the weekly journal entries for the semester are presented in Appendix B and help facilitate the examination of both ethics and leadership topics. By answering these questions, students are better prepared for class discussions. For this session there is initial discussion of general leadership topics (state of leadership in our country/organizations, and whether leaders are "born" or "made").

### *Week 3 – Ethical Reasoning: Implications for Accounting/Leadership Foundations*

Class begins with student presentations of the cases from Chapter 4 of Mintz and Morris (2017) that deal with topics that include the application of accountant obligations and rules of conduct under the AICPA Code of Conduct, along with revenue recognition rules. The various ethics cases covered in this course help address both the second course objective (recognize ethical issues and dilemmas and offer values-based decisions) and the fourth course objective (explain and justify values-based decisions in response to ethical situations). A format for the case presentations and list of weekly cases and their topics is included in the Case Assignments section. All students in each group have a speaking role in that week's presentation and a group grade is assigned. For shorter cases, more than one case may be assigned to a particular group. Students read Chapter 1 of Mintz and Morris (2017) "Ethical Reasoning: Implications for Accounting" and class discussion focuses on integrity as the basis of accounting and ethical theories, including deontology, utilitarianism, and virtue ethics, thereby addressing the third course objective (understand major ethical theories and how they apply when resolving ethical dilemmas). The leadership component of this class (a continuation of Lesson 1) focuses on Part II of the Wren (1995) textbook "What is Leadership" with an examination of different definitions of leadership and processes of learning about leadership.

### *Week 4 – Cognitive Processes and Ethical Decision Making/Leadership Theories*

Class begins with student presentations of cases from Chapter 1 of Mintz and Morris (2017) that deal with personal conduct in the accounting workplace, including accepting a job offer, maintaining professional relationships at the firm, eating time, and admitting mistakes. The professional judgment and decisions of accountants are the focus of this class. Students read Chapter 2 of Mintz and Morris (2017) "Cognitive Processes and Ethical Decision Making in Accounting" and class discussion focuses on Rest's Four Component Model of Ethical Decision Making, Kohlberg's Stages of Moral Development, professional skepticism, and a model for making ethical decisions. This class includes Leadership Lesson 2 and students read Part III "Historical Views of Leadership" and Part IV "Modern Views of Leadership," Chapters 18–21. Topics include transformational and transactional leadership, the relationship between leadership and ethics, and tasks associated with leadership. During this class discussion centers on how transformational leaders raise others to "higher levels of motivation and morality." Students usually agree that while it may be easier to function as transactional leaders in the workplace, they would rather work for and aspire to be transformational leaders, who they regard as more effective.

*Week 5 – Organizational Ethics and Corporate Governance/The Leaders*

Class begins with student presentations of cases from Chapter 2 of Mintz and Morris (2017) that deal with responding to client pressure to act unethically, proper revenue recognition at year end, and addressing improper conduct by fellow employees. Students read Chapter 3 of Mintz and Morris (2017) "Organizational Ethics and Corporate Governance." Ethical decision making in business is the main subject addressed in this class; special attention is paid to the Ford Pinto case and the Johnson & Johnson Tylenol case, two business ethics cases profiled in the chapter. Other topics include corporate governance, stakeholder theory, agency theory, organizational codes of ethics, and whistle-blowing. Leadership Lesson 3 is included in this class with the examination of traits and personal factors, and students read Part IV, Chapter 22, and Part V "The Leader" of the Wren (1995) textbook. Leadership traits discussed include leadership drive, leadership motivation, honesty and integrity, self-confidence, cognitive ability, and knowledge of the business. This discussion provides another opportunity to reinforce the importance of leaders being honest and persons of integrity and the significance of establishing trust as a leader.

Personality preferences are also discussed in this course. If available, the MBTI is used for students to learn about their personality preferences and how they interact with others in the workplace. The MBTI can frequently be obtained from the College or University Career Center or Counseling Center. There is frequently not enough time for the MBTI review during the Week 5 Class, so it is usually addressed in the "Catch-Up" session in Weeks 10 or 11. During that session, students receive their MBTI results and learn about the differences in personality preferences.

In this Week 5 class students also select their leader/ethical case research topic for the leader and case they will examine in their semester research papers and class presentations. The Leader/Ethical Case Research Assignment is provided in Exhibit 3. Students have discretion in who they select; a list of some of the past semester topics are provided in Exhibit 4. The individuals identified in Exhibit 4 include both people who have made ethical mistakes (David Duncan, Rita Crundwell, Bernard Ebbers, Dennis Koslowsky, Andrew Fastow) and moral exemplars who have made the correct ethical decisions under some challenging circumstances (Arthur Andersen, Timothy Flynn, Cynthia Cooper, Joseph St. Denis).

## *Week 6 — Fraud in Financial Statements and Auditor Responsibilities/Followership*

Class begins with student presentations of cases from Chapter 3 of Mintz and Morris (2017) that deal with individual versus group ethical behavior, IRS whistle-blowing on tax cheats, and the Union Carbide Bhopal, India tragedy. Students read Chapter 5 of Mintz and Morris (2017) "Fraud in Financial Statements and Auditor Responsibilities." The focus of this class is the auditor responsibilities and accounting fraud and includes audit opinions, auditing standards, the fraud triangle, and fraud risk assessment.

The main leadership concept examined is the concept of followership, as students read Part VI "The Followers" of the Wren (1995) textbook for Leadership Lesson 4. In this class students realize and appreciate the relationship between followership and ethical behavior. Students typically conclude that frequently followers who behave like "sheep" may be more prone to act unethically due to pressure from their boss or other superiors. The "exemplary followers" who critically think about situations are more likely to make the correct ethical decision. Students also learn about their followership roles as new hires at accounting firms and other organizations, including the responsibility to develop their expertise and judgment as accounting professionals.

*Week 7 — Legal, Regulatory, and Professional Obligations of Auditors/*
*Leaders and Followers Together*

Class begins with student presentations of cases from Chapter 5 of Mintz and Morris (2017) that deal with material misstatement of earnings, revenue recognition issues, internal control problems, and audit client considerations. Students read Chapter 6 of Mintz and Morris (2017) "Legal, Regulatory, and Professional Obligations of Auditors." Regulatory issues and obligations are the main topics of this class, including Board of Directors' and managers' responsibilities, auditor liability and typical defenses, the Securities Act of 1933, the Securities and Exchange Act of 1934, additional coverage of the Sarbanes-Oxley Act, and the Foreign Corrupt Practices Act.

Students read Part VII "Leaders and Followers Together" of the Wren (1995) textbook for Leadership Lesson 5. The main leadership concept examined is situational leadership, with specific focus on how it applies to accounting firms. For example, when students begin their careers as new accountants and auditors, they can expect to receive specific instructions and close supervision. This situation will change as their "follower readiness" develops over time and eventually tasks will be delegated to them as more seasoned professionals. Discussion also focuses on the need to clearly communicate expectations, to effectively train and develop individuals, and to properly evaluate performance.

*Week 8 — Earnings Management/Leadership Environment and*
*Organizational Culture*

Class begins with student presentations of cases from Chapter 6 of Mintz and Morris (2017) that deal with violation of the Foreign Corrupt Practices Act, auditor negligence, auditor resignation from an engagement, and insider trading by accounting professionals. Students read Chapter 7 of Mintz and Morris (2017) "Earnings Management." Earnings management, financial restatements, and "financial shenanigans" are the main subjects addressed during this class.

For Leadership Lesson 6 students read Part VIII "The Leadership Environment" of the Wren (1995) textbook and "Leadership and Organizational Culture: Lessons Learned from Arthur Andersen" (Kelly & Earley, 2009). Organizational culture is the main leadership topic addressed and students learn about the importance of an ethical culture in an organization. Specific attention is also paid to how leader actions impact the ethical culture of an organization, thereby addressing the last course objective (gain an understanding of moral leadership and the actions they as leaders can take to foster ethical decisions and an ethical organizational climate).

### Week 9 — Ethical Leadership and Decision Making in Accounting/Leading Individuals and Groups

Class begins with student presentations of cases from Chapter 7 of Mintz and Morris (2017) that deal with earnings management techniques and manipulation of accounting earnings. Students read Chapter 8 of Mintz and Morris (2017) "Ethical Leadership and Decision-Making in Accounting." This class focuses on reviewing prior ethics and leadership concepts, including transformational leadership, followership, organizational culture, and ethical leadership.

Leadership Lesson 7 focuses on Part IX "Leading Individuals" and Part X "Leading Groups" of the Wren (1995) textbook. Leadership topics include motivation (Maslow, Herzberg) and bases of power, including French and Raven's five bases of power, and groupthink. Students gain insight into the motivation associated with ethical and unethical behavior, along with the power bases that can potentially impact moral decisions. Students also learn about the potential for groupthink in an accounting firm due to pressure, self-censorship, and "mindguards," when a partner or another senior executive expresses a particular point of view on a subject.

### Week 10 — Giving Voice to Values/Moral Leadership

Class begins with student presentations of cases from Chapter 8 of Mintz and Morris (2017) that deal with misrepresentation of earnings and a difficult client. One focus of this class is a review of Giving Voice to Values by Mary Gentile, which is used across the graduate curriculum. For Leadership Lesson 8 students read Part XI "Skills of a Leader" and Part XIII "Practicing Moral Leadership" of the Wren (1995) textbook, along with "Ethical Leaders in Accounting" by Kelly and Earley (2011). Topics include essential leadership competencies, moral leadership, individual moral development, and universal human values and help address the final course objective (gain an understanding of moral leadership and the actions that they as leaders can take to foster ethical decisions). The Kelly and Earley's (2011) paper reinforces the idea that in many cases accounting professionals have acted ethically when presented with challenging circumstances. The ethical leaders provide examples of conduct to aspire to for students entering the accounting profession.

*Week 11 – Catch Up/Leader/Ethical Case Research Presentations*

This class provides an opportunity to "catch up" with any topics that still need to be addressed from prior classes. As mentioned, if the MBTI is used during this semester, this class provides an opportunity to learn about personality preferences and receive their MBTI results. For large classes, students begin their Leader/Ethical Case Presentations during this class.

*Weeks 12–15 – Leader/Ethical Case Research Presentations*

During these classes, students present their ethics cases and leader profiles, reinforcing concepts of moral exemplars and unethical actions taken by different leaders. Students maintain their reflection journals on what they learn from these presentations, which tends to keep students engaged and helps them make connections with prior course material.

# APPENDIX B: REFLECTION JOURNAL WITH FOCUSED LEADERSHIP AND ETHICS QUESTIONS

The following questions are based on readings from Wren (1995) *The Leader's Companion (TLC) — Insights on Leadership Through the Ages* and Mintz and Morris (2017) *Ethical Obligations and Decision Making in Accounting.* The following are recommended questions for the reflection journal:

What did I learn from this class?

What were the concepts where I found agreement/disagreement?

Massey and Van Hise (2009) and Mintz (2006) contain other examples of useful reflection journal questions.

*Week 2 Questions* — Based on Readings in Part 1 of Wren's (1995) TLC:

1. In our society today, is there a "crisis of leadership"? Provide an example to support your position.

2. Are leaders "born" or "made" (or can leadership be taught)?

3. Does servant leadership apply to accounting ethics?

Please read Chapter 4 of Mintz and Morris (2017) (M&M). Answer questions 4, 5, and 6 (pp. 253–254) and submit them to the SAKAI Drop Box.

*Week 3 Questions* — Based on Readings in Part 2 of Wren's (1995) TLC:

1. Pages 28–30 provide a list of 10 reasons why colleges are "bashful about teaching leadership." Discuss one or two that you agree with.

2. Do you agree with Bass' definition of leadership on p. 38?

3. Is the Bass definition of leadership (p. 38) superior to the definitions provided on pp. 41–42? Why or why not?

Please read Chapter 1 of Mintz and Morris (2017) (M&M) (pp. 1–42). Answer questions 6, 7, 11, and 25 (pp. 43–46).

*Week 4 Questions* — Based on Readings in Parts 3 & 4 (Chapters 18–21) of Wren's (1995) TLC:

1. For Part 3, Chapters 12–16 — Historical Views of Leadership. Provide two examples of how leadership is related to ethics.

2. For Chapters 19–20: Identify either a transactional or transformational leader from today and describe why that person is either transactional or transformational.

Please read Chapter 2 of Mintz and Morris (2017) (M&M). Answer questions 1, 19, 25 (pp. 89–92) and submit them to the Drop Box.

*Week 5 Questions* — Based on Readings in Chapter 22 and Part 5 of Wren's (1995) TLC:

1. For Chapter 22: Using Kotter's approach, identify a modern day or historical leader, explaining the reasons for your selection.

2. For Chapters 23–24: Select a modern leader and comment on that individual's traits. Do they contribute to his or her success?

3. Do you agree with Kotter's differences between management and leadership? Please explain your answer.

Please read Chapter 3 of Mintz and Morris (2017) (M&M) (pp. 111–162). We will focus on two of the cases in the chapter, the Johnson and Johnson Tylenol case and the Ford Pinto case. Answer questions 1, 10, and 11 (pp. 163–164) and submit them to the Drop Box.

*Week 6 Questions* — Based on Readings in Part 6 of Wren's (1995) TLC:

1. For Chapter 31: In today's business environment, is enough attention placed on followership? Why or why not?

Please read Chapter 5 of Mintz and Morris (2017) (M&M) (pp. 269–309). Answer questions 2 and 11.

*Week 7 Questions* — Based on Readings in Part 7 of Wren's (1995) TLC:

1. For Chapter 32: Do you agree with Hersey and Blanchard's situational leadership discussion? Cite one strength and one weakness.

Please read Chapter 6 of Mintz and Morris (2017) (M&M) (pp. 339–376). Answer question 14.

*Week 8 Questions* – Based on Readings in Part 8 of Wren's (1995) TLC, along with *Leadership and Organization Culture: Lessons Learned from Arthur Andersen* by Kelly and Earley (2009).

1. Given the actions by leaders at Arthur Andersen, was the demise of the firm to be expected? Do you agree that Andersen should have been indicted?

2. What are the implications of Andersen's demise for other large accounting firms?

3. Other than the leaders who we will examine in our research papers, name a leader who influenced the culture of his or her organization (positively or negatively) and describe the impact.

Please read Part VIII in Wren (1995). After reading Chapter 38, please write a paragraph that describes the organizational culture for the student body at our College.

Please read Chapter 7 of Mintz and Morris (2017) (M&M) (pp. 405–458). Answer questions 1 and 9.

*Week 9 Questions* – Based on Readings in Parts 9 and 10 of Wren's (1995) TLC:

1. For Chapter 44: Do you agree or disagree with Herzberg's Two-Factor Theory? Provide an example to support your position.

2. For Chapter 45: See the discussion of five bases of social power. Name a leadership position that you have held during your lifetime. What Power Base(s) contributed to your success in this position?

3. For Chapter 47: Assess the potential for groupthink in a large accounting or other business firm. How can it be prevented?

Please review Chapter 8 of Mintz and Morris (2017) (M&M) (pp. 503–525). Answer questions 3 and 14.

*Week 10 Questions* – Based on Readings in Parts 11 and 13 of Wren's (1995) TLC:

1. In Chapter 61, James MacGregor Burns discusses moral leadership. Identify a modern leader who practices or provides a good example of moral leadership and another modern leader who does not serve as a good example of moral leadership.

2. In Chapter 62, what are the implications of Bandura's Social Learning theory (SLT) for organizational leaders? Name one specific action for leaders suggested by SLT.

3. In Chapter 63, do you agree with the Heinz Board of Director's decision to not fire ANY of the employees involved with the improper income transfer practices?

4. Do you agree with Kidder's Universal Human Values? If not, what is missing?

Please read the first five pages of *Ethical Leaders in Accounting* (2011) by Kelly and Earley posted on SAKAI and skim the remaining pages of that chapter. Do you consider any of the profiled leaders a "hero" in the accounting profession? Please explain your answer.

*Weeks 11–15 Journal* — No specific reflection journal questions assigned — students maintain journals based on what they learn from the Leader/ Ethical Case Research Assignment class presentations. This tends to promote active learning and facilitates students making connections with prior course material.

# A WISDOM-BASED ACCOUNTING ETHICS COURSE

Michael K. Shaub

## ABSTRACT

*The purpose of this chapter is to describe an accounting ethics course whose purpose, in part, is to short circuit the process that leads to foolish ethical decisions by professional accountants. In addressing how to make ethical decisions, the course deliberately includes processes intended to develop wisdom and to impede reflexive decisions that reflect the five fallacies of thinking. The approach described represents an active, engaging approach to increasing dialogical and dialectical reasoning in students' pursuit of wisdom through individual selection of outside reading, engaging speakers, and the use of ethics accountability groups. The course is adaptable to large and small class settings where the professor desires extensive interaction among students, and it creates an environment designed to help students develop self-chosen principles to guide their professional lives. Students take responsibility for developing self-determined principles to guide their professional*

Advances in Accounting Education: Teaching and Curriculum Innovations, Volume 20, 181–216
ISSN: 1085-4622/doi:10.1108/S1085-462220170000020008

*lives. Clearly identifying these principles provides students a basis for resisting ethical compromises in their careers. The course focuses students on developing wisdom and recognizing the weaknesses in a purely calculation-based moral reasoning.*

**Keywords:** Wisdom; accounting ethics; ethics education; moral reasoning; accountability; five fallacies of thinking

The accounting ethics course discussed in this chapter is the culmination of a seven-year process of seeking methods of building wisdom into young accountants, enabling them to become capable of handling a broad variety of ethical issues through a systematic reasoning process that emphasizes long-term thinking, accountability, and the broader impact of ethical decisions on others. While there is some consensus that accounting ethics education is warranted and important (Blanthorne, Kovar, & Fisher, 2007), it is critical to engage students in a way that will affect future decisions.

Recent headlines have carried numerous stories of successful people, many of them in the accounting profession, who have sacrificed promising careers because of foolish decisions. These decisions have in many cases destroyed shareholder value, but in almost every case they have changed the trajectory of the decision maker's life. Often people are mystified that successful people could make the kinds of choices that derail a productive life. But Sternberg (2003a) would say that this behavior happens quite frequently; in fact, successful people are often the ones most susceptible to these decisions.

Success tends to validate a leader's thinking, and it may serve to make that leader less willing to accept others' counsel, which seems increasingly inferior to their own plans. This leads to failures in dialogical thinking, or taking into consideration the concerns of others. Also, success creates the expectation of success, and the attendant performance pressures to continually prove that one is making good decisions. This tends to shift decision-makers into a short-term focus, short-circuiting dialectical thinking. Dialectical thinkers engage in rational discussion with those who disagree, testing the impact of ideas on long-term outcomes, but the daily pressures in the business world tend to focus a

CEO on quarterly earnings and an audit firm senior manager on keeping clients and making partner.

Failures in dialogical and dialectical thinking indicate a lack of wisdom guiding leaders' decisions, and they make leaders subject to what Jordan and Sternberg (2006) identify as the five fallacies of thinking: egocentrism, omnipotence, omniscience, invulnerability, and unrealistic optimism. As a result, intelligent, creative individuals who have a history of success find themselves faced with unprecedented personal and professional failures, and often with no real strategy for overcoming those failures.

The purpose of this chapter is to describe an accounting ethics course whose purpose, in part, is to short circuit the process that leads to these types of decisions by professional accountants. In addressing how to make ethical decisions, the course deliberately includes processes intended to develop wisdom and to impede reflexive decisions that reflect the five fallacies of thinking.

I have delivered this course to class sizes ranging from 140 to 218 because we have a large five-year accounting program at our university, and it is offered to students returning from spring semester auditing internships in a six-week condensed format. But the course would likely be even more effective in smaller settings, since it is reasonably labor- and writing-intensive.

The chapter is organized as follows. The next section describes more fully the goal of the course, which is developing wisdom in accordance with Plato's three concepts of wisdom. This is followed by a discussion of the five fallacies of thinking, which represent explicit failures in exercising wisdom. Sections describing the course structure and course activities are followed by a section discussing the contribution of the activities to the development of each of Plato's three concepts of wisdom. Next, I describe outcomes using actual comments from course evaluations, followed by concluding comments.

# COURSE GOAL: WISDOM

While the demand for accounting ethics classes has been growing over the past decade, culminating with California's recently passed requirement of 10 semester hours of ethics in a 150-hour accounting program, correspondingly creative approaches to these courses have not arisen. There is some recent evidence that a substantial number of students see limited benefit to accounting ethics courses, perhaps because they are seen as regulatory boxes that must be checked. For example, Hurtt and Thomas (2011) find that though recently certified CPAs were generally positively inclined toward the three-semester-hour accounting ethics course required by Texas law, they largely felt that the issues covered were not ones they encounter in their career. Cases, coverage of independence issues, "open group discussions" related to ethics, and guest speakers were seen as providing the greatest benefit.

As of February 2016, 13 states require at least a three-semester-hour accounting ethics course in order to be licensed, and 24 others require licensees to take an ethics exam after passing the CPA exam. In addition, some states have an ethics continuing education requirement. The biennial continuing education course required by Texas law after CPA certification received, on average, largely neutral evaluations about its worth. However, enforcement actions against CPAs in Texas have dropped significantly since the law's implementation (Hurtt & Thomas, 2011), providing support for implementation of accounting ethics education requirements, or at least arguing against any repeal of current requirements.

While accounting ethics education requirements as stringent as California's are not likely to be generally accepted, university level accounting ethics courses appear to be here to stay. An important question for the accounting profession is how to make those courses valuable enough to warrant their place in the accounting curriculum. This requires a strategy that has the potential to impact accountants' behavior once they are in the profession. The course discussed in this chapter focuses on building wisdom into young accountants, enabling them to be capable of handling a wide variety of ethical issues through a systematic reasoning process that emphasizes long-term thinking, accountability, and the broader impact of ethical decisions on others. I modeled this approach after Sternberg's (1998) Balance Theory of Wisdom. In this model, he uses as a starting point (Sternberg, 1998, p. 347) the dictionary definition of wisdom as the "power of judging rightly and following the soundest course of action, based on knowledge, experience, understanding, etc." (Webster's New World College Dictionary, 1997, p. 1533). While accounting students are intelligent, they sometimes lack the knowledge, experience and understanding to make wise decisions. While an ethics course cannot provide all of these, it has the potential to accelerate their development.

The attempt to understand wisdom has been approached philosophically and psychologically (Sternberg, 2003a). Examples of philosophical approaches include those of Aristotle and Plato, with the latter's dialogues providing a three-fold concept of wisdom (Robinson, 1990):

> ... as (a) *sophia*, which is found in a contemplative life in search of truth; (b) *phronesis*, which is the kind of practical wisdom shown by statesmen and legislators; and (c) *episteme*, which is found in those who understand things from a scientific point of view. (Sternberg, 2003a, p. 394)

The accounting profession can address all three of these, with s*ophia* a likely approach to an accounting ethics education, *phronesis* best demonstrated in accounting practice, and *episteme* potentially contributed through accounting ethics research.

The accounting ethics course provides the opportunity to introduce students to all three of these philosophical approaches, however. When an instructor focuses an entire course on questions of how to live life, the contemplation necessary for *sophia* has the potential to take place. This is less likely to be true of an isolated case in an introductory or intermediate accounting course. Discussion of real life cases or the political implications of ethical decisions exposes students to the reality of how difficult it is to live with the kind of *phronesis* that influences others' choices well. The ethics course also provides ample time to introduce relevant accounting ethics research and, in some cases, to participate in the development of new knowledge by conducting research in the classroom, increasing students' *episteme*.

Sternberg argues that creativity is rooted in intelligence, that a certain level of intelligence is required in order to be creative. However, intelligence is a necessary, but not sufficient, condition for creativity. In addition, many people who are intelligent are not wise, largely because they do not think dialogically nor dialectically, and thus they fall prey to the five fallacies of thinking: egocentrism, omnipotence, omniscience, invulnerability, and unrealistic optimism (Jordan & Sternberg, 2006). Wisdom involves balancing intrapersonal, interpersonal, and extrapersonal interests to achieve a common good, similar to the tenets of stakeholder theory (Freeman, 1984). It requires the ability to think dialogically, taking into account others' interests and viewpoints, and dialectically, testing their ideas against those who disagree and focusing on long-term effects, not just short-term outcomes.

## THE FIVE FALLACIES OF THINKING

Jordan and Sternberg (2006) identify the five fallacies of thinking as egocentrism, omnipotence, omniscience, invulnerability, and unrealistic optimism. These fallacies seem to arise out of a focus on self-interested behavior, behavior which is considered normative under the dominant moral theory taught in business schools, agency theory (Jensen & Meckling, 1976, 1994). On the other hand, Sternberg (2002) claims that purely self-interested behavior lacks wisdom.

This is an interesting contradiction, and one that is not often explicitly discussed in accounting research. Jensen and Meckling (1994) argue that people should engage in self-interested behavior, and that it is irrational to do otherwise. While Adam Smith saw self-interested behavior as descriptive, it cannot readily be said that he endorsed it as normative. In fact, in *The Theory of Moral Sentiments* Smith explicitly stated, "The wise and virtuous man is at all times willing that his own private interest should be sacrificed to the public interest of his own particular order or society" (1966, p. 346). This is consistent with Sternberg's (2003b) definition of wisdom as involving dialogical thinking, taking into account others' interests rather than being purely self-interested.

Falling prey to the five fallacies of thinking leads to foolish choices (Sternberg, 2006), what Shaub and Fisher (2008) refer to as "stupid" behavior. Not recognizing one's limitations is fundamental to succumbing to these fallacies.

*Egocentrism* means that a person thinks only of himself, ignoring the rights and interests of others. Though normative under agency theory (Jensen & Meckling, 1976), an exclusive focus on self-interest exposes the self-interested person to consequences that might not be anticipated. This is in part because the focus on self-interest as rational (and, by implication, on considering others' interests as irrational) has reclassified agency theory as a normative approach to ethical decision-making rather than a positive or descriptive approach. Ghoshal (2005, pp. 81–82) claims that the reason that agency theory continues to dominate the business school landscape is because it can be "elegantly modeled," even though the evidence from a long series of studies does not support its implications for the effects of independent directors, CEO/chair role separation, and stock options on corporate governance.

*Omnipotence* is the sense that one can control all circumstances, including random events. This fallacy evidences itself in many financial risks taken that seem, in retrospect, inexplicable. Andy Fastow exuded this characteristic in the movie *Smartest Guys in the Room* when he was making a presentation to Merrill Lynch regarding Enron's special purpose entities. His response to one Merrill Lynch representative's comment that they were having difficulty picking holes in his presentation was simply, "Good," accompanied by a knowing smile. AIG's CEO Hank Greenberg has been accused of unwittingly destroying his firm through running a "fiefdom" that allowed him to manufacture earnings through sham transactions when the market turned against him (Barr, 2011). When Greenberg was removed as CEO after his confrontation with New York Attorney General Eliot Spitzer and AIG had to be bailed out, he still maintained that he would have been able to unwind AIG's bad deals prior to the housing crisis if he had been left in power.

*Omniscience* is the belief that one understands everything there is to know about a matter, or that one understands more than others and need not take into account their perspectives. This belief short circuits dialectical thinking and leads to an unwillingness to take objections to questionable strategies seriously. For example in the KPMG tax shelter case, partners were deliberating whether to adopt the aggressive tax shelters and market them to clients because of their uncertain status under IRS regulations. One partner's e-mail was explicit about the calculation driving the decision:

> **First the financial exposure to the Firm is minimal.** Based upon our analysis of the applicable penalty sections, we conclude that the penalties would be no greater than $14,000 per $100,000 in KPMG fees. Furthermore, as the size of the deal increases, our exposure to the penalties decreases as a percentage of our fees. For example, our average deal would result in KPMG fees of $360,000 with a maximum penalty exposure of only $31,000.

> This further assumes that KPMG would bear 100 percent of the penalty. In fact, as explained in the attached memo, the penalty is *joint and several* with respect to anyone involved in the product who was required to register. (pbs.org, 2004)

These types of memos, which are increasingly common with the prevalence of e-mail and text messaging evidence being introduced at trial, underestimate the potentially negative response of readers and jurors to ethical calculations. This response is one of the omitted variables in some people's ethical calculations.

This omniscience also seems to reflect itself in the rise of the influence of "quants" in the financial markets, those few with the higher knowledge to understand certain complex transactions. As an *Economist* article indicated, the occurrence of "black swans" (extreme events) in financial markets is much more frequent than would be predicted by standard probability models. But the "hubris of spurious precision" demonstrated by these quants led during the recent financial crisis to inappropriate risk-taking and its attendant problems (Valencia, 2010).

*Invulnerability* is a sense that one is immune from the harm that can result from behavior choices. Sometimes it arises from the overconfidence that accompanies a string of successes. It also can be a result of people underestimating others' ability to detect unethical behavior. Also, the natural delay between an act and its detection, especially when that act is unique or new, may lead to a feeling of being untouchable. Invulnerability may also be tied to a sense of omniscience, as it apparently was in the KPMG case.

> So why would savvy professionals (five of the indicted former KPMGers are lawyers), knowing they were skating close to the line, write such damaging stuff? New York Law School professor Tanina Rostain, who has studied KPMG's shelter business, chalks it up to a sense of "invincibility" that was part of the culture. "They just thought they were smarter than the IRS and would never get caught," she says. (Novack, 2005)

*Unrealistic optimism* evidences a less sinister type of folly than the other four fallacies, but it arises from the same type of thinking. Some creative people are unrealistically optimistic, since creativity requires a willingness to buck the system in order to put forth a novel idea. What Sternberg (2003a, p. 387) calls "successful intelligence" is important for the creative person to determine whether that new idea will actually work within societal constraints. But unrealistic optimism is much harder to criticize than are the other four fallacies.

## COURSE STRUCTURE

I have taught the accounting ethics course described here over six weeks, meeting four days a week, but instructors could easily modify it for a 15-week semester[1] or a 10-week quarter. The opening week of the course focuses on ethical theory and developing a common language for understanding ethical issues. The second week generally focuses on some of the biggest scandals to impact the accounting profession, helping students to make sense of stories they have heard and the potential impact of ethical decision-making in their careers. The next two to three weeks vary somewhat from semester to semester based on the speakers who visit the classroom and topics in the news. This period is also when there is significant coverage of topics important to regulators, such as integrity, objectivity, the state code of conduct, and SEC compliance.

I generally administer a mid-term exam in the fifth week of the course. It counts for 20% of the course grade and is comprehensive regarding the material we have covered in the course to that point. I believe that it is important for students to have some command of the facts of prior cases, in addition to being able to apply ethical principles in hypothetical settings and being able to interpret the moral reasoning driving different decisions.

The last week to week-and-a-half involves group presentations that allow the ethics accountability groups to give back to the class. I always spend the last day of class trying to offer some perspective on life and career, tying together many of the thoughts we have addressed throughout the course.

Table 1 provides a sample course calendar from a recent semester.

### Ethical Leaders in the Course

Prior to the course, I contact the students who are on their audit internships and ask for volunteers to serve as ethics accountability group (EAG) leaders. Because I use groups of four or five, I need 35–45 volunteers to serve in this role. I am encouraged to find that I consistently have more volunteers than I need, even though I am deliberately vague about what the expectations are. I offer very little reward for serving in the role other than the experience that it provides. I select several of the capable leaders to serve as course facilitators, who are particularly helpful in accumulating ideas from the small groups to contribute to the large class discussions. They can also help to reinforce ideas with, and get feedback from, group leaders for my benefit. This can be helpful if some group leaders feel like they have inadequate direction from me about my expectations, but are not yet comfortable enough to approach me about it. And since the course is only six weeks long, it is important for me to get feedback quickly. The individual group leaders sometimes need help in raising the level of discussion in the ethics accountability groups, and occasionally need advice in how to encourage participation.

## COURSE ACTIVITIES

### Freedom to Choose Source Materials

In the spring of 2009, I made a conscious decision to create an atmosphere of freedom, giving my students almost complete discretion about what their

*Table 1.* Sample Course Schedule.

| Date | Topic | Pre-Class Reading | In-Class Presentation | Turn In |
|---|---|---|---|---|
| Monday, March 30 | Introduction | | | |
| Tuesday, March 31 | How We Make Ethical Decisions | | Presentation: How We Make Ethical Decisions | |
| Wednesday, April 1 | Ethical Reasoning/Judgments | Hunt-Vitell model article | Presentation: Four Obligations of an Audit Professional, Part I | |
| Thursday, April 2 | Moral Courage/Ethical Intentions: Independence, Integrity and Objectivity | Bazerman article; M&M Chapter 4, pp. 190–196 (full text); Mintz article on virtue | Presentations: Four Obligations, Part II Threats to Auditor Independence | |
| Monday, April 6 | WorldCom, Cynthia Cooper, and Virtue | Behind Closed Doors article; Time Person of the Year Cynthia Cooper article; M&M Chapter 2, p. 78 (full text); David Myers WSJ article | David Myers video | WERS #1 |
| Tuesday, April 7 | *Smartest Guys in the Room* – the story of Enron | David Duncan articles | Video: Smartest Guys in the Room | |
| Wednesday, April 8 | Discussion of Enron HealthSouth introduction | Amoruso, Roberts and Trompeter paper | | |
| Thursday, April 9 | *Dr. Ronny Daigle's* HealthSouth case | HealthSouth materials online; M&M, pp. 199–200, 239–241 | *Dr. Ronny Daigle* Dress: *Business Casual* | HealthSouth case group solutions |

**Table 1.** (Continued)

| Date | Topic | Pre-Class Reading | In-Class Presentation | Turn In |
|---|---|---|---|---|
| Monday, April 13 | Gullibility and wisdom: Madoff, Stanford, Kurt Barton, and assorted other Ponzi schemes | Greenspan article Time article on Ponzi schemes New Era article Allen Stanford article M&M Chapter 3, pp. 128–131 | Presentation: Gullibility, Wisdom and Professional Skepticism New Era Philanthropy Video | WERS #2 ESEM #1 |
| Tuesday, April 14 | Guest Speaker: *Helen Sharkey* | *Dress: Business Casual* | *Helen Sharkey* | |
| Wednesday, April15 | Insider Trading | Fortune Galleon Article Galleon-Goldman Link KPMG Insider Trading M&M pp. 196–198, 361–364 | Presentation: Insider trading | ESEM #2 |
| Thursday, April 16 | Whistleblowing | M&M Chapter 3, pp. 91–92, 131–137 Roger Boisjoly and the *Challenger* Disaster article The Dark Side of Whistleblowing | Presentation: Whistleblowing | |
| Monday, April 20 | Stockholder versus Stakeholder Theory Texas Code of Conduct Sarbanes-Oxley Act | M&M Chapter 3, pp. 107–109 M&M Chapter 4, pp. 203–213 M&M Chapter 6 The Social Responsibility of Business is to Increase Its Profits | Presentation: Stockholder versus Stakeholder Presentation: Regulatory Ethics in the Accounting Profession | WERS #3 |

**Table 1.**  (*Continued*)

| Date | Topic | Pre-Class Reading | In-Class Presentation | Turn In |
|---|---|---|---|---|
| Tuesday, April 21 | Mid-term exam | | | |
| Wednesday, April 22 | Guest Speaker: *Dr. Kelly Richmond-Pope* | All the Queen's Horses: The Rita Crundwell Story | *Dr. Kelly Richmond-Pope Dress: Business Casual* | |
| Thursday, April 23 | *Dr. Richmond-Pope*, Day 2 | Whistleblowing Whistling While You Work Case | *Dr. Kelly Richmond-Pope* Whistling While You Work | *Dress: Business Casual* |
| Monday, April 27 | Ethics Accountability Group meetings/Class Discussion | | | WERS #4 |
| Tuesday, April 28 | EAG Presentations Groups 1–6 | | | ESEM #3 and #4 |
| Wednesday, April 29 | EAG Presentations Groups 7–16 | | | |
| Thursday, April 30 | EAG Presentations Groups 17–23 | | | |
| Monday, May 4 | EAG Presentations Groups 24–30 | | | WERS #5 |
| Tuesday, May 5 | EAG Presentations Groups 31–40 | *CLASS WILL MEET AT 3:00* | | |
| Wednesday, May 6 | Our Final Conversation | | | Ten Principles |

M&M = Mintz and Morris, WERS = Weekly Ethics Reading Summary, ESEM = Ethics Speaker Evaluation Memo.

outside reading would be for the course. My intent was for students to develop principles to guide their professional lives based on their values, not my values. Therefore, it made sense to me to allow them choice, particularly once we had covered some fundamentals of ethical theory and ethical decision-making. Students are required to report the time they spend reading each week, but the only constraint on the source is that it has to have ethical content. As one might imagine, this has led to a great diversity of reading material (see examples in Exhibit 1). Students are also permitted to

***Exhibit 1.*** Examples of Diversity of Readings Within Accountability Groups.

*Reading selections:*

There are two forces largely at work in the Weekly Ethics Reading Summaries. In many cases, the summaries serve to refine or reinforce an already-present ethical viewpoint. Almost as often, they present ideas/questions other students in the group had never previously thought about. This leads to interesting discussions and to a higher probability of dialectical reasoning. Below are two actual examples of the readings adopted by the members of Ethics Accountability Groups, along with their literature classifications.

*Diversity in topic and time period* — 2012, EAG 3

1. *Nausea*, Jean Paul Sartre (1938)

    Contemporary Literature and Fiction, Philosophy

2. *IBM and the Holocaust*, Edwin Black (2001)

    Company Business Profiles, World History

3. *The Hunger Games*, Suzanne Collins (2008)

    Teen Science Fiction and Fantasy

4. *Ordering Your Private World*, Gordon McDonald (2007)

    Christian Living, Religion and Spirituality

*Diversity in topic* — 2012, EAG 18

1. *Cleaning Up*, Barry Minkow (2005)

    Biographies & Memoirs, Business & Investing

2. *The Runaway Jury*, John Grisham (2012)

    Mystery, Thriller, & Suspense

3. *Outwitting the Devil*, Napoleon Hill (2011)

    Business & Investing, Self-Help

4. *Boys Will Be Boys*, Jeff Pearlman (2008)

    Biographies & Memoirs, Sports & Outdoors

change their ethics readings during the course of the semester, as long as they report that change to me. Often students change their readings from hearing what other class members are learning from their readings.

## Ethical Accountability

I have historically found it difficult to effectively communicate the importance of ethical accountability to my students. Most ethical decisions in accounting are made at an individual or small group level. For example, young auditors typically have to make ethical choices in consultation with a senior, manager, trusted friend on the audit staff, or mentor within the firm. Encouraging students to trust others enough to discuss ethical issues with them before they make important decisions has been a challenge.

So I assign students to EAGs at the beginning of the course. Because I teach the course in a relatively large auditorium style classroom, I encourage the students within a group to sit close to one another to facilitate in-class discussions. From the outset of the course, students report attendance daily and outside reading hours weekly to the EAG leader. This serves to reduce the anonymity that is typical of a large class.

## Weekly Ethics Reading Summary (WERS)

On Mondays, students bring a hard copy 300-word summary of what they have learned from their outside ethics reading the prior week (see Fig. 1). Meeting in their EAGs, the students read each other's summaries and annotate them with written comments in the margins. These annotated reading summaries are then handed in for grading. I am impressed by the significance of the interaction that these comments reflect, with many of the groups representing a wide diversity of viewpoints. It is also very interesting to see group members learning from one another and, as mentioned above, often shifting their ethics readings based on insights gleaned from reading group members' summaries. This exercise is an example of the critical thinking technique of summing up recommended by Bonk and Smith (1998). In fact, according to Bonk and Smith (1998, p. 278):

> As recent progress in learning theory indicates (Bruer, 1993) a few additional minutes allocated to sharing one's summary and receiving peer or class feedback can further enhance these knowledge gains.

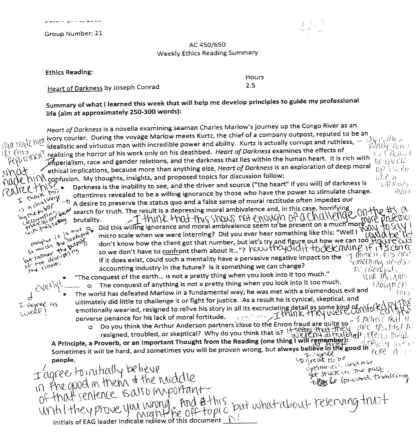

Fig. 1.   Example Weekly Ethics Reading Summary.

The annotation process itself forces the other students in the group to contemplate what the group member is trying to communicate and form a reaction to the writer's arguments. This is an application of the thesis/antithesis/synthesis process in dialectical reasoning, and provides immediate feedback to students as they are developing their principles to guide their professional lives. There is at least some anecdotal evidence of significant knowledge gains demonstrated by interactions in these EAGs. Exhibit 2 provides an example of comments from two groups that seem to indicate application of material learned in the course.

***Exhibit 2.***   Anecdotal EAG Comments Evidencing Knowledge of
Accounting Ethics Course Subject Matter.

1. *Laughing Without an Accent*, Firoozeh Dumas (2009) – 2012, EAG 22
   a. Biographies & Memoirs, Travel
   b. "This is just like a conversation we had in class. Sometimes the situation may seem frivolous; nonetheless, there are still virtues, duties, and consequences we must consider."
   c. "Kant's categorical imperative comes to mind. It appears society has chosen to all be unethical together."
   d. "… also reminds me of [name of insider trader]'s rationalization due to the fact that 'everyone' was trading inside info."
2. *Circle of Greed*, Patrick Dillon and Carl Cannon (2010) – 2012, EAG 22
   a. Professional & Technical, Business & Investing
   b. "Reminded me of ethical decision-making process – judgment, intention, behavior – it takes behavior to truly make an ethically sound choice."
3. *Enron: The Smartest Guys in the Room*, Bethany McLean and Peter Elkind (2004) – 2012, EAG 23
   a. Business & Investing
   b. "So this is just like the trade-off between long-term and short-term interest … So we should not ignore the long-term impact when making decisions."
4. *Decision Points*, George W. Bush (2011) – 2012, EAG 23
   a. Biographies & Memoirs, Literature & Fiction
   b. Identified example of how to "not be an ethical egoist."

I grade each WERS using the rubric presented in Exhibit 3, with 20 points assigned to content, 10 points to grammar and structure, and 10 points to peer evaluation. EAG leaders perform peer evaluation each week on a randomly assigned group's papers using the rubric in Exhibit 4.

*Capstone Project – Ten Principles*

The individual capstone project involves developing and justifying 10 or fewer principles to guide the student's professional life. This is consistent with Kurfiss's (1988) idea that critical thinking requires a "clearly worked out value system." The "working out" of a value system comes from practicing dialogical and dialectical reasoning, rather than simply adopting untested presuppositions. Most of these students have an internship experience prior to the course, so they have some framework within which to develop these principles. It is rewarding to see how many of the students actually adopt principles that arise out of the readings of others in the EAGs, but are impactful enough that they adopt them.

## *Exhibit 3.* WERS Grading Rubric.

**20 points on content**

**Goal: Make your reading meaningful to the others in your group, communicating concisely how it benefited you.**

Communicating what you read, but also what you learned or what it means — 15 pts

Other contributions — 5 pts

- If possible, applying it to your life or career — but you don't have to force it
- Generates questions and discussion comments in the group
- Cumulative learning over weeks of reading
- Ties to material covered in class
- Communicates the book's unique contribution to your moral reasoning
- Points toward your Ten Principles to Guide My Professional Life

**10 points on grammar and structure**

**Goal: Write in a way that your writing does not distract from the meaningfulness of what you have learned and what you are trying to communicate. You do not want the reader distracted by your grammar.**

Punctuation

Spelling

Subject-verb agreement

Changes of tense in your writing

Writing actively, not passively

Possessive — singular/plural

Ending sentences with prepositions

**10 points on peer evaluation**

Each week the EAG leader for another group will read your WERS and provide an evaluation according to the following rubric. They will read the WERS on Monday night and provide me a grade Tuesday morning.

| Criteria | Description | Points |
|---|---|---|
| Important Lesson | Did the student write an insightful thought from the reading that could help in developing a moral principle? | 20 |
| Stimulated Discussion | Do you see evidence of comments and discussions arising from the WERS? | 20 |
| Moral Reasoning | Did the student evaluate the reading for moral content? Does it include an analysis of the book's views on ethics? | 20 |
| Effective Summary | Did the student provide a clear summary of the reading? Were you able to understand the basic content of the reading? | 20 |
| Writing Style | Was the writing style concise? Was the WERS written in a way that did not distract from what was being communicated? | 20 |

***Exhibit 4.*** WERS Peer Evaluation Rubric (Performed by EAG Leader of a Different Group).

| Criteria | Description | Point Value |
|---|---|---|
| Important Lesson | Did the student write an insightful thought from the reading that could help in developing a moral principle? | 20 |
| Stimulated Discussion | Do you see evidence of comments and discussions arising from the WERS? | 20 |
| Moral Reasoning | Did the student evaluate the reading for moral content? Does it include an analysis of the book's views on ethics? | 20 |
| Effective Summary | Did the student provide a clear summary of the reading? Were you able to understand the basic content of the reading? | 20 |
| Writing Style | Was the writing style concise? Was the WERS written in a way that did not distract from what was being communicated? | 20 |

Name: _____

Your Group Number: _____

Group Number Being Evaluated: _____

| Name | Topic | 1 | 2 | 3 | 4 | 5 | Total |
|---|---|---|---|---|---|---|---|

Since the capstone project is based on the individual's values, half the grade is based on the *reasons* for the chosen principles, the quality of supporting arguments given for including each principle in the ones they have identified as critical. The other half of the grade is for grammar, punctuation, and structure of the written document, and the clarity of its communication.

A common argument against teaching ethics is that students' values are fully formed by the time they reach college. I judgmentally selected 10 capstone projects from each of the first four semesters I taught the course and analyzed the sources of the principles. Forty-six percent of the principles were learned in class, 27% were from the student's background, 25% were learned in EAG discussions, and 2% were learned during an internship. An example capstone project is included in Fig. 2.

## *Speakers*

Speakers are particularly helpful in promoting *phronesis*, or practical wisdom. I have observed this happening in two specific ways. First, I invite speakers who I intend to have target the practical application of ethical decision-making. They address topics such as independence problems with Big 4 firms, whistleblowing, insider trading, and preventing versus participating in financial frauds. Second, speakers often are good storytellers. Storytelling is a common way for cultures to pass on values, and some of the stories told by my speakers have clearly had a big impact on my students. In one semester, 71 out of 188 students (38%) said that one speaker's story was the most impactful event in the course, and another 33 (18%) cited her key takeaway, which she had in common with a second speaker.

## *Ethics Speaker Evaluation Memos*

The accounting ethics course has a history of including a number of outside speakers which, especially in a large classroom, may lead to a relatively passive learning style. As an alternative to that approach, students in my course initially evaluated guest speakers using a form designed around concepts they learned in the early part of the course (see Exhibit 5). Much as auditors are required to do with clients, students were required to evaluate the types of assertions that the speaker made and categorize them according to the type of ethical theory and the stage of ethical decision-making (Rest, 1986). They were also required to assess the persuasive quality of the assertions made and to identify when the assertions were largely unsupported. These forms are an example of the reviews and guided questioning suggested by Bonk and Smith (1998) as critical thinking techniques.

Because of the demands of evaluating these forms in order to provide feedback, I have chosen a new approach to speaker evaluation which seems to address my intent more efficiently. I now require students to submit a three-sentence summary evaluation on the next class day after a guest

Group 3

ACCT 650
5/1/14

**Nine Principles to Guide My Professional Life**

1. Do not let money guide your decisions.
2. The more power a position has, the more important it is to behave ethically.
3. Develop your moral framework now, before it is too late.
4. Focus on duties rather than consequences.
5. Maintain a healthy level of professional skepticism.
6. Strive for veracity and do not fall into a pattern of lies.
7. Be content in all you do and do not be envious of others' success.
8. Always hold yourself accountable.
9. Respect others.

*Fig. 2.* Example Ten Principles Project (Page 1 of 4).

Support for My Nine Principles:

1.  **Do not let money guide your decisions.** It seems the desire for money was at the root of all of the scandals and fraud we studied in class. Greed in one's professional and personal life can be detrimental. If I let money become the main factor in my decision-making, I could be more inclined to make an unethical decision if it promises more money as an outcome.

    Source: Class readings and cases

2.  **The more power a person has, the more important it is to behave ethically.** Unethical decisions can be made at any level in a company, but higher power positions such as executives have the ability to influence and affect a greater number of people. Therefore, one must consider the scope of their influence and assume the responsibility of making ethical decisions. This was especially apparent in my reading, The Wolf of Wall Street. Powerful individuals such as judges and police officers constantly let Jordan Belfort off the hook for his crimes and bad decisions. These individuals needed to consider the effect on society it had when they turned a blind eye. Like Uncle Ben from Spiderman wisely said, "With great power comes great responsibility".

    Source: The Wolf of Wall Street

3.  **Develop your moral framework now, before it is too late.** Weston Smith attempted to drill this principle into our heads. His story and experiences inspired me to sit down and think about exactly what I stand for. He warned that if we do not have a clear moral and ethical code now, it will be too difficult or too late to develop one when the time comes. He advised us to be cautionary and make our "ethical plans" now, even if we do not anticipate being involved in an ethical dilemma.

    Source: Weston Smith's presentation

4.  **Focus on duties rather than consequences.** Duties inspire loyalty and steadfastness, which usually lead to ethical decisions. Consequences, be they positive or negative, inspire selfish thinking, which usually leads to unethical decisions. In order to be successful in my career I must adopt a sense of duty

*Fig. 2.    (Continued)*

to my profession, to my company, etc. and stick with it. I will be motivated by duties instead of consequences when I am faced with an ethical dilemma.

Source: Readings and class discussion

5. **Maintain a healthy level of professional skepticism.** This is something that is important as an auditor but can carry into other professions as well. It is important to reasonably question the information given to you and to never take anything at face value. As we have discussed in class, gullibility is a frequent excuse for individuals committing fraud. In order to prevent getting caught up in something because you accepted things as they appeared, it is necessary to be professionally skeptical and have a questioning mind.

Source: Class discussion

6. **Strive for veracity and do not fall into a pattern of lies.** My parents always stressed truth and honesty when I was growing up. I remember getting in severe trouble when I was younger for telling a lie, and that punishment only grew the longer I had been keeping the lie a secret. Many cases we studied spiraled out of control when the perpetrator fell into a pattern of lies and dug too deep of a hole to get out of. This is a principle I want to carry over into my professional life. As an auditor it will be my job to ensure the public is provided with fairly presented financial statements, and so I will constantly be searching for truth. However this principle applies to all professionals, not just auditors. A huge component of credibility is one's track record of honesty. If I wish to remain credible and held in high esteem, I must always strive for veracity.

Source: Personal background

7. **Be content in all you do and do not be envious of others' success.** Envy often goes hand in hand with greed, which often leads to fraud or other unethical decisions. In the Bible, it states that we must never envy our neighbor or covet what they have. James 3:16 even says, "For where jealousy and selfish ambition exist, there will be disorder and every vile practice." I think a solid foundation of ethical thinking lies in always being content with

*Fig. 2.* (*Continued*)

where you are at any moment. It is healthy to want to advance in life but it is also important to remember that we are exactly where we are meant to be. If I base my happiness or success on how it compares to others' happiness or success, I will live an unfulfilling life and could fall into the trap of unethical decision-making.

Source: Christian teachings

8. **Always hold yourself accountable.** Helen Sharkey warned us of the dangers of failing to hold oneself accountable for one's actions or decisions. It is important to own up to decisions you make and take full responsibility for your mistakes. In my opinion, accountability coincides with integrity. I must remember that if I go along with someone else's decision, it then becomes my decision. I must carefully consider the effects a decision could have before I commit to it and I must hold myself accountable for my actions should negative effects arise.

Source: Helen Sharkey's presentation

9. **Respect others.** I have been taught by my parents to respect others regardless of background, race, gender, etc. I also live my life by the Golden Rule that states "Treat others as you would like to be treated". This rule can be found in the Bible as well as almost every other religion's teachings. This also goes along with Kant's Categorical Imperative. If I disrespect others then I am allowing them to disrespect me back and cannot expect them to respect me. I have always believed that an ethical decision considers the wellbeing of others. Therefore, in order to make personal ethical decisions I must always respect others.

Source: Personal background

*Fig. 2.* (*Continued*)

**Exhibit 5.** Ethics Speaker Evaluation Memo Evaluating Ethical Assertions.

1. How did the speaker appeal to *duties or rules* that need to be complied with? What duties or rules?

What was the reason given by the speaker for assuming the duty or complying with the rule?

2. How did the speaker appeal to a *consequentialist calculation*?

What was the calculation and was it a reasonable estimate? What was left out?

3. How did the speaker appeal to a *virtuous character*?

What was the reason given by the speaker that this virtue is more important than self-interest?

The speaker focused on (give specific examples):

*Ethical Recognition or Sensitivity*:

*Ethical Judgments*:

*Ethical Intentions*:

*Ethical Behavior*:

| Evaluation | Strongly Disagree | | | | Strongly Agree |
|---|---|---|---|---|---|
| I found the speaker's arguments convincing. | 1 | 2 | 3 | 4 | 5 |
| The speaker made many unsupported assertions | 1 | 2 | 3 | 4 | 5 |

The speaker's overwhelming appeal was to (circle one): Duty or Rule Calculation Character

speaker's appearance. These three sentences include a statement of the speaker's basic argument, the basic ethical reasoning underlying that argument, and an assessment of the persuasiveness of that argument. Either form, however, gives the student the opportunity to think through the ethical decision-making model in evaluating the quality of the speaker's arguments.

Over time the course has been able to attract a variety of impactful speakers. One speaker in the spring of 2013 had just decided to tell the story of her role in a major financial scandal that sent her to prison as a new mother, even though her role was at a relatively low level compared to some of the other executives involved. The most common comment from students was, "That could be me." The supportive response of students face-to-face and in subsequent notes has given the speaker courage to tell her story more broadly. This unexpected, but welcome, outcome of the course was featured in a television news story in a major city shortly thereafter. Students were visibly impacted when their actual supportive notes were pictured on the screen, and voices read specific portions of the notes to supplement the story. This is one example of students learning to give others moral courage.

## Videos

Many videos are available on the market covering a wide variety of topics relevant to an accounting ethics class. Many of these videos are available at no cost, including the **PBS** Frontline series. Instructors can purchase some videos with case discussion questions as well. But much like the speakers, these videos have the potential to enliven students' imaginations and make them think differently about ethical issues, including raising professional skepticism in some cases.

## Codes of Conduct

Those states requiring ethics courses may mandate coverage of specific topics or code of conduct issues important to state law. Learning to comply with state law and to relate to the jurisdictional officials who provide CPA licensing are both worthwhile outcomes of an accounting ethics course. In some locales, it may be impossible to get an accounting ethics course approved for credit with the state board of accountancy unless it explicitly accomplishes those compliance goals. This is, perhaps, the ultimate application of the practical wisdom shown by Plato's "statesmen and legislators."

## Group Presentation

I require every EAG to develop some sort of presentation, role playing scenario, video or other similar project. The only instruction given is as follows: "This presentation must be relevant to this course, but it may be as creative as you would like it to be." Bonk and Smith (1998) and Davis

(1992) suggest that "creative dramatics" can be useful as a creative thinking technique. But these presentations are the chance for the students to give back to the class as a whole, to provide a practical takeaway that is memorable for their fellow students. It is the short-term application of what they have learned in the course.

I use a standard evaluation process for the presentation similar to what I would in any other accounting course. I assign points for creativity (20), communication skills (30), coordination (10), content (30), and the conclusion (10). Each student evaluates all other presentations as well on a 1−7 Likert scale for impact, indicating strengths and weaknesses as feedback for presenters. Each day students vote for the best presentation of the day, which receives a two-point bonus above my assessed grade. The second favorite presentation receives a one-point bonus. Performing these evaluations engages the students in the presentations and gives me objective feedback to insure fairness in grading.

## Ethics Coffees

Generally once a week I meet any students who are interested for coffee and informal ethics discussions. Typically, 5−20 students show up, and the discussions are wide ranging, covering everything from moral philosophy to practical career matters. These optional meetings provide an additional opportunity to personalize the large classroom setting without a large investment by the instructor, and it seems to stimulate the commitment of a critical subset of students to the course.

## Ethics Kudos

I make ethics kudos forms available to students. They are asked to indicate on the forms when they notice something positive happening in the class, allowing me to receive better input from students on the quality of EAG discussions and the influence that students had on each other. This is also an opportunity to provide students with positive reinforcement when they notice something good happening ethically, rather than simply focusing the course on criticizing ethical failings. Students are very familiar with the challenges and perils of whistleblowing by the time they complete the course; the ethics kudos form allows them the chance to engage in "positive whistleblowing."

# CONTRIBUTION OF THE ACTIVITIES TO WISDOM DEVELOPMENT

My course admittedly includes a wide variety of activities. Others could easily develop a course around a subset of these activities depending on the instructor's priorities in wisdom development. The purpose of this section is to describe what activities are most useful in developing each of Plato's three concepts of wisdom, as well as identifying those exercises most effective in enhancing dialogical reasoning and dialectical reasoning. Table 2 provides a delineation of the activities that stimulate dialogical and dialectical thinking under each of the three concepts — *sophia, phronesis,* and *episteme.*

## *Developing Sophia*

*Sophia* is really the heart of the accounting ethics course, and the incremental contribution of the classroom to the student's intellectual and moral development. Six weeks are set aside for intense consideration of issues that are largely never discussed in other courses or in the workplace. The course focuses on taking advantage of these opportunities for reflection to develop both dialogical and dialectical thinking.

I have specifically designed two course activities to develop students' dialogical reasoning in the context of *sophia*, their interaction in EAGs and

***Table 2.*** Course Activities: Organized by Plato's Concepts of Wisdom and Type of Reasoning They Develop.

| | Dialogical Thinking | Dialectical Thinking |
| --- | --- | --- |
| Sophia: A contemplative life in search of truth | Classroom discussion<br>Ethics accountability groups<br>Weekly Ethics Reading Summaries (WERSs) | 10 Principles<br>Outside ethics reading for WERSs<br>Writing WERSs<br>Google docs |
| Phronesis: Practical wisdom | Ethics coffees<br>Q&A with guest speakers | Ethics speaker evaluation memos<br>Google docs<br>HealthSouth case<br>10 Principles<br>In-class videos |
| Episteme: Scientific understanding | Lecture<br>Week one discussions<br>Group presentations | Questions from students after group presentations |

the broader classroom discussion. Students sit in their accountability groups every day, so they regularly interact over the topics in the course. I allow students to choose their outside ethics reading for the course. On Mondays, they read each other's Weekly Ethics Reading Summaries and annotate those summaries with comments. I grade the annotated summaries, and the grades on five summaries represent 25% of the total course grade. After annotating the summaries, the groups discuss commonalities and differences in their readings and in what they learned that week. Each group provides one idea or question that came up in their discussion to share with the whole class. The next portion of class is devoted to discussing as many of those ideas as we can as an entire class. Both these exercises create substantial dialogue in the classroom setting.

Dialectical reasoning in the contemplative context of *sophia* is produced by at least three activities: the development of Ten Principles to Guide My Professional Life, the weekly reading that is the source of the Weekly Ethics Reading Summary, and a Google doc that is updated each week by the student in anticipation of developing the 10 principles.[2] Students record their thoughts in a Google Docs document for my review on a weekly basis. The purpose of the document is to build toward the development of personal ethical principles, but the by-product is that the students are writing down the results of thoughtful contemplation rather than having those thoughts disappear within a few minutes. The weekly reading and Google doc updating performed by students allow them to test their ideas against competing ideas, wrestling with the ideas in their outside reading book in hope of coming to a resolution that synthesizes those perspectives.

### Developing Phronesis

Teaching practical wisdom in a classroom is challenging, because *phronesis* is primarily developed through experience. What students can do is share their experiences with one another, and the timing of my accounting ethics class promotes this sharing, since the overwhelming majority of my students have just completed a 10-week internship, almost all of them with a Big 4 public accounting firm. They are able to share stories of the ethical pressures that they encountered in their first few weeks on the job. In fact, I have been surprised at their willingness to enlighten others in the class about some problematic issues for young professionals that exist in the firms. These students share their mistakes and uncertainty quite openly in class; perhaps that is because it is a safe environment in which to communicate uncertainty or admit a mistake. They also tell stories of when they have walked away from opportunities to act unethically.

Considering the practical wisdom of phronesis contributes to both dialogical and dialectical thinking. Besides the classroom interaction, dialogue is encouraged through Q&A sessions with guest speakers and through weekly ethics coffees for smaller groups of students outside the classroom. However, a wide variety of classroom activities engage the students in thinking dialectically about practical wisdom. The Google doc leading to the Ten Principles contributes to this goal, since the desired outcome of the project is a set of principles that a student would know how to practice in a professional setting. In addition, students work through a detailed case involving one of the major scandals to understand the practical implications of ethical failures, as well as watching memorable in-class videos. Finally, the students prepare an evaluation memo for every outside speaker that requires them to evaluate what the speaker said, the fundamental ethical argument made by the speaker (duty, calculation, or virtue), and the argument's persuasiveness. This forces students to explicitly consider the strength of others' arguments in reaching conclusions about how to apply what they say.

### Developing Episteme

Week one of the course helps the students get a sense of the importance of understanding an ethical decision-making structure both through lecture and classroom discussion. The model discussed in the course, based on work in the psychology and marketing literatures, provides a common language for ethical decision-making that we use throughout the course.

My approach to ethics theory, or *episteme*, is to provide the class with a theoretical ethical decision-making model during the first week of class based on Rest's (1986) four-component framework, as modeled by Hunt and Vitell in their stream of work in marketing ethics. Hunt and Vitell (1986, 1993, 2006) model ethical decisions as combining deontological (duty) and teleological (outcomes or ends) evaluations. I use the 1986 version of the Hunt-Vitell model which includes Rest's four-component sequence: recognition/sensitivity, judgment, intention, and behavior. Rest's work is built on the foundation of Kohlberg's (1969) ethical theory, and each developed a measure of moral maturity based on a justice orientation.

As we discuss these different approaches to ethics, I lecture and assign readings that will familiarize the students with the philosophical underpinnings for duty, rights, and virtue ethics. We also discuss the tensions between the theories, and the ways in which they integrate with one another (e.g., one person's rights may result in another person's duties). We also discuss the concept of a profession, defined by the International Federation of Accountants' Code of Ethics for Professional Accountants (IFAC, 2005) as:

1. Mastery of an intellectual skill through training and education;
2. Adherence to a common code of values and conduct, including being objective; and
3. Acceptance of a duty to society as a whole (usually in return for restrictions in the use of a title or in the granting of a qualification) (Knechel, Salterio, & Ballou, 2007, p. 734).

The course's focus on duty and on developing wisdom seems consistent with this definition of a profession.

By laying this foundation in week one, we have a common language with which to discuss issues that arise in the course. However, because of the wide variety of outside readings chosen by students, over the course of six weeks we discuss a variety of philosophers, from Aristotle to Augustine to Confucius. A full semester course might call for two or three weeks focusing on ethical theory on the front end of the course, and might provide additional opportunity to examine the philosophical underpinnings of ethics.

## OUTCOMES

One of the ways the development of dialogical and dialectical reasoning from the course became evident was through student evaluation comments. Students consistently used terms that reflected their developing ability to engage in dialogue about ethical issues, as well as the dialectical tension that came from testing their ideas against others' in order to reach conclusions. Exhibits 6 and 7 include essentially all the spring 2015 student evaluation comments that were not primarily assessments of the instructor, but were comments on the course itself. Exhibit 6 comments primarily reflect development in dialogical thinking, and Exhibit 7 comments are dialectical in nature.

Dialogical comments include phrases like:

- encouraged open dialogue,
- listened,
- accepted differing viewpoints,
- allows freedom to develop own opinions,
- respectful of all opinions,

***Exhibit 6.*** Course Evaluation Comments Indicating Dialogical Reasoning Spring 2015.

---

"Did not push his opinion but encouraged open dialogue."

"This was a wonderfully stimulating course, and I think that you did a fantastic job fostering discussion without swaying anyone or pushing your own personal views. Most interesting class that I have taken since I joined the business school. And most influential."

"Very interactive, lots of class discussion, interesting speakers."

"Intriguing, respectful of all opinions."

"I can honestly say it is a joy coming to class and talking ethics."

"The group participation during class was a strength."

"I thought the class discussions, but even more the small accountability group discussions were of great value in making me think."

"This course is the most interactive class that I have ever had at [the university]. The curriculum forced students to reflect, read and listen in ways I have never had the opportunity to before."

"I appreciated classroom discussions so much but wish we had smaller class sections to engage more and hear more opinions." (There were 197 students in the class.)

"Allows us to learn from each other."

"Open discussion created an interesting environment for collaboration."

"Ethics groups [a strength]."

"The discussion is great! Really challenges you to think."

"I liked the class discussions and I think they contributed a lot to the overall effectiveness of the course."

"Stimulated great learning from peers."

"Learned a lot and it stimulated a lot of great thought and conversation."

"Great discussions, really made you think."

"Intellectually stimulating! Love our discussions!"

"Engaged discussion."

"Love ethics coffees!"

"Discussions on Mondays were great!"

"Good class discussion and interesting outside speakers."

"Great interaction."

---

- class discussions (and, even more, small accountability group discussions) were of great value in making me think,
- most interactive class that I have ever had, and
- appreciated class discussions so much but wish we had smaller class sections to engage more and hear more opinions.

*Exhibit 7.*   Course Evaluation Comments Indicating Dialectical Reasoning
Spring 2015.

"Challenged me to think about both sides to an argument and not be so closed minded."

"This course was awesome, and so much was learned. The speakers added a special atmosphere that taught valuable lessons to future professionals."

"I loved how you listened and accepted differing viewpoints. You were extremely patient and always challenged us by asking questions."

"Very intellectually stimulating and applicable to life and the working world."

"Fantastic course. Finally a course that challenges and intellectually stimulates students."

"He is very objective and allows students the freedom to develop our own opinions and encourages discussion and dissent."

"Tell us your opinion more! We want to hear it!"

"Lots of thought provoking questions/soul-searching, if you will."

"Really makes you think about who you want to be/are."

"Challenged me to think outside the box."

"Very intellectually challenging and thought provoking."

"It challenged us intellectually and gave us several ways to look at life."

"Good way to stimulate thinking."

"Made me think critically on ethical issues presented in the business world today."

"The strength of the course was the guest speakers in my opinion. They stimulated my learning and allowed me to see ethics from a different perspective."

"The course was very inspiring. It was the first time that I started to think about the questions that I never thought would bother me."

"Challenged me to think more intellectually."

"Challenged me to create a set of values."

"Gives tools to use in career to overcome persuasions/temptation to act in an unethical manner."

"Very intellectually stimulating. Made me think a lot."

"Encouraged me to develop my own ethical groundwork."

"I enjoyed the open-endedness of the course and how it challenged all of us to think about our own principles."

"Really makes you think about the consequences of our actions."

"Really made me think about my choices."

"One of the most intellectually challenging courses I have ever taken."

"Understanding the importance of one's moral code."

"Posed difficult/intellectual questions."

"Very engaging and thought-provoking course."

"He challenged us intellectually and encouraged us to engage in class discussions."

"Brought in outside examples to solidify concepts, allowed us to see things from others' perspectives."

"This course really challenged me to be open minded as well as solidify who I am and what my values are."

"Very engaging and thought provoking."

"Eye opening to see how much damage you can do in the corporate world."

"Teaching really stimulated my thinking because you taught from personal experience rather than just purely theory."

"Really challenged me to think about who I am, and who I want to be."

"I thought the course did a good job at getting students prepared to face ethical dilemmas in the professional world."

"Challenged us to think every class."

"The course continually makes you think past the norm and challenges your morals to make them stronger."

"A perfect way for students to process their internships."

"Intellectual stimulation [a strength]."

"Encouragement of thinking in a new way."

"Forces students to answer tough questions and creates guidelines and a strong foundation on our moral principles and values!"

"Encouraged thought provoking questions."

"Was very informative and really helped to change my perspective on what 'ethics' really is."

"Inspires us to learn and develop ourselves."

"Ethics is a very thought provoking course, one that every business student should take."

"Great at not forcing his opinions on his students, allowing us each to develop their own principles."

"Didn't favor anyone or any topic."

"Challenged peoples' thoughts and views."

---

Dialectical comments often include phrases like "really made me think," "intellectually stimulating," or "challenged me to think outside the box."

Categorizing these phrases was actually an interesting exercise, as it became evident that increased dialogue inside and outside the classroom stimulates a dialectical environment where people hold their views in tension with others. This dialectical tension carries into the outside reading and students' Weekly Ethics Reading Summaries, where students consider four other people's ethical viewpoints, as well as testing their own worldview against their source reading. This comes through in student comments like "encourages discussion and dissent," which reflects both dialogical and dialectical reasoning in the classroom.

Besides the desire for smaller class sections described in the dialogical comments above, students' negative comments included limited integration of the textbook into the course, excessive outside reading for a six-week course, and too many small assignments. I have addressed some of these comments by first reducing, and then eliminating, the use of a textbook, as well as by discontinuing some of the minor assignments, such as commenting on blogs.

## CONCLUSION

This chapter describes an accounting ethics course that intentionally includes activities designed to stimulate dialogical and dialectical reasoning in the hopes of short-circuiting the types of foolish decisions that reflect the five fallacies of thinking in professional accountants. The intended outcomes are to enable students to develop wisdom as they clearly identify the principles that will guide their professional lives.

However, thinking dialogically and dialectically, as well as becoming more others-centered and a better listener, does more than develop young accountants' wisdom. These characteristics are at the heart of client service, strategic thinking, and leadership. This process has the potential to develop the types of leaders for the accounting profession that will assure that it continues to have a significant role in a free society's financial markets.

Certainly there are many potentially effective approaches to an accounting ethics course, and the one described in this chapter may not be appropriate in every context. But expanding creative approaches to developing wisdom has the potential to make young accounting professionals less susceptible to the fallacies of thinking that can undermine their careers and their personal lives. Even modest successes in this effort would help to ensure that accounting ethics courses warrant their place in the accounting curriculum.

## NOTES

1. I am currently revising the course to be delivered in a full semester format for a somewhat smaller group of about 60.

2. Technically, students develop 10 *or fewer* principles. They are not required to develop 10.

# REFERENCES

Barr, C. (2011). AIG, Hank Greenberg and the omnipotent CEO myth. *CNNMoney Online*. Retrieved from http://finance.fortune.cnn.com/2011/04/24/aig-hank-greenberg-and-the-omnipotent-ceo-myth/. Accessed on August 29, 2013.

Black, E. (2001). *IBM and the Holcaust: The strategic alliance between Nazi Germany and America's most powerful corporation*. New York, NY: Crown.

Blanthorne, C., Kovar, S., & Fisher, D. (2007). Accounting educators' opinions about ethics in the curriculum: An extensive view. *Issues in Accounting Education, 22*(3), 355–390.

Bonk, C. J., & Smith, J. S. (1998). Alternative instructional strategies for creative and critical thinking in the accounting curriculum. *Journal of Accounting Education, 16*(2), 261–293.

Bruer, J. T. (1993). *Schools for thought: A science of learning in the classroom*. Cambridge, MA: The MIT Press.

Collins, S. (2008). *The hunger games*. New York, NY: Scholastic Press.

Davis, G. A. (1992). *Creativity is forever* (3rd ed.). Dubuque, IA: Kendall/Hunt Publishing.

Freeman, R. E. (1984). *Strategic management: A stakeholder approach*. Boston, MA: Pitman.

Ghoshal, S. (2005). Bad management theories are destroying good management practices. *Academy of Management Learning & Education, 4*(1), 75–91.

Grisham, J. (2012). *The runaway jury*. New York, NY: Penguin Random House.

Hill, N. (2011). *Outwitting the devil: The secret to freedom and success*. New York, NY: Sterling Publishing.

Hunt, S. D., & Vitell, S. (1986). A general theory of marketing ethics. *Journal of Macromarketing, 6*, 5–16.

Hunt, S. D., & Vitell, S. (1993). The general theory of marketing ethics: A retrospective and revision. In N. C. Smith & J. A. Quelch (Eds.), *Ethics in marketing* (pp. 775–784). Homewood, IL: Irwin.

Hunt, S. D., & Vitell, S. (2006). The general theory of marketing ethics: A revision and three questions. *Journal of Macromarketing, 26*, 143–153.

Hurtt, R., & Thomas, C. (2011). Ethics education for CPAs in Texas: Is it working? *Today's CPA, 39*(July/August), 32–35.

International Federation of Accountants (IFAC). (2005). IFAC Code of Ethics for Professional Accountants.

Jensen, M. C., & Meckling, W. H. (1976). Theory of the firm: Managerial behavior, agency costs, and ownership structure. *Journal of Financial Economics, 3*(October), 305–360.

Jensen, M. C., & Meckling, W. H. (1994). The nature of man. *Journal of Applied Corporate Finance, 7*(Summer), 4–19.

Jordan, J., & Sternberg, R. (2006). Wisdom in organizations: A balance theory analysis. Unpublished manuscript, Dartmouth College.

Knechel, R., Salterio, S., & Ballou, B. (2007). *Auditing: Assurance & risk*. Mason, OH: Thomson South-Western.

Kohlberg, L. (1969). Moral stages and moralization: The cognitive-developmental approach to socialization. In D. Goskin (Ed.), *Handbook of socialization theory and research* (pp. 347–480). Chicago, IL: Rand McNally.

Kurfiss, J. G. (1988). *Critical thinking: Theory, research, practice, and possibilities*. Washington, DC: Association for the Study of Higher Education.

McDonald, G. (2007). *Ordering your private world*. Nashville, TN: Thomas Nelson.

Minkow, B. (2005). *Cleaning up*. Nashville, TN: Nelson Current.

Novack, J. (2005). Smoking e-mails. *Forbes.com*, October 3. Accessed on February 21, 2010.

pbs.org. (2004). *Tax me if you can*. Retrieved from http://www.pbs.org/wgbh/pages/frontline/shows/tax/schemes/3.html. Accessed on March 16, 2016.

Pearlman, J. (2008). *Boys will be boys: The glory days and party nights of the Dallas Cowboys Dynasty*. New York, NY: HarperCollins.

Rest, J. (1986). *Moral development: Advances in research and theory*. New York, NY: Praeger.

Robinson, D. N. (1990). Wisdom through the ages. In R. J. Sternberg (Ed.), *Wisdom: Its nature, origins, and development* (pp. 13–24). New York, NY: Cambridge University Press.

Sartre, J. (1938). *Nausea*. Paris: Gallimard.

Shaub, M. K., & Fisher, D. G. (2008). Beyond agency theory: Common values for accounting ethics education. In D. Swanson & D. Fisher (Eds.), *Advancing business ethics education* (pp. 305–328). Charlotte, NC: Information Age Publishing.

Smith, A. (1966). *The theory of moral sentiments*. New York, NY: Augustus M. Kelley.

Sternberg, R. (1998). A balance theory of wisdom. *Review of General Psychology*, 2(4), 347–365.

Sternberg, R. (2002). Successful intelligence: A new approach to leadership. In R. E. Riggio, S. E. Murphy, & F. J. Pirozzolo (Eds.), *Multiple intelligences and leadership* (pp. 9–28). Mahwah, NJ: Lawrence Erlbaum Associates.

Sternberg, R. (2003a). WICS: A model for leadership in organizations. *Academy of Management Learning and Education*, 2, 386–401.

Sternberg, R. (2003b). *WICS: A theory of wisdom, intelligence and creativity synthesized*. New York, NY: Cambridge University Press.

Sternberg, R. (2006). How could I be so stupid? *USA Today Magazine*, July, pp. 70–72.

Valencia, M. (2010). The gods strike back. *The Economist*, February 13, pp. 3–5.

Webster's New Collegiate Dictionary. (1997). Springfield, MA: G. & C. Merriam Co.

# INDEX

Printed in the United States
By Bookmasters